Also by W. Hugh Missildine:

YOUR INNER CHILD OF THE PAST

Also by Lawrence Galton:

FREEDOM FROM BACKACHES
(with Lawrence W. Friedmann, M.D.)
FREEDOM FROM HEART ATTACKS
(with Benjamin F. Miller, M.D.)

Your Inner Conflicts– How to Solve Them

W. Hugh Missildine, M.D.
Lawrence Galton

SIMON AND SCHUSTER   NEW YORK

DESIGNED BY ELIZABETH WOLL
MANUFACTURED IN THE UNITED STATES OF AMERICA
PRINTED BY MURRAY PRINTING COMPANY
BOUND BY THE BOOK PRESS

2   3   4   5   6   7   8   9   10

LIBRARY OF CONGRESS CATALOGING IN PUBLICATION DATA

MISSILDINE, W. HUGH
    Your inner conflicts—how to solve them.

    1. Self-love (Psychology).   2.   Parent and child.
3. Psychotherapy—Cases, clinical reports, statistics.
I. Galton, Lawrence, joint author. II. Title.
BF697.M55   1975   158′.1   74–11370
ISBN 0–671–21836–0

To
BARBARA GALTON
who not only lent moral encouragement
but played a vital creative role in
the writing and editing of this book

Contents

8   *Contents*

10   *Contents*

Preface

This book attempts to take you on a voyage of self-discovery and self-realization so that you can live with yourself and others more fully, more freely and more comfortably.

All of us carry within ourselves the child we once were. In the conflict between that still-living child and our adult selves lies the source of much adult distress and unhappiness. Here, in this conflict—which we can readily examine for ourselves, without need for penetrating any murky depths of unconsciousness and without need for psychiatric jargon—we can discover specific influences and interferences in our lives.

That was the concept first presented eleven years ago in the book *Your Inner Child of the Past*. In the intervening years, there have been additional thousands of opportunities to test the validity of that concept, to add to and refine it and to evolve practical methods for dealing with internal conflict.

Beyond considering the inner child and our need to be a good parent to that child and to ourselves, the thrust of this present book is toward answering the question "How?"

We are grateful to the innumerable patients whose struggles, insights and growth have contributed toward answering the question. It is our hope that you can identify yourself in this book and that with its help you can understand yourself better, throw off the internal forces that limit you and grow toward becoming your own unique self.

In a therapist-patient relationship, the therapist can serve only as guide; the patient must do the work. Our hope is that this book can be guide or auxiliary guide to helping you to help yourself.

This book is complete in itself; in going beyond *Your Inner Child of the Past*, it incorporates the basic material to be found there.

W. Hugh Missildine, M.D.
Lawrence Galton

part I

Being a Loving Parent
to Oneself

chapter 1

What Kind of Parent Are You to Yourself?

Children and adults differ in many obvious respects. Although one difference is crucial, most of us give it little if any thought. Children have parents who guide, direct and provide the emotional atmosphere for them. Adults, on the other hand, must assume the functions of guiding and directing themselves and of creating their own emotional atmosphere. They must be parents to themselves.

This may seem like a fairly obvious fact but it is culturally overlooked, with large groups, whole populations, having no concept of self-parenthood. Spoken aloud, the words "I am parent to myself" sound strange, even bizarre.

Yet the way we treat ourselves in adult life is critical for our mental health, happiness and productivity. It affects everything we feel and everything we achieve or fail to achieve. *If we do what comes naturally, we tend to treat ourselves in adult life as we were treated when we were growing up. We re-create the old home atmosphere of long ago.*

We have a powerful built-in tendency to do this. It's almost as if a great flywheel inside keeps pulling us back to the old atmosphere. Particularly when we are tired, ill, overloaded with responsibility or under stress, we go home. And going home means treating ourselves as we were treated back in childhood.

Old Borrowed Attitudes

We can write sentimental songs about the homes of our childhood. But, realistically, most homes, though we like to think of them as near-ideal, only seem so in nostalgic retrospect.

Our parents were human, with problems of living. They carried many of those problems with them from their own home backgrounds. They faced others engendered by the social and cultural situation of the time, still others provoked by the economic situation and perhaps some by the marital situation. Because of their problems, they saw us, as children, askew. And because they saw us askew, they had attitudes that at times were hurtful to us, not because they had any desire to hurt us but simply because that was the way it was.

When certain attitudes are hurtful to us as children, they can become even more hurtful if we internalize them and use them on ourselves when we grow up. For in adult life, when we veer toward treating ourselves as our parents treated us, we are jammed up with ourselves twenty-four hours a day in a small area, smaller than a phone booth. Almost always, as children, we could get away at least temporarily from our parents. But we cannot, as adults, get away from ourselves and from our parenthood to ourselves.

Unless we examine how we treat ourselves—the kind of parents we are being to ourselves—we may live almost constantly with hurtful borrowed attitudes, and we may call those attitudes the truth about ourselves.

But they are not the truth, have nothing really to do with us now, and when we apply them it is because we are unaware of what we are doing. We apply them automatically but they can be pervasively harmful, sometimes even disastrous.

As adults, most of us view life in two ways. We see ourselves and the world through a realistic window of the present, and all appears, in that view, to be logical, reasonable, understandable. But we also look at things through the colored glasses of our past home life—and, when thus seen, we ourselves, our spouses, our work, our bosses and our friends no longer seem reasonable or understandable; our view is distorted and everything we see seems to be distorted.

Confused by the distortions of view, we react in ways that may be hurtful to us or to those around us. The distortions and reactions become habitual. We find ourselves saying resignedly: "This is the way I am!" But this is the way we are because we are unaware of what is making us this way.

If we look for the hurt caused by such distortions and reactions, we find it in the extreme in prisons and mental institutions. Short of the extreme, it is all around us: in broken marriages; in the vast numbers of people who seek help for psychosomatic illnesses; in the alcoholics, the obese, the angry, the fearful, the unproductive, the people stuck in jobs below their true capacities; in books never written, symphonies never composed, pictures never painted.

All through our adult lives, many of us experience feelings we find inappropriate, unreasonable, undesirable. We make a plan and get no satisfaction when it is realized. We are disturbed to find ourselves sometimes feeling embittered toward someone who loves us. We suspect, without evidence, that we have been victimized by a shopkeeper. We endow a child with a lovingly selected gift and fly into a rage, expressed or unexpressed, because the child is not profusely grateful.

We wish to be friendly and, unaccountably, find ourselves saying things that could hardly be better calculated to alienate. We sometimes are surly on what should be happy occasions and erratically amused on what should be sad occasions.

We don't like these feelings and reactions; we don't understand why we have them; we are ashamed of having them; we may berate ourselves for having them. Because we have them, we regard ourselves as somehow different, perhaps neurotic. Or, shaken by them, we may try to project the blame for them onto family, friends, fate, even the weather. As they keep recurring, we become increasingly disturbed and may feel ourselves alone, separated from others.

Yet, much of our loneliness and discomfort stems from carrying into our self-parenthood one or more old borrowed attitudes. It is not that we are unworthy or strange or victims of a severe and dark neurosis.

The Emerging Picture

In twenty-five years of working with more than 5,000 patients, I have had repeated opportunities to observe how strong the distortions that come from borrowed parental attitudes can be and how much unhappiness they can cause. I have seen the unhappiness begin to be manifested in children; develop further in adolescents; and then, in adults, both young and old, take a toll in anxiety, depression, fears, loneliness, marital discord, sexual difficulties, career failures and compulsive, often self-defeating, striving for success.

People should not have to live this way. Hopefully, at some future time, certain principles of child raising may be universally used—in particular, a simple cardinal principle of mutual respect about which I shall have much more to say—and we will not have to play "catch up."

But now we do have to play "catch up." We have to understand the need to be good parents to ourselves and to understand the role of borrowed parental attitudes in contravening this. We have to look for those attitudes in ourselves and, aware of their presence and seeing clearly their influence, set about not necessarily extirpating them entirely (for that is neither possible nor essential) but bringing them under our control.

And, fortunately, for this, we do not have to delve into murky areas—although I must confess that I thought so for a time.

When I began to practice medicine in a small Iowa town just before World War II, I did the usual things a family physician does. There were babies to be delivered, broken bones to be set, sniffles and sometimes more serious infections to be dealt with.

But it soon became apparent, as it has to many family physicians, that people are much more concerned about family relationships and personal emotional hurts than about their splinters, sprains and bellyaches. To be sure, when they sought help, it was for some physical problem. But then, often, they got to talking about their emotional troubles. I had no answers; although I quickly became convinced that for me emotional problems were much more important in the everyday practice of medicine than physical problems, I was not trained to deal with them.

Entering the Army just before World War II, I happened to be at Pearl Harbor just after the Japanese attack. There, and then later in Guadalcanal and Luzon, where I served as infantry battalion surgeon and then division artillery surgeon, there were physical casualties to be helped; there were also emotional casualties.

After the war, convinced by my experiences overseas as well as in Iowa that emotional problems were of prime importance and that I wanted them to be my concern, I took four years of psychiatric training at The Johns Hopkins Hospital, Baltimore: two years of it in the treatment of emotional problems in children, two years in treatment of adult problems. And, with the intention of becoming a psychoanalyst, I went through 300 hours of personal, training analysis.

In 1949, a child psychiatrist was needed in Columbus, Ohio, to start a child-guidance clinic in connection with the outpatient department at Children's Hospital. When I went to Columbus, it was with no idea of how the experience there—with both children and adults—would lead me away from practicing psycho-analysis.

Duly, the guidance clinic, called the Children's Mental Health Center, was started. In 1953, an inpatient facility for psychiatrically disturbed children, the Columbus Children's Psychiatric Hospital, was also set up. At both facilities, I saw many children and troubled parents—children with behavior problems and parents having a difficult time coping with them. In private practice, I was also seeing some children and, in addition, many adults.

We had a problem at both the center and the hospital. Our staff members—pediatricians, psychiatric social workers and others—were of diverse backgrounds, including dyed-in-the-wool Freudians, neo-Freudians and advocates of other theoretical schools. We had to present cases to each other, discuss them and arrive at methods of treatment and follow-up. And, for that, with our babble of tongues, our differing backgrounds, we had to find a common language—otherwise we made no sense to each other.

We could agree among us that many, if not most, of the

disturbances in the children we saw came from breakdowns or disturbances in parent-child relationships. We could conceive what might be the ideal parent-child relationship—centered about the mutual-respect principle, to be dealt with more completely later. Given the mutual-respect principle, we could without great difficulty see how infringements of it led to problems for our patients. We could evolve an approach to child guidance that we could agree upon and talk about, that made sense to everybody and that helped our young patients.

And then I found that the same approach was no less valid for my adult patients. The pathogens for the children—the parental attitudes and the child responses that produced emotional turmoil in the young—were pathogens for troubled adults as well. Only now they were pathogens because the adults were inflicting them upon themselves, carrying over old parental attitudes into their adult lives.

It no longer seemed to me that psychoanalysis was the sine qua non, the only way, or best way, or most practical way, to get at the roots of emotional disturbances. I dropped it.

In bare outline, the concept that I have seen work many times, that I present to patients and in lectures to medical students at the Ohio State University College of Medicine, is simply this: Whether we like it or not, we are not just adults living wholly in the present. We are also the children we once were, still living with some, even much, of the home atmosphere, the emotional environment in which we were raised. We think we have outgrown the past but we have not. We were exposed to parental attitudes, perhaps all of them well intentioned but not all of them valid and truly applicable to us. But we were exposed to them for many years; they very much impinged on our lives as children; we developed certain attitudes and reactions in response to them. The child within us has not died. Nor have the attitudes, the good and the bad.

The bad—arising from our parents' own problems—now have become our ever-nagging though rarely realized hindrances, preventing us from living life as we should and could live it, as we have the capacity and desire to live it.

We can find and do something constructive about those

carryover attitudes if we try. It has been my experience that often, with very little help, many people who have long been gripped by seemingly ineradicable fears and anxieties, feelings of loneliness and alienation and feelings of being inadequate or worthless can discern for themselves the true causes of their problems and can keep them from dominating their lives any longer.

Let me illustrate how exciting the chase can be and how the seemingly imponderable can be made to make sense, which is the very first important step.

Examples

Laura

Laura is an attractive, intelligent twenty-five-year-old woman with what appears to be a promising career ahead as a designer. She has been married two years and separated for one of the two. Shortly after their marriage, she and her husband, Charles, had begun to have sex difficulties and had found themselves growing apart. On a summer vacation she met and had an affair with an older man who persuaded her to leave her husband. But she came home after a brief interval to work things out.

Things didn't work out, she told me. She felt her marriage was no good; she wanted someone to love; she was currently having another affair but felt upset because the man, whom she liked very much, had had to go away on an extended trip and she was certain he did not miss her as much as she missed him.

Her husband, she told me, had a weight problem and she was repulsed by it. Charles had been her first boyfriend, the first person with whom she had had sex. Because of her strict upbringing, she had felt guilty in high school about that. Her husband, she said, is "too kind; that just makes me feel guilty." He is affectionate toward her, hasn't much of a temper, thinks she is overly tense and nervous. He came from a home where the father was friendly and lenient, the mother kind and concerned, and both enjoyed "doing" for him, yet Charles wasn't spoiled and worked quite a lot while growing up.

Laura herself came from a somewhat different family. She didn't know her father well. He was a quiet man, concerned with his career, remote from the family, strict, often critical. "I never got any praise for the good marks I got in school; he didn't appreciate ever the gifts I got for him for Christmas. My parents let me know they resented any money they spent on me."

Her mother was critical of both Laura and her brother. "We had our work to do at home; it was very hard to please her. After my first year of college, they cut off financial support for me and I had to get a government loan and work, and still owe on my education." Laura also told me: "I am a hard worker. I get angry easily but don't show it. I never have spent much money because I feel guilty about it. I turn against myself if I get just three pounds overweight."

Her husband was glad to come to see me. A friendly, personable, well-built, muscular man, he wasn't obese at all. "I am very much in love with Laura," he told me. "I wasn't upset before, but I am now. I don't understand what my wife is doing; the way she is living her life upsets me very much. I don't understand where she is going. She is attracted to men who aren't going anywhere. All I want is for her to be straightened out. Her parents have never shown her any love. After we got married, the sex part just wasn't any good any more; she doesn't respond."

So here, then, is an attractive woman, married to an attractive and successful man who loves her and is kind, considerate, understanding even though she runs around with other men. She is upset, depressed.

On the face of it, it doesn't seem to make any sense. But it does when you put together the pieces from her past life that are still very much at work in the present. For here is a woman who as a girl was criticized repeatedly by her parents, who couldn't please them no matter how hard she tried. They reacted to her destructively, even cutting off her money in college. Because she was often the object of parental criticism, she is self-critical, turns against herself even when she gains a few pounds. She gets depressed easily. She was resentful of her parents, the figures in her home life as a child; she is resentful now of her husband, the person in her current home life. And the more resentful she feels, the more depressed she becomes and the more she longs for love.

She learned as a girl that you can't get anything from people in the family except criticism and injustice. She found, as a high school girl, that she could get understanding, affection and love if she went outside the family—to Charles. But when they married and established a home, he was suddenly *in* the family and now this same man who loved her became a post on which she hung a lot of old feelings from her past.

She picked on his weight when, in reality, he had no weight problem; it was a peg, not a valid one, for her child-of-the-past feelings. Aware that it isn't valid, she feels guilty about it; it doesn't make sense to her adult of the present. And her guilt makes her feel depressed, and the more depressed she gets, the more she longs to find the "solution" she found in adolescence— another man. She is a sucker for any man who will look at her, and many will because she is an attractive woman.

She has to understand that as a parent to herself now she is treating herself with the old borrowed critical attitudes of her past home life. That when she does so, she cannot see her husband clearly. That she cannot bring up one part of her past home life without bringing up all parts of it—and she is seeing her husband distorted, not in fact as her husband at all but as a home figure to whom she assigns attributes of her parents to which she reacts with emotional hurt. And that this is likely to be true with any man with whom she shares a home.

She has to recognize this and then, without self-criticism of any kind, has to begin to treat herself in her own way, not her parents' way. And while it takes some effort to do this, it can be done; it is feasible to do. In fact, she is doing it.

Sandra

Sandra is a twenty-year-old woman who came to see me because of a phobia. "I have a death phobia," she told me. "It underlines everything I do. I think about death all the time."

She is a music student, about to graduate from college, has been living for the past year with her fiancé and is very much in love with him, as he is with her. He too is in music.

When I asked her to talk about herself, she told me: "I'm afraid of failure. I won't even attempt something unless I'm assured of success. I think too much. I don't have a temper.

"War things and medical programs bother me. I was terrified of bugs as a child. Airplanes used to bother me, too, and storms. My mother used to cuddle me and comfort me when I was fearful. When I was afraid, my sister would call me stupid. I scold myself for being afraid. I often feel that I'm a burden to people. I sometimes get depressed.

"I think the fear of death will always be there. I wish I could turn off this part of my mind. I wish there were traumas to explain all this, but I've never had any traumas. When I get a headache, I'm always sure it is fatal. Then I worry that I will die, which makes the headache worse. Everything makes me think of death. I have to divert myself in the evening constantly—by eating, watching television, practicing my music or masturbating. I feel constantly that I'm coming a minute closer to death. What a waste of time to think of that all the time. But thinking this is a way of life with me."

Questioned about her family, Sandra told me that her father had been a sensitive, sweet person who enjoyed doing things for her and whom she adored. He had died suddenly just before she had graduated from high school. Her mother?

"A saint—a real saint," Sandra said. "She is kind, patient, never critical. When I was at home, my mother always enjoyed doing things for me and giving me things."

Here, then, is a young woman who came from a loving home, who is in love and is loved in return, who is bright, is intelligent, is attractive, has a deep interest in music and yet is an emotional cripple. Why should she suffer so much from, and devote so much of her attention to, an almost overpowering fear of death?

We had to examine closely her childhood, the parental attitudes to which she was exposed and the child of the past she carries with her now. She grew up in a good family with wonderful parents who made the mistake of catering to her. When she had fears as a youngster, her mother cuddled her and did everything possible to shield her from the fears. But, as Sandra could recall after we had talked at some length, her mother would be exasperated with her when she was fearful.

What it really came down to was that Sandra had been subjected to three principal practices as a child: overindulgence, including coddling of her fears; oversubmission to her fearful whims; and overt belittling on the part of her mother—and sister as well—shown through exasperation and resentment toward her fears.

Now, as an adult, Sandra had continued to treat herself with the same attitudes and practices. She coddled her fears, which only tended to strengthen them. She belittled herself resentfully. Her long-term pattern of being indulged, both by herself and by her mother, stood in the way of developing self-discipline. Her lack of self-discipline made it virtually impossible for her to control herself, particularly when she was fearful.

She had to face the fact that as long as she continued to treat herself indulgently, she would have fears; they and indulgence had always gone hand in hand.

There was nothing really mysterious about her phobia about death. It had grown out of her past conditioning and was being continued because she had continued to follow the conditioning. She would have to develop discipline. She would have to let the fears come, understand their origin, make sure she didn't belittle herself about them and then continue to do what she was going to do, whether she had fears or not. As an adult, she couldn't let the child inside force her to make activity decisions based on fears.

Not long afterward, Sandra decided to do what her fiancé had long urged: get married. She became so busy with the wedding plans that, she told me in some surprise, she was thinking less and less about her fears. That was a good indication that when her adult of the present took over from the child of the past, she could dispel the fears.

She is now much better. She is not driven by fears as she was before she started to treat herself with methods other than the old home methods of childhood. She still tends to slip back occasionally into old indulgent, self-critical ways and to become a little fearful, but she can quickly abort the relapses.

Bill and Bob

Bill, in his late twenties, is a college and professional-school graduate, with a good job in his chosen profession, married to an attractive and affectionate woman. He is hard-working, is doing well in his job, loves his wife and two young children. But he finds life humdrum, dull and tasteless, and he doesn't know why. He is self-critical, barks orders at himself, forces himself to get going, often feels depressed.

It doesn't make sense until we see that he is treating himself with the same perfectionistic, arm-twisting, order-barking attitudes that were present in his early home life. His almost-constant tendency to be critical of and unable to please himself is borrowed virtually intact from his past home background, where he was ordered about, barked at and criticized. And his self-criticism makes life dull and unsatisfying. Characteristically, whenever we turn on ourselves to any extent, the spark and color go out of things. If we beat on ourselves a little more critically when we fail at something, we get a heaviness in the chest and a tear in the eyes. And, with still more beating, we have a difficult time getting started and find that we have trouble sleeping, and our appetite falls off. And if we continue this self-punishment long enough, we become clinically depressed.

Bob is thirty-five, a bachelor, unhappy with himself and his life. He wants marriage but has never been able to bring himself to it. He often criticizes himself and has known many women and invariably has become critical of them. He worries about his failure to find someone whom he can marry, can't understand why he is unable to do so. But, in essence, he can't do so because he is living with old, borrowed, critically perfectionistic attitudes toward women instilled in him by his mother when he was growing up. Her indulgence of him was accompanied by a conviction that no woman would ever be worthy of "her boy." And what Bob has done for years, without recognizing it until recently, has been to search constantly for the nonexistent perfect woman and become bored with every woman who proves to be human.

Becoming Better Parents to Ourselves

If they are sought, attitudes carried over from long ago are to be found behind the emotional disturbances manifested in a wide variety of problems of living: marital and career difficulties, psychosomatic disorders, difficulties with interpersonal relationships, discontent with a life that seems incomprehensibly dull and unrewarding.

At some time or other, every one of us has observed an irritable child browbeating an embarrassed parent. It is just such a conflict that is going on inside many of us although we are not aware of the conflict or of the combatants in the internal struggle: on the one side, the child we were in the past, carrying over attitudes and reactions from childhood; on the other side, the adult we are today, embarrassed by these carryovers and so often frustrated by them.

But we need not remain helpless in the face of them. We can learn to identify the carryovers; we can very often do this on our own; they are not difficult to identify. And, having identified them, we can learn to control them, to set effective limits on them, and this too we can very often do on our own.

Effort, I must emphasize, is required. But it is effort, I have found, that is far from impossible for most of us.

Sigmund Freud developed the concept—a monumental breakthrough for which we all can be grateful—that human beings in adult life are influenced by what happened when they were children. His work dealt largely with infantile sexualism. He focused on the libido, the life force, and how it moved through various stages of development—oral, anal, oedipal—and how it might be perverted or stopped as the result of a child's relationship with a parent.

But this is only a small part of the whole picture. Freud arrived at his focus on infantile sexuality without the benefit of any significant body of knowledge about children, at a time when child psychiatry was a nonexistent discipline and without, to that point, ever having seen a child patient. He was chiefly guided by insights based almost entirely on limited observations of adults.

But as time has gone on, as both children and adults have been studied with increasing intensity, as new techniques of therapy have been tried and the results have been scrutinized, Freud's concepts have been modified. The importance of emotional attitudes and their constant interplay between children and parents has become apparent.

I had occasion, even in my first years of psychiatric practice, to become aware that some of Freud's best-known concepts of infantile sexuality were not necessarily applicable to my patients' problems. They did not explain the problems or lead to any helpful resolution of them.

Thus, for example, according to Freudian psychoanalytic theory, character is "fixated" at the "anal stage" by overattention to this area of the anatomy, particularly when a child is two to three years old. As a result, the theory holds, the individual later takes pleasure in mean, compulsive, sadomasochistic withholding activities. But I have known many patients who directly contradict this. One had congenital megacolon (Hirschsprung's disease), which meant that he was born without the normal nerve supply in the large bowel and could not eliminate normally. From birth, he had required enemas. Every few months, moreover, he had to have his bowels cleaned out surgically. With all the poking, prodding and fussing with his little behind all his life, is he an "anal" character? On the contrary, he is a loving, generous, happy person because his relationship with his mother was sound.

In our everyday lives as adults, in the attitudes we take toward ourselves and others and the problems we face, we can be influenced for the good by sound parent-child relationships in the past. When we are influenced for the bad, it is not so much, or at all, because of libidinal factors but because of unhappy, crippling parent-child relationships and the attitudes we carry over from them.

Understandably, the "unconscious" is something that over-awes, dismays, frightens many people. In books and articles, it has often been portrayed as a deep, dark internal "lake" of grotesque feelings that somehow rule us, make demands we must satisfy, overpower us, are beyond our control.

I am not talking here—and will not be anywhere in this book—about the "unconscious." I have long since given up talking to patients about it. I have never found it of value or necessary for helping anyone to understand why he or she is having problems, why he or she has troubled feelings.

It is parental-attitude carryovers we must be concerned with—and you know them. Every patient I have ever seen has been able to recall them. All of us can, with little difficulty, remember the attitudes our parents displayed toward us in our childhood. We may only dimly remember our reactions to those attitudes—because we may not have permitted those reactions to be expressed for fear of losing acceptance within the family. But the parental attitudes that led to them we do not forget. It is all the more difficult to forget them because we are actually apply-ing them now as adults.

We have no need to consider any mysterious "demons" of the "unconscious." We have to look at the borrowed attitudes of the past—at the "inner child of the past" who puts them to work within us. We have to become a good, and knowing, parent to this inner child and to ourselves so that no longer can there be interference with our adult goals and satisfactions.

There is nothing mysterious about any of this. We do have to do some searching but that can be adventurous as well as ultimately rewarding.

Self to Self: The Most Critical Transactions

There are some today who believe that much of what makes us unhappy, of what stands between us and our adult goals and expectations, lies in our faulty transactions with other people. There are some who even believe that the fault arises because we sometimes do not deal with others entirely on an adult-to-adult basis; at such times, our childish attitudes and our borrowed parental attitudes become involved. And they believe that in dealing with others we must be alert to recognize and control such childish and parental attitudes; in effect, we must practice transacting with others while exercising the control.

It seems to me that there is validity in that. But I believe firmly that it is our transactions with ourselves that very largely go to the heart of the matter and that we can transact effectively with others once we learn to transact effectively with ourselves.

You are already transacting with yourself because you are acting as a parent to yourself, willy-nilly; we all must do this. But, as we have noted, we tend to use on ourselves the same attitudes our parents did and even to use the same techniques they used to comfort or punish us. If those attitudes and techniques—which we shall define clearly in detail—painfully limit our opportunities and satisfactions as adults, we don't have to continue them. We can learn to become better parents to ourselves. We can understand parental attitudes and techniques and the childhood feelings they aroused, and we can mature now by accepting them for what they are, setting limits to them and becoming able to live our own way. And as we improve the transactions within ourselves, we can expect, almost certainly, that our transactions with others will improve and we will be as happy with and gratifying to others as we are with ourselves and our new-found abilities.

chapter 2

The Inner Child of the Past

One of the most pervasive misconceptions about human growth and development to be found in our culture is that we move from childhood to adulthood and the two are separate and distinct, joining only briefly at some point in time, after which the child is gone and only the adult lives on.

All of us have reason to know better. We become aware, every so often, that something reminiscently childish intrudes. We are busy with adult activities and thoughts. They are, or seem to be, in the forefront much of the time. But occasionally we have a feeling or urge, or we actually do something, and the thought crosses our mind: "That was childish."

On such occasions, some of us may even have a feeling of dismay. To even think of something childish, we may consider, is reprehensible, a reflection on our adulthood and worth. How could we, as mature persons, long since outgrown childhood, entertain such a thought? Where could it have come from? And, not understanding, we may become self-contemptuous.

"The dreams of childhood—its airy fables; its graceful, beautiful, humane, impossible adornments of the world beyond: so good to be believed in once; so good to be remembered when outgrown." So Charles Dickens wrote in his *Hard Times*.

And we do often remember them—and other childish feelings. We don't leave those feelings behind once and for all. Many of us, in fact, are dominated to some extent, and some of us to a great extent, by the feelings of childhood. They are present in all of us. We cannot eliminate them, cut them out and thereafter be free of them.

But we can recognize them, understand them and—when necessary—control them so that they are not permitted, when they might exert detrimental influences, to dominate our lives.

When childhood feelings do exert detrimental influences, they may do so in either of two broad ways. They may batter down our self-esteem, leading us to be unduly self-critical, self-abusive, self-belittling. When they do this, they become the prime barriers to the achievement of our adult goals. Or, they may lead to problems of self-control, of inability to discipline ourselves as adults must and as the achievement of even the simplest of adult goals requires. Sometimes they may cause us to be both self-belittling and undisciplined.

In psychology and psychiatry, it has long been known that a decisive determinant of personality is how one looks upon and feels about oneself.

How an individual deals with others, what he does and does not do, what he feels he can and cannot do, the dreams he dreams, the goals he sets for himself, his whole approach to life—all are influenced greatly, even primarily, by how he feels about himself.

Yet a man who feels himself to be ineffectual, weak and even stupid and a woman who feels herself to be unattractive and awkward are rarely as ineffectual, weak and stupid and as unattractive and awkward as their feelings convince them they are.

Almost invariably, such feelings are not objective, not determined by realistic appraisals. Rather, they are carryovers from childhood, and they are carried over in the "inner child of the past" all of us have.

That "inner child" is a product of parental attitudes to which we were exposed, our reactions to those attitudes and our feelings about our reactions.

The child is always with us; the feelings are, too. They are a real, living part of us. But they need not dominate us if we understand their origins and our almost automatic use of them.

The feelings, in the final analysis, are the results of a parent-child relationship back in the past that was something less than ideal. Before we can consider what is less than ideal and what are specific, noxious parental attitudes, we must consider what might be the ideal parent-child relationship.

Mutual-respect Balance

Although there have been many attempts to define the ideal parent-child relationship and some have been quite complex, it can, so far as I am concerned, be defined very simply. It is a relationship in which respect is given to the rights of both parents and child to live their lives in their own unique ways, to practice the skills and pursue the satisfactions of their age levels, so long as what they do does not infringe on the rights of another to do the same. Hopefully, in such a relationship, limits are set with sufficient firmness to preserve the rights of each on an ongoing basis.

This is a shirt-sleeve rather than fancy definition. It is much like the definition of a democratic society, allowing for individual uniqueness, differences in capacity, differences in interests, desires and goals between individuals and within the same individual at different times—only limited by one ban: no infringement on the rights of others.

Such a mutual-respect relationship has in it three elements. In addition to the first—respect for, caring for and fostering and preserving the flowering of the unique individualities of parents and child—and the second—limits placed where the behavior of one infringes on rights of others—there is the element of conflict: the recognition of its inevitability.

There is no such thing as a conflict-free relationship between parents and child. Hopefully, the conflicts are centered about infringements. Infringements always occur in parent-child relationships. They occur in adult relationships but are more common in those between parents and child because a child is an immature being whose job is to experiment with various kinds of behavior, to determine what is permissible and what not. Hopefully, parents will feel and say: "Look, my child, you chug along in your own unique way and we will love it unless and until you infringe on someone else's rights, at which time we will limit you."

In the preschool years, more interdiction is needed—to the extent that a toddler must be kept from unwittingly hurting himself. He needs to be warned about and kept from exposing himself to common dangers such as light sockets, potentially harmful medications, busy streets. But, hopefully, not long after the preschool years, interdiction is confined largely to preventing interference with others' rights.

If, through the growing years, a child is accepted by his parents at each stage of development without unrealistic expectations about his behavior or achievement, if he is firmly but not belittlingly limited when his actions infringe on others' rights and if he is gradually, progressively, called upon to participate in and help with the ongoing work of the family, he will, as an adult, tend to be self-respecting, responsible and respectful of others. He will carry with him parental attitudes that are useful in helping him achieve goals and satisfactions of adult life.

But most of us grew up in homes where the ideal of mutual-respect balance was not fully achieved. For various reasons, our parents had at least occasional difficulties in keeping us as children in individual perspective. They may have expressed toward us attitudes that were harmful.

With departures from mutual-respect balance, a child reacts: he may be hurt and show the hurt, or have fears, or become excessively demanding, or display temper tantrums, or develop psychosomatic disorders.

Parental Pathogens

Certain parental attitudes are pathogenic, or damaging. They make for departures from mutual-respect balance. They may produce obvious harm in a child but the damage does not stop there. With repeated exposure to such attitudes, a child internalizes them and grows up to use them upon himself as an adult.

When an adult does this, treating himself with parental pathogenic attitudes, the "child of the past" within him tends to respond much as he did as an actual child when they were inflicted originally. Now the adult, although outwardly an adult, is also a hurt-inflicting parent to a reacting inner child and becomes a hurting adult with inner pain.

The pathogenic attitudes are fairly characteristic, as are the usual responses to them. Often more than a single pathogen was present in our childhoods, and some of us as adults visit upon ourselves a combination of hurtful attitudes.

Let's consider them here just briefly, for we will be looking into them later in greater detail and considering then, too, how specifically they can be modified. But perhaps even with the brief discussion here you may begin to suspect that one or more were present in your early home life and may have contributed to difficulties you face today.

Overcoercion

Perhaps the most common pathogenic parental attitude, overcoercion involves constant direction, supervision and redirection of a child with an almost endless river of instructions and anxious reminders, without adequate regard for the right and the need of a child to pursue his own activities and interests in his own way.

The child may submit, learning to rely excessively on outside direction. Or he may resist, either directly or passively; he may dawdle, daydream, forget, procrastinate or use other forms of resistance.

Later, in adulthood, the overcoerced child may continue to rely unduly on outside direction, or he may order, direct and admonish himself much as did his parents. And the child of the past may rebel against the overdirection now just as the actual physical child once did, and the adult may dawdle, daydream and procrastinate even as he urges himself on. He may complain of always being tired; he may lack ability to make decisions; he may put things off until forced to meet a deadline and may then hastily turn out a mediocre job. He is the victim in adulthood of the old pushing-resisting cycle of his childhood.

Oversubmission

Almost as common as the overly coercive is the parent who submits to a child's whims, demands, temper and impulsiveness. Perhaps out of a concern for surrounding the child with loving care, the parent who is oversubmissive disregards his own rights and makes the child "boss," himself becoming slave.

The child's response to such a parental attitude almost invariably is to become more demanding, more impulsive, more insistent upon having his demands fulfilled, more given to temper tantrums when the demands are not met. He has difficulty in considering any rights of others.

Since the child rarely if ever has had "no" said to him and made to stick, since no limits were placed upon his immature impulses, he has little if any concept of limits and becomes unable to say "no" to himself as an adult. So he may eat too much or drink too much or smoke too much; he may lose his temper quickly; his thoughtlessness, stemming from great difficulty in keeping in mind the rights and dignity of others, often antagonizes others, jeopardizing his adult relationships in marriage, at work, in social intercourse. And he often finds that his impulsiveness sets up roadblocks and makes necessary detours that impede the achievement of his adult goals.

Perfectionism

Perfectionism is a pathogen commonly found among "successful" people who are never content with their achievements, who must strive endlessly, pathetically, fruitlessly for still greater "success," for perfection.

Perfectionism is created in a child reared in a home where the prevailing attitude is one of conditional acceptance—that is, where the parents accept the child only when his performance is unusual, "beyond his years." Unless the child demonstrates behavior and achievements calling for greater maturity than he has or can comfortably manifest at the time, the parents withhold acceptance.

The child responds to such an attitude with excessive striving and with abnormal, overserious preoccupation with physical, intellectual or social accomplishments. At the same time, he grows up with a feeling that he can never meet the standards his parents have set for him and he therefore feels unworthy. He may keep striving for achievements beyond his capabilities or give up in the belief that nothing he can do is worthwhile and he himself is not worthwhile.

As an adolescent, preoccupied with achievement, he may be able to accept himself only sporadically when his performance reaches unnaturally high levels. As an adult, he tends for the most part to belittle himself and his efforts, to be disappointed in himself and his achievements, even though his accomplishments, as viewed objectively by others, are found to be satisfactory and even more than satisfactory. For him, life rarely has any color or sparkle; he is often depressed.

Overindulgence

Some parents constantly shower a child with presents, privileges and services, often without any expression of desire for them by the child and without regard for his actual needs. While an overly submissive parent waits for and accedes to a child's demands, the overly indulgent besieges the child with "treats" without the child's asking.

Sooner or later, the child's response to the inundation, the ever-overflowing cornucopia, is characterized by boredom and blasé behavior. At the same time, he loses initiative and spontaneity, and his capacity for persistent effort suffers.

As an adult, the overindulged person tends to be self-indulgent and to blame others or "life" if he no longer receives goods and services without effort. He may attach himself, in dependent fashion, to anyone who will be as indulgent as his parents were. Yet, though he wants to restore and maintain the indulgent atmosphere of his childhood years, if he succeeds in doing so, he will react much as he did as a child—with boredom, blasé behavior, peevishness and apathy.

Punitiveness

Punitiveness is a common parental attitude that often is combined with overcoercion and perfectionism or another pathogenic attitude. In parts of our culture, punitiveness—the actual physical punishment of a child—is even considered essential for proper "disciplining" and "training."

Some punitive parents vent personal hostility and aggression on a child. More often than not, it is the parents' own subjective feelings rather than any error or infraction of rules by a child that determine the excessive punishment. Generally, punitive parents have had the same treatment themselves as children and may believe sincerely that it is needed.

But a child who is punished excessively reacts with behavior that invites punishment, has longings for retaliation and is self-devaluating. Which of these characteristics will be prominent in adulthood depends largely upon what associated attitudes his parents displayed toward him in childhood. If the parents were neglecting (see below) as well as punitive, he will tend to be retaliatory in the main, fiercely desirous of revenge, in part at least because he lacks ability to enjoy human relationships. If his parents were affectionate while being punitive, he may punish himself by placing himself in punitive situations as an adult and may carry over an inordinate amount of self-criticism and feelings of guilt. If his parents combined punitiveness with submissiveness, he may tend to retaliate on impulse and then shortly afterward may experience contrition for what he has done.

Neglect

Neglect is often found in homes where parents are frequently absent or busily preoccupied and where little consideration is given to the child's right to have the parents' interested assistance at each level of his development. The children of the prominent and the financially successful can be victims of neglect; so can the children of parents overwhelmed with work, poverty, alcoholism and other problems. Death and divorce may be factors.

A child neglected in early life often lacks the ability to form close and meaningful relationships, first as a child, and then later as an adult. Because no one was interested enough to set limits on him as a child, he has difficulty setting limits on himself as an adult. Because, from his viewpoint, no one looked upon him as a meaningful human being in childhood, he has trouble, as an adult, in seeing himself in healthy perspective, in establishing a self-identity that would enable him to relate to others. He tends to gratify his impulses at the expense of others.

The partially neglected child grows up with resentment and disappointment in adult relationships that do not and cannot satisfy like the all-protecting and all-giving parent relationship that the child longed for but didn't have.

Rejection

Fortunately, this parental attitude—which grants the child no accepted place in the family—is not very common. A child so treated may look upon himself as isolated and helpless; he may develop bitter, hostile, anxious feelings as a consequence; and, also as a consequence, he may suffer from severe self-devaluation.

As an adult, the rejected person remains bitter and hostile.

He also may have, inside, a great longing to be cared for by someone else, to be dependent. But he may be so upset by the side-by-side existence within him of tumultuous dependent and hostile feelings that he cannot relate comfortably to anyone. He may suffer, too, from intense fears (of death and disease, for example) and from generalized anxiety.

Excessive Responsibility

Because of economic circumstances or problems within themselves, some parents foist responsibility on a child at an early age, responsibility that is excessive in view of the child's age. A mother, upon the death of her husband, looks to a thirteen-year-old son to carry on the farm work. In wartime, children may be displaced from their homes, separated from parents, and an oldest child may be given the responsibility of taking care of the little ones.

In these and other situations, a child may take on a burden beyond his years and carry it out well, but not without missing out on and hungering for things that are normal at his age: child play and the reassuring feeling that someone older is taking responsibility for and watching over and caring for him. The child laden with premature and excessive responsibility may or may not feel resentment; he is likely to do so if he considers the responsibility to be unfair and he is not given acceptance and praise.

But even without resentment, there may be a serious effect that he carries with him throughout childhood, adolescence and adulthood. He may go on to assume more responsibilities than are really necessary, may always feel hard-pressed and may never get around to giving himself carefree times because of an inability to play and relax and even a nagging anxiety that develops whenever he tries to play and relax. Beyond restricting his own personal life, the drive toward always assuming excessive responsibility and always being unable to ease off and play may affect his relationships with others, particularly with spouse and children.

Should Parents Be Blamed?

However much pathogenic parental attitudes account for limitations on our capacities and achievements, there are dangers in blaming our parents for our problems, including the likelihood that they do not properly deserve the blame.

Commonly, very young children view their parents as god-like beings but then, as they grow older, recognize that however wonderful the parents may have truly been, they were still human beings with their share of imperfections and frailties that go with humanness.

In my own experience with thousands of parents—the over-coercive, oversubmissive, punitive, neglectful and others—I have found few who were not concerned about their children, who did not love them and who did not try to the best of their ability to provide for them. But the best of their ability was limited, often severely limited, because of their own victimization by the pathogenic attitudes handed on to them by their own parents and by their own "inner child of the past" who dominated them as adults. I have been impressed, too, by how often a parent victimized by a parental pathogen and now making his or her own child a victim of it has come for help, recognizing that something was wrong and hurtful.

It may seem logical to pin blame on parents: After all, did they not hold the harmful attitudes, create the emotional atmosphere of one's childhood? They must be to blame! If so, then grant them that they should be commended for the positive, helpful attitudes they passed on. And grant them, too, that if they could have done better, almost all of them would have done better.

There is no grace in turning our parents into scapegoats. There is no comfort in it. And there may be added harm to ourselves.

A preoccupation with placing blame begs the question of what we can now do to help ourselves. It can materially hinder helping ourselves. Blaming parents often can be a way of expressing feelings of hostility and aggression from childhood, a way of continuing childhood, a way of not becoming good parents to ourselves because we will not abandon the idea that everything was up to them and now we can do nothing about our problems because of their failings.

For some of us, too, any idea that blame must be placed on parents frightens us off from insightful examination of our present problems and what we can do about them. The mere fact that parental failings, pathogenic attitudes, need to be recognized and understood may make us regard any effort to solve our problems as disloyal.

Our purpose in identifying our child of the past, the child within us now, the parental attitudes involved in creation of that child and operating within us now, is not to build a case against our parents but rather to help ourselves become free of the damaging, limiting influences and effects such attitudes have produced.

chapter 3

The Essence of What We
Have to Do

All of us have heard and perhaps have even used the familiar saying "That's the way I am!" There is a prevailing concept that we have our formative years—a period covering childhood and adolescence, and perhaps even very early adulthood, when we are molded—and, thereafter, for better or worse, the shape of our personality and even of our life has been established.

The essence of what we have to do is to discount that saying. If we say it and believe it, we are stuck with what we are and with continuing to get hurt. But if we say, instead, "The way I react is only part of me, a part that incorporates some mistaken attitudes about me in the first place," we can begin to understand why we are the way we are and understand, too, that whatever our age, we are not inevitably doomed to continue to be that way. We can begin to treat ourselves in our own way, a rational way that is more respectful of our individuality.

Realistically, we must recognize that we can learn to treat ourselves in our own way, we can become good parents to ourselves; but we never get rid of the tendency to return to treating ourselves with old home attitudes.

To some people, this may seem discouraging, but it should not be. We never get rid of dust once and for all. Just because we don't and must expect to dust today and perhaps a week from today is no reason for discouragement. It's a fact of life that we have to deal with dirty dishes three times a day; we adjust to the fact.

We can adjust, too, to the fact that we carry within us old parental stereotype attitudes we use on ourselves and confuse with the truth and that our job is to cut through these stereotypes, to recognize them for what they are—garbage from the past—and to determine that we are not going to use them on ourselves any longer but rather that we are going to treat ourselves in our own way as we have a right and need to do as adults. And we can adjust to the fact, too, that these stereotypes have been recorded, in effect, on a tape* that is within us and there is no button to turn off, once and for all, the old recording. We can expect to hear it play from time to time but that does not mean that we always have to believe it and act on it.

Treating Ourselves in Our Own Way

What do we mean by treating ourselves in our own way?

You will recall that we talked about the good parent-child relationship as one in which mutual-respect balance was present.

If we are good parents to ourselves in adult life, to our present selves and our child-of-the-past selves, we can respect everything we think and feel. We don't become critical of ourselves—don't moralize, berate or undermine ourselves because of any thoughts or feelings we have. But we do apply two questions to everything we think and feel. If we express or follow through on a thought or feeling, will we be infringing upon somebody else's rights or dignity? And, if expressed, will there be any infringement on our own adult goals, any hindrance to our getting to where we want to go and achieving what we want to achieve?

If the answer to either question is yes, we don't give the thought or feeling expression. We swallow it. But we don't scold

* An additional discussion of "childhood tapes" can be found in T. A. Harris, *I'm OK—You're OK* (New York: Harper & Row, 1969).

or criticize or diminish ourselves because of the thought or feeling. We simply insist that we will not express it no matter how much it kicks around inside. We take the kicking and say, "Sorry, but this is not to be expressed."

The Two Hindrances

To treat ourselves in our own way, to be good parents to ourselves, two things are essential. We must respect ourselves and our thoughts and feelings, considering them and separating out those that deserve expression and those that do not. And we have to set limits and swallow or control those that do not deserve expression.

For some people, the prime problem is control. They are not accustomed to control. Their inner child, dominating them, demands expression for almost any thought or feeling. And the resulting impulsiveness leads to mistaken action and often to remorse.

On the other hand, some people have no difficulty with control but have great difficulty with self-respect. They castigate themselves and critically undermine themselves for their thoughts or feelings. They are the self-belittlers, and their sufferings from lack of self-esteem can be intense.

We shall be dealing in detail in Part II with self-belittlement, the many ways it manifests itself and takes its toll, the particular parental attitudes that foster it. We shall be dealing similarly in Part III with problems of self-control.

Responsibility to Self

"In this incredibly complex world, each of us needs to examine ourselves—our motivations, our goals," Dr. Roy Menninger of the Menninger Clinic has observed. "As a search for a clearer idea of what we stand for, toward what we are headed and what we think is truly important, this kind of continuing self-scrutiny can help to stabilize us in a world of explosive change."

And Menninger has also underscored what we are so much

concerned with in this book: "A close look at ourselves contributes to that sought-after capacity for autonomy, and gives us
greater ability to make wise and useful choices, to exert some
control over our own destiny."

It has been observed frequently that it is not easy to look
closely at ourselves. But it seems to me that the difficulty has
been that we do not know really what to look for and have had
no guidance to help us know.

Many of us may recognize that we have a deep responsibility
to ourselves and this involves at the very least as close an
examination and deep a commitment as we give to the everyday
problems that confront us. Some of us, especially when prodded
by crisis or worry, do try to look into ourselves and review ourselves and ask questions.

We may ask ourselves: What are my goals? Toward what
am I aiming? Are my objectives realistic? Are they for real—
would I truly value them if I achieved them?

We may also ask ourselves: Am I properly using my time
and energy? Am I too often busy, busy with things that are not of
prime importance to me—to the detriment of those that are?

At least to this extent, some of us do try to step back and view
and review ourselves with more or less success.

But even more important, in the final analysis, is an understanding of who we are and why, of what we have become and
whether this is what we should be, of the self-to-self interactions
we have, of the child of the past within us and the parental
pathogens the child may be bearing, and the conflicts between
the child of the past and the adult we are that keep us from
being the adult we should and could be.

"We have met the enemy—and they is us," Pogo remarked in
his inimitable fashion. Not quite true. Close to the truth. The
enemy is not ourselves but rather what we carry within us. And
even that is not quite accurate either. For the enemy within us is
an enemy only if we don't recognize him. Once recognized, the
enemy—the inner child of the past with the parental pathogen or
pathogens he carries—becomes no enemy to be vanquished but
only a force to be respected and controlled.

It does take courage to face ourselves, to look within, to

gain understanding. Any status quo, however hurtful it may be, has elements of comfortableness in it. We may fear to upset the status quo—our "this is the way I am" fatalism—because of some vague fear of what we may find if we do the upsetting. To conquer this fear and to act does take courage.

Yet the fact is that we really need have no fear that we will come upon hobgoblins, buried secrets that had better remain buried, horrifying atrocities committed upon us or of our own commission.

part **II**

Self-belittlement

chapter 4

Self-belittlement: What Is It?

No matter who we are—college student, housewife, business-person, factory worker—all of us have an image of self, a way we habitually think of ourselves, that is crucial to our emotional health, our physical health and our effectiveness and productivity.

Some of us suffer from one form of distorted self-image: a view of ourselves as superior to others, possessed of rare genius, unable to do wrong. We may be either snob or dictator: snob if we feel we are better than everyone else and dictator if we also assume the right to infringe on other people's rights. Often snobs and dictators are successful if success is measured in terms of achievement or of imposing will on other people. But in terms of happiness and fulfillment as human beings, their lives leave much to be desired.

Much more common as a form of self-image distortion, however, is self-belittlement. A large army of us—and I include myself among them—tend to turn against ourselves, to regard ourselves scornfully. Our appearance, our conversation, our behavior, our achievements are never as handsome, as clever, as proper or as worthwhile as we feel they ought to be. No matter what we do, our performance is somehow unacceptable to us.

We view ourselves almost as a different breed. We hurt—with a pain that those not so afflicted have a hard time understanding.

Telling ourselves how terrible we are, we go around with a heavy emptiness in our chests. We restlessly seek peace of mind. We read self-help books. They often tell us not to be so hard on ourselves. "Be more friendly to yourself," they advise. We recognize that treating ourselves more kindly would probably help. But how can we be artificially kind to ourselves when we are honestly so disappointed in what we are and do? So we return again and again to the old familiar habit of viewing ourselves with scorn because our shortcomings seem to us so obvious.

Self-belittlement—the uncomfortable condition of feeling unacceptable to oneself—is always painful. It never serves a useful purpose. Few attributes of personality are more hazardous. Although it is rarely recognized as such, self-belittlement is the primary menace to mental health today.

An occasional feeling of inferiority or inadequacy may be experienced by everyone since no one can excel in everything. But when feelings of inadequacy or inferiority become dominant, they produce chronic unhappiness and interfere with efficiency and social adjustment.

Self-devaluation takes root in the powerful emotional atmosphere of childhood, where parental attitudes play on a child's receptive, immature personality and produce a self-belittling response. And it may then flourish in an achievement-oriented society that does not tolerate failure or the unwillingness to "make it."

We have to learn all we can about any tendency we have toward self-belittlement and understand how, specifically, we can cope with it. Achieving healthy self-regard is an essential pursuit. If you already have it, you are indeed fortunate. You may not need to dwell on this part of the book for yourself but you can use it to understand those around you who are not as fortunate emotionally.

Forms of Self-belittlement

Self-belittlement manifests itself in several ways, some of them fairly apparent. But there are subtle varieties as well.

Direct Self-deprecation

This is the most common form. It may involve repeated severe self-criticism. You may find yourself saying habitually to yourself: "I was so stupid," "What I did was so silly," "Why must I be so lazy?" "That proves I am really inadequate." The words *stupid, silly, ridiculous, ugly, dumb, inadequate, unworthy, bad, sinful* and *lazy* should have no place in the vocabulary we use in thinking of ourselves, but for many of us they do.

Almost anything can be turned into a critical club over your head if you allow it to be. "My nose is too long," "I am too fat," "I am all thumbs," "I can't remember names," "I'm not good at speeches," "I never was any good at math," "I'm tongue-tied at a party" and "I'm OK until the boss calls me into his office and then I can't think of anything" are a few examples.

We all have our deficiencies and difficulties. But telling yourself that you are unworthy because of some deficiency or difficulty doesn't help in any way. Self-criticism and self-belittlement only make you depressed and miserable. Moreover, they tend to keep you from dealing constructively with a deficiency or difficulty about which you are so scornful of yourself.

Unfavorable Comparison

This is another common form of self-belittlement. The self-belittler makes unfavorable comparisons of himself with others, always coming out second best.

You may say to yourself: "I'm no good in comparison with this other person (brother, sister, father, business partner, spouse, good friend) who is so much more (beautiful, competent, energetic, intelligent) than I am" or "I wish I could be as good as Dick . . . he's so intelligent, incisive, self-confident and popular" or "I'm in love with Mary but there's no hope . . . I'll never be good enough for her."

The more you put someone close to you, or someone you know or would like to know, on a pedestal—essentially assigning vast superiority to him or her because you assign vast inferiority to yourself—the more of a gap you place between the two of you and the more you come to belittle yourself in comparison. And the price you often pay for such idealization of another and deprecation of self is a twisted relationship that makes it impossible for the other person to be close to you.

Distrust of Self

With this third type of belittlement, there is a feeling of inadequacy in regard to the future rather than the present. You may say: "I'm doing all right now, but just wait till next week (or exam time, or when I make that speech, or when I take that new job); I am certain to be inadequate then, to goof up."

Such self-belittlement usually makes more for feelings of anxiety rather than depression. It spoils the present; it makes the future more difficult than it need be.

Projection

Sometimes self-devaluation may seem to come not from within oneself but from outside. You may project onto others the feelings you have about yourself so that it seems that they, not you, have these feelings.

You may say: "They think I am stupid, ugly, incompetent, lazy" or "They look upon me as clumsy, foolish" or "They will be laughing behind their hands when I make that speech or suggestion."

You react to those around you as if, indeed, they had such feelings about you without bothering to find out whether they really do. And your hurt is compounded; your own basic self-belittlement, recognized or not recognized for what it is, is multiplied by the number of persons to whom you impute belittling attitudes toward you.

Choosing Inferiority

Our very life styles sometimes bespeak our self-deprecation eloquently. Perhaps, for example, your job position reflects your inner feeling of "I am inferior—I deserve no more than this job" and yet the job may be far below your true capacity. Some of us choose marital partners who devaluate us.

You may shift from one form of self-belittlement to another, employ several simultaneously or at various times express all of the modes. All are painful, destructive. All keep you from being free to grow and develop in the way you were meant to.

Example

Let's look in on a fairly typical self-belittler. Mrs. Roberta Williams is a tall, slim, well-dressed woman whose story, as she told it to me in my office, was essentially this:

"I have been depressed and unhappy for a long time, find it difficult to get up in the morning and face the day, and I know I am often irritable and hard to live with. I have a good husband and fine little girl of five. I've had problems with my mother ever since childhood and I don't want my reactions toward her to color what I do with my husband and daughter.

"When I married my husband, I felt a sense of freedom for the first time in my life. He is an architect, well liked in his firm, kind to me, very understanding. But I cannot get rid of my depressed feelings.

"My father is a good man, hard worker, quiet and, I think, lonely. When I was a child, he and Mother would argue. She would accuse him of being unfaithful. I would worry about how I was going to keep the family together. By about six, I was actually afraid of my mother.

"She was strict, correct, would teach me the Bible with one

hand and whip me unmercifully with the other. Even now I have an unhealthy approach to Christianity. Our church was strict. I won't want to teach a religion of fear to my daughter. My mother would whip me or use church doctrine to make me feel guilty. I worry about raising my child; I don't know what normal is.

"My parents held grudges. I always tried to get them to talk to each other. Fighting and conflict bother me. It's often hard for me to have a good time; I feel guilty about it. I wish I could relax and have some fun at least once in a while.

"I get angry with myself. I have a hard time making even simple decisions. I feel that I am existing, not living. I procrastinate and then I fuss with myself. I never smile or get a kick out of things. I even resent my little girl sometimes, and this really bothers me. Lately, I've not wanted to talk to anybody. I feel that I'm a drag on my husband. I tell myself to quit complaining because I really have it so good."

That is Mrs. Williams—damaged severely in her self-regard in her childhood years. It serves no purpose to blame her mother, who did what she thought was best according to the strict, moralistic rules of her own upbringing.

Mrs. Williams now has gradually been able to free herself of her mother and her mother's critical methods, which she was using on herself. Especially when she is tired or ill, she will always have some tendency to treat herself with her mother's methods, but for the most part she has slowly learned to treat herself in her own way, which is more respectful. No longer does she automatically inflict upon herself old, borrowed, punishing methods that have no real relationship to objective evaluations of herself now.

What Mrs. Williams had to do—and we will be dealing with the specifics later and see them applied to other illustrative cases—was what we all have to do. We have to assess our self-regard to determine if it is functioning satisfactorily or has been damaged. We have to recognize what influences can damage it in childhood and continue to do so when carried over into adult life. We have to work, with an understanding of those influences, at repairing the damage and then make certain that our rebuilt self-esteem, now normal and healthy, is kept that way through adequate daily nourishment.

Recognizing Self-belittlement

Self-belittlement can resemble other feelings, but it is fairly easy to recognize if we have guidelines. It can be differentiated from feeling sorry for oneself, from honest appraisal of the quality of one's work and behavior and from guilt, loneliness, grief and humility.

Feeling sorry for yourself can be a self-respecting matter. You may realistically recognize that you are having a hard time and feel sorry that you are. Feeling sorry for yourself can be useful if it serves as an impetus to work out of a difficulty or if it helps you get the assistance you may need. It is hurtful if you use it as an excuse to do nothing about your difficulties or to cling dependently to someone else for never-ending reassurance and support. However, self-belittlers use feeling sorry for themselves as a club. "I'm just feeling sorry for myself," they say scornfully, then proceed to call themselves weak, inadequate and so on.

You can honestly appraise your appearance, your behavior and the quality of your work without belittling yourself. I remember reading the letter of a college athlete to his family in which he made this refreshing appraisal: "Our opponents found a big hole in our line. That hole was me." But he did not go on about what an awful person he was because of it. You can practice to become better in the skill or job you have chosen without need to castigate yourself or apologize for being an interested continuing learner.

Very few people are beautiful enough to win beauty contests, but most of us can be attractive if we are well groomed, interested, alert, kindly and generous. There is no reason to berate ourselves because we lack great beauty or talent.

Guilt is the painful feeling of being unacceptable to one's group because of having done something that infringed on group standards, customs or morals. Guilt is a tool by which individuals are kept in line with a group's goals and purposes. The discomfort of guilt furnishes the stimulus for an individual to seek to right a wrong he has done or make restitution so he can once again live in the security of group acceptance.

A guilty person may be self-belittling—but, on the other hand, a self-belittler may not, in fact, be guilty at all. The self-belittler may not have infringed in any way on group standards or morals. He may, in fact, feel outside of a group that actually accepts him. A guilty person can make amends and be relieved of his unhappy inner feeling, but the self-belittler continues to be unhappy without relief so long as his self-belittlement hammer pounds away inside no matter what he does to make amends.

Loneliness is the uncomfortable feeling that comes to an individual who, by force of circumstances, has too few opportunities for gratifying interpersonal exchange. The self-belittler, too, is lonely but for a different reason. Self-belittlement creates a barrier that others can penetrate only with great difficulty. When someone knocks on the personal door of a self-belittler, there is often a sign on the door, "Out to lunch," and the self-belittler retreats into the back room of his personal life for intense self-belittlement and further loneliness. The person on the outside, the knocker at the door, becomes discouraged and goes away, not because he found the self-belittler unattractive or unworthy but because he found him unavailable.

Grief is that empty, desolate feeling that comes from loss of a loved one. The grief-stricken person may be temporarily self-belittling as well as sad, indecisive, apathetic and even inert. But grief is dissolved with time and with opportunity to talk about the lost loved one with sympathetic, supportive people. The self-belittler has some of the symptoms of the grief-stricken. But the symptoms go on and on in the self-belittler while they are only temporary for the grief-stricken but self-respecting.

Respectful humility is the inner feeling of being no better than others but as infinitely worthwhile as anyone. Self-belittling is the feeling of not measuring up to the worthwhileness that others possess.

For many years, I have been confronted in my office with a virtually endless flow of patients who tell of their painful symptoms, who have been brought finally to seek help because the pain has become almost unbearable. They tell me about how they cannot stand themselves and hate themselves, about their past home lives and how persons back there criticized and compared them unfavorably with others so often in the name of discipline. I have seen thousands of problem children, too, and many adolescents in trouble, and I have come to recognize parent-child difficulties that, when left unmodified, turn children and adolescents into self-belittlers before one's eyes.

chapter 5

Symptoms of Self-belittlement

The symptoms of self-belittlement are varied. You may have one or many. Here is a list of them.

Depression

Everything seems dull and lackluster. You regard the future as well as the present without zest or enthusiasm and without hope. You have difficulty in getting started in the morning, in facing each new day. At times during the day there may be a heavy oppressive feeling in the chest. You sigh often. Food has little appeal. You have little interest in sex. You often find that you have difficulty with sleep and that you wake up in the night and cannot readily get back to sleep. You may often feel like crying. You may experience a pervasive kind of stifling of initiative, ambition, productivity and creativity.

Alienation

You feel that you are on the outside of a circle within which things are happening, life is going on, people are participating and interacting happily and rewardingly—all people but you. You feel that you have nothing to say to people and that they strain themselves unwillingly to spend time with you or speak with you. You feel cut off—in a bleak, empty, painful, hopeless world of self with a wide gulf separating you from others.

Inertia

You may have a feeling of being mired down, without zip or spring, always tired. Small tasks are big burdens for you; you know they must get done but you find even the thought of doing them oppressive and it seems to you that you must make unduly great efforts even to bring yourself to get started doing them.

Hunger for Love and Acceptance

You want acceptance very much but find yourself never quite satisfied even when you get it. You face every situation with a nagging doubt: "Will I do all right and be accepted?" When you actually are accepted, when someone tries to show you that you are, you feel uncomfortable and may doubt the other person's sincerity.

Because you have little in the way of acceptance supplies within you, you feel empty and seek—often and feverishly—to find such supplies on the outside. I use the term "acceptance supplies" to indicate those attitudes that we get from within ourselves or from others that contribute to a feeling of worth and belonging.

Inner acceptance supplies include satisfaction in your work, satisfaction in goals and values to which you have committed yourself and appropriate commendations and compliments from within. Outer acceptance supplies include respect, admiration, compliments, friendship, expressions of love—all those things given by others that help to make you feel good about yourself.

But if you are self-derogatory, you are short on or lacking in inner acceptance supplies; you cannot commend yourself or even accept anything you do or feel as worthwhile. And any acceptance supplies available to you from the outside often bump up hard against the self-critical wall you have erected so they do not really get through to help fulfill your need.

Irritability

Since the people you depend upon for love never quite can provide the fulfillment you need, you may turn on them irritably for not providing more fulfillment. You are touchy, feel slights when none is intended. You may exhaust the patience of a loved one who cannot help coming to feel that, touchy and irritable as you are, it is hopeless to try to get through to you. And when the loved one then stops making his or her previous all-out effort and gives you less of the acceptance supplies vital for you, you feel more irritable, more self-critical, more alienated and more depressed.

Not all self-belittling people display irritability. Some feel they are to blame for the inability of the loved one to fulfill them. And this feeling only goes to prove to them how unacceptable they are, and they become more self-critical and depressed, and the wall between them and their loved ones becomes even thicker.

Anxiety

Most habitual self-belittlers feel anxiety much of the time. Anxiety is a kind of dread that something bad is going to happen. A self-critical, anxious person reacts much as does a child who anticipates being called on the carpet by a stern parent. The anxiety flows from an anticipation of criticism. As a self-belittler, you may even criticize yourself for feeling anxious in a situation that does not warrant the amount of dread or fear you have. And the chiding you give yourself fulfills the prophecy that led to anxiety in the first place—the prophecy of some chiding to come.

Deterioration of Personal Care and Work

When self-belittling produces a feeling of hopelessness and the corollary feeling of not caring that so often accompanies hopelessness, interest in appearance may decline. You may select dull, shapeless clothing and give less attention to hair grooming and other details of personal care. You take no pride in yourself, feeling that there is nothing to take pride in. Your work may be done haphazardly; you may let important tasks slide along uncompleted; you may miss appointments. Not caring any more, nothing seems important or worth effort.

Psychosomatic Symptoms

In turning against yourself, you may alter not only the psychologic but also the physiologic balance in your body. Physical symptoms, many and varied, may develop.

Anxiety releases the powerful hormone adrenalin into the bloodstream from the adrenal glands atop the kidneys. So does anger. The emotions of anger and fear and the release of adrenalin they trigger are responses to critical situations that originally served to make animals physiologically ready to meet those situations, to fight an enemy or flee from him.

When you turn against yourself in anger or become anxious in anticipation of self-scolding, the adrenalin may pour into your bloodstream and produce several responses. Your heart beats faster, your breathing becomes more rapid, your mouth becomes dry, your digestive processes stop so less blood need flow to the gastrointestinal tract and more can go to brain and muscles to aid you in fighting or fleeing.

If you don't fully understand the emergency adrenalin outpouring and the responses it produces, you can misinterpret what you feel and start worrying that you have heart trouble because of the rapid breathing and pounding of the heart or stomach trouble (indigestion) because blood has been shunted away temporarily to muscles.

Self-belittlement also can cause undue fatigue since, in addition to your ordinary work, you are carrying on a civil war within you. Self-belittlement also can cause muscle tension—for, with anger or anxiety, the muscles are readied for fight or flight but aren't used for either, and their tensed readiness is continued. Such muscle tension is a frequent cause of headaches and backaches.

These are common symptoms of self-belittling. They hurt entirely too much. Now that we have reviewed the symptoms, we are ready to look more closely into the sources of pervasively harmful injuries to self-esteem.

chapter 6

Family Sources of Self-belittlement

If you have the self-belittling habit, any one of several parental pathogens or combinations of pathogens is the most probable major source of it. Let's consider a few examples.

Don

At forty, Don was a competent, hard-working research scientist yet was extremely self-critical, largely isolated and unable to get any satisfaction out of life. He had difficulties associating well on the social level. Deep personal attachments were almost impossible for him. Although he could make friends, he couldn't keep them, and sometimes his antagonisms took him away from people with whom he had begun to have some feelings of close attachment. Personal relationships seemed stifling to him. He had met a woman eight years earlier and they had been engaged and disengaged many times. He admired her glamorous looks but deplored her flamboyance and lack of studiousness. He was frequently hurt by her as she humiliated him in front of others and went for long periods without speaking to him.

Don had a compulsion to work and to be perfectionistic; nothing he did ever seemed adequate to him. "I criticize myself constantly," he said. "I withhold approval of myself. I don't have confidence."

Don grew up with what he called "the world's worst self-belittling" about his physical condition. He had been sickly as a baby; throughout his childhood, he had been skinny, under-muscled. "I used to be so ashamed of my body; I would roll my sleeves down because I was skinny. I was picked on by other boys."

In high school, he decided to build himself up physically and went in for weight lifting. He was pleased with the results, continued the weight lifting while in the Army and afterward largely sacrificed social life to keep building himself up physically.

There was antagonism between Don's parents. His father had a drinking problem; his mother, always sickly, was critical of the father. The father never gave the boy approval. Although Don did well in school, he was criticized for any average grades; only the best would do. His mother fussed over Don, kept the boy from having any fun, insisted that he do many chores beyond what should have been his normal allotment because his younger brother wouldn't do as good a job of them. She was critical of him. Even at age forty, Don was still being told by his mother what to do and how to do it, and he accepted her criticisms because he wanted to avoid arguments.

Here was a man who had internalized a perfectionistic pursuit of achievement, anxious overcompensation for physical inadequacy, his mother's critical overcoercion. He had brought the parental attitudes and standards into his adult life as self-attitudes. These borrowed attitudes and criteria forced him to work extra hours rather than pursue pleasurable recreational activities. They had even pushed him toward a woman who bossed and belittled him, thereby reinforcing the parental pathogens he was using on himself.

Phyllis

I have seen many hundreds of patients victimized by punitive parental attitudes that they internalized during childhood and later inflicted on themselves in various ways.

One woman we can call Phyllis had been punished physically almost daily in childhood by her father, who misguidedly but stubbornly had determined "to teach her better." At seventeen, she met a man who told her he loved her, and his expression of love, because she had never had any from her parents, gave her a sense of triumph and vindication. Like so many of the punitively treated, Phyllis had longed for retaliation, and now she wanted to announce to her parents that she was leaving them to be married. But, fearful of her father, she eloped instead.

It wasn't long before she discovered that her husband could be as punitive as her father, calling her names and beating her. For a time, she thought that the names her husband called her were suitable; they were compatible with the low esteem in which she held herself. She had punished herself inside by her self-criticism; she had also punished herself outside, as it turned out, by choosing and staying with a punitive husband. But, after eight years, she had had enough of all the beating and name calling and she divorced him.

After her divorce, she got a job in a department store and even then continued to punish herself by doing extra work both in the store and in her tiny apartment, refusing dates and invitations to social affairs—until finally her loneliness and bleak life became intolerable. At that point, she began to have lunch with co-workers and through them met other people. She became attracted to one man who was considerate of her feelings and treated her with love and respect. She married him.

But after eight months of this marriage, she became seriously depressed. It was at this point that she came to see me. She described herself as no good, worthless, unworthy of her husband, who was so good and kind to her, never spoke angrily to her and never pushed her around.

Once again, her inner child of the past was expressing itself.

With an internalized need for punitive self-belittlement, she had first married a man who beat her; after divorcing him, she had punished herself with extra work; and now, in her second marriage to a kindly, considerate man, she did not feel "at home" and was beating on herself by feeling unworthy and had become depressed.

Until she recognized that her depression was a form of self-punishment, that she was using her husband's kindness to trigger her own punishing self-belittlement and that she could, with some effort, learn to respect and value herself, she was automatically dominated by her child of the past and the internalized punitive parental attitude.

Marianne

At twenty-three, Marianne complained of "this ridiculous self-consciousness that poisons everything." She characterized herself as capable, intelligent, but often defensive, self-centered and irresponsible. She was, she said, "bitterly disappointed in myself."

Particularly in recent months, she said, she had come to feel that she was not effective in anything and had "dropped out of everything," and although she was trying to "get back in" she had not been able to make it.

A year earlier she had experimented briefly with drugs and had recognized that she couldn't handle them. Her mother had hated it when Marianne had told her about the drug experimentation. The mother had thought the daughter was living an alien life and there had been a loss of rapport, which Marianne had felt deeply.

On further inquiry, it turned out that Marianne had quit college and had thought many times of wanting to return; she had dropped out of three jobs in the last three years; she had a typing job now, which she didn't like; she had a boyfriend, whom she respected and adored, and yet that relationship was not going well. Nothing was going well! "Why," she demanded, "should I be such a drag?"

Marianne's parents were intelligent, cultivated people. Both her mother and her father, an executive in a large corporation, were warm and loving. They had never been scolding or critical. They had shown their love for her by doing for her and by giving her advantages. They had high moral standards but they also had been oversubmissive.

Marianne had internalized her parents' permissiveness so that she had difficulties with self-control. She had also internalized her parents' high achievement and moral standards. And, because her self-permissiveness did not give her sufficient self-discipline to attain these standards, she turned on herself critically and belittlingly even though criticism as such was not part of her past home life.

Marianne had to learn that turning on herself belittlingly, far from being helpful in achieving self-control, only made her depressed and all the more impulsively rebellious. She had to have practice in firmly but not self-critically saying no to herself whenever her impulsiveness infringed on her goals as an adult.

Mildred

Mildred, an attractive, somewhat fragile-appearing young woman, sought help because of both physical and emotional turmoil. For the past five months she had been under medical treatment for colitis but there had been no relief and she was scheduled to enter a hospital for further tests within a short time.

Mildred had a one-and-a-half-year-old baby, a good-natured child, whom she loved very much, as did a neighbor who took care of the child during the day while Mildred worked. "I work and it bothers me," Mildred said. "I can't sleep at night because I keep thinking about my work." She had been on the job as a secretary for three years. Her employer had had a secretary before her who had been with him a long time and had been very efficient. Mildred was trying to measure up to the former secretary's standards and many times would go in to work early, stay in during lunch hour and take her job home with her, sometimes working most of the evening. "I've always been conscientious," she said.

Her husband, a twenty-six-year-old engineer, was a hard worker, a calm, unexcitable man, affectionate and close to the baby and to Mildred. She confessed to nagging him because, although he made good money, he had no job security or any insurance. Somewhat hesitantly, Mildred also admitted that she could not love her husband or make love to him the way she wanted to. "I'm all tense and can't relax—and then making love is painful. I'm not the woman I should be for my husband. Other women don't have this problem and if something in me doesn't change, he will probably look around for someone else and I wouldn't blame him."

Asked to characterize herself, Mildred said that she was a conscientious person with a heavy guilty feeling, always criticizing herself, self-conscious about her looks and feeling she was ugly (she was not), compelled to keep everything in her home spotless and to work hard at it.

Mildred had been born out of wedlock and she and her mother had lived with her grandparents, who adopted her when she was three years old. Her mother died when she was eleven, but Mildred didn't know she was her mother then, having always called her "Sis."

Mildred and her grandmother didn't get along well. Her grandmother could make her feel guilty not only during childhood but even now. The grandmother, Mildred explained, would never let her "be in things" when she was in high school and kept telling her she was going to get pregnant like her mother did. Although Mildred was valedictorian in high school and wanted to go to college, her grandmother wanted her to stay home and look after her, but Mildred went to college anyway although she couldn't enjoy it.

Mildred was never free to go home to her grandparents without getting a continuous lecture about how ungrateful she was. Her grandfather was a quiet man who seldom said a word, dominated by his wife. The grandmother kept saying and, Mildred reported, does even now: "After all we did for you, giving you a home and all . . ."

Mildred's problems are representative of those that can develop when throughout childhood and adolescence a girl is subjected to belittling, punitive overcoercion. Out of such a situation, any one or a combination of the following may occur in adult life: a driving need to try to please a parent or other authority figure such as a boss; self-belittling with periodic periods of depressed feelings; psychosomatic difficulties; sexual difficulties. In some cases, there may even be choice of a spouse who will treat the self-belittling person with the same attitudes the mother or other authority employed during the early years. Not infrequently, too, without being aware of it, a self-belittling woman, upon becoming a mother, encourages demanding, disrespectful behavior in one or more of her children. Such behavior then provides an atmosphere similar to what she experienced during her own childhood and adolescence.

These are just a few examples of how parental pathogens can be the sources for self-belittlement. In addition to perfectionism, overcoercion and oversubmission, other pathogens that can provoke loss of self-esteem include distrust, neglect and rejection, and we shall be considering these later.

chapter 7

Cultural Sources of Self-belittlement

Certain elements in our culture contribute to self-belittlement. I would like to consider these with you because, with an understanding of them, it is often possible to minimize or sidestep their belittling power.

Achievement Worship

Achievement can and should be a byproduct of self-respect. If you like and respect yourself, you have an inner drive for useful work—and if you have trained yourself to have a certain amount of self-discipline, the drive will be constructively directed. When you feel right with yourself, doing a good job is more gratifying than doing a poor one; doing good work each day adds to self-esteem.

But in our culture, the concept of achievement often seems to be distorted. Achievement tends to be viewed as the sole criterion for assessing individual worth. The person becomes subordinated to achievement that is no longer what it should be: the natural expression of a person's energy, skill and self-respect.

For example: It is New Year's Day. The scene is a stadium

where two college football teams are battling for a bowl victory. It's the final quarter; the score is tied; one team kicks; the ball goes into the end zone. The receiver, believing he can make a long gain, runs out of the end zone, confronts several onrushing tacklers and, to avoid being tackled, circles back. But the tacklers are faster than he anticipated and drop him. Instead of advancing his team's chances of winning, the receiver, by being tackled in his own end zone, adds to the other team's score by two points in the closing minutes of the game.

In achievement terms, he goofed. He may have made a slight mistake in judgment. Another time, in the same situation, he might well have advanced his team's cause by outrunning his would-be tacklers.

His team went on to win but the newspapers reported that our receiver felt so humiliated that he could not bring himself to talk about that play for four days.

And we expect this! We expect a young man to agonize over something that wasn't even a clearcut mistake in judgment. His action almost made his team a loser; we applaud "winners" and look down upon "losers." We don't stop to think that for every winner there must be, by definition, a loser. We pay lip service to "how you play the game" but the dominant sport ethic, in Vince Lombardi's famous observation, is that "winning isn't everything, it's the only thing." To be a loser means to be a lesser person, a somewhat tainted, inadequate person, in our culture.

This orientation—to win is to achieve, and to lose is to fail—permeates almost everything we do. It is evident in our schools, with teachers and parents urging children to get better grades, to be at the top of their class. Boys have to be winners in athletics from Little League on. Little girls have to be pretty and popular and have to win over others to become cheerleader, baton champion or queen of this or that. In business, the slogan is "beat the competition"; it is also "beat the other fellow" to the promotion. On the golf course or tennis court, winning becomes more important than the recreation. Social events become a means of achieving social status rather than opportunities to exchange human warmth, humor and understanding.

Competition can be useful and fun. It's the notion that a

person is less worthwhile if he happens to lose to which I object. Can't we somehow learn to acquire merit without putting someone else down, without stepping on someone else's self-esteem?

We can, if we choose, work toward a culture concerned with the self-esteem of all. We should seek ways by which everyone can acquire merit without the need for humiliating another. But we first have to recognize the vital importance of maintaining the self-esteem of all.

Moralizing

A vast stream of moralizing emanates from our mass media, churches and parental attitudes. Behavior is almost continuously rated as good or bad. In movies and on television, good guys forever chase bad guys—on the Western prairie or through crime-ridden city streets. Churches have come a long way, but we still often emerge from them feeling guilty and steeped in sin.

The simplistic good-bad framework is hardly adequate for understanding and dealing with children. For instance, docile, even abnormally docile, behavior in a preschooler may be labeled by parents as "good" while normally aggressive or negativistic behavior in a toddler often is termed "bad." Thus, within the good-bad framework, a child may be approved of for abnormal and disapproved of for normal behavior for his age level. Nevertheless, parents often use this framework for evaluation.

And they often use belittling control when they judge the behavior "bad." It is usually not enough, in our culture, for a parent to say *no* firmly to a child's immature behavior and, when necessary, isolate him temporarily when he infringes on the rights of others. Somehow, the parent feels he must go on to say, "You're bad, naughty," or use another similarly belittling statement. *Bad, naughty, silly, ridiculous, stupid, I'm ashamed of you* and *I'm disappointed in you* are part of the verbal barrage so commonly directed toward children. Subjected repeatedly to the barrage, a child may grow up ashamed of or disappointed in himself, harboring a feeling of being unacceptable and given to using the same barrage on himself.

Twisted View of Childhood

Children, without adult responsibilities, live carefree lives, happy lives, lives free of problems. A ridiculous view? Yet that view of children and childhood is common in our culture.

No small part of parental exasperation with children arises when, in the view of parents, a child who has led a carefree life all day complains about some small chore or responsibility after the parents have worked hard all day to provide for the child's welfare and even to give him pleasures and comforts. It is not unusual to hear a parent say: "Can't you even pick up your belongings and put them away? After I've worked all day to give you a good home, you complain!"

That attitude of disappointment, if expressed continually, must create feelings of inadequacy and guilt in a child that eventually resound in adulthood.

Our cultural view of childhood is distorted. Children do not have carefree lives. They have to adjust to parental attitudes that are often difficult to adjust to; and they have to contend with their immaturies and lack of knowledge, which keep getting them into difficulties. If we hold the view that childhood is carefree and as a result express derogatory attitudes toward children, we contribute to building a foundation for later self-belittlement.

Prejudice

Prejudice—a false belief taught or fostered by a particular culture that remains unmodified despite rational proof to the contrary—contributes to self-belittlement.

Among the most common prejudicial attitudes are those that belittle members of minority groups. For them, the difficulty of maintaining self-respect is increased. Blacks, Jews and homosexuals have long been targets of prejudice. And while advances are being made in combatting prejudicial attitudes directed at these groups, we have only begun to scratch the surface.

Other prejudices are rampant. Terms like *hippie, longhair, establishment, square, loser, neurotic*—all put individuals into stereotype categories that are hurtful and belittling. We all have personal problems enough in maintaining our self-respect without having to bear the additional, invalid group-stereotype problems imposed by prejudice.

Reinforcements of Parental Pathogens

Perfectionism

A subtly confusing aspect of perfectionism is that it may seem desirable. In a nation of strivers and doers, the cultural heritage tends to reinforce the excessive striving of the perfectionist, everyone seems to approve it, and the façade of achievement may make it more difficult for the perfectionist to recognize the source of his misery and inner emptiness.

Moreover, perfectionistic parents tend to be supported by the educational system, which often goads children to compete and stimulates greater effort. There is some similar support from church teachings and urgings of children to be better—and some church teaching may be looked upon as calling for a kind of perfection achievable only by a saint, not a human, even though in reality no church expects its members to be or become saintly.

Oversubmissiveness

For several decades, a common theme in thousands of well-intentioned lectures, articles and books devoted to child rearing has been that too often mothers fail to give children all the "love and security" they should have. But what has not been emphasized sufficiently has been the need to provide love and security without oversubmission.

Many mothers have gone out of their way to keep their children smiling and happy—without understanding fully, or at all, the need to set limits. If, by nature, a child must test and explore his world, find out what he may and may not do, he must also depend upon parents to show him the limits. There has been a strong, not healthy, cultural push toward oversubmissiveness.

Punitiveness

Occasionally, we hear of children brutally beaten by parents punitive to the extreme. While there is no cultural support for the extreme, nevertheless some less punitive parents may look about and see punitiveness practiced not only by other parents but by schools, armed forces and prison systems.

Neglect

While a neglectful attitude toward children receives no direct support from our culture, still, insofar as the culture contributes to preoccupying many parents with material success and social advancement, it indirectly supports a breakdown of family closeness and loss of opportunity for children to have all the vital contacts they need with parents. Neglect, as we know now, is not simply a physical matter.

Rejection

Our cultural emphasis on material success may also sometimes contribute to the rejection of children. A child coming at a time of family financial problems may suffer rejection. If there are marital difficulties, parents may view children as chains and may adopt a rejecting attitude. Our cultural stress on physical beauty, often to the exclusion of other considerations of individual attractiveness, may contribute to the rejection of a child whose physical appearance is disappointing to parents.

part III

Self-control

chapter 8

Self-control Difficulties

If we were perfect parents to ourselves in adult life, we would be automatically respectful of ourselves rather than automatically self-critical and self-belittling—and we would also have control, realizing the need and having the power to set limits. And our self-respect and self-control could feed and augment each other.

But many of us were brought up in an environment that left us, as adults, with an inability to say *no* to ourselves and make it stick.

Characteristics of Those With Self-control Difficulties

It's natural, as we've seen, for a child to be impulsive, to "live for the moment," to want to try this, do that, say this. Immaturity and lack of knowledge make impulsiveness almost inevitable in a child, and to no small extent the impulsiveness can contribute to learning and eventual maturity if the child is shown when and how it may be necessary for him to control it.

But if the child does not learn self-control in the early years, if no limits are set for him and he has no practice in setting limits on himself, he grows up to become an adult who tends to set no

limits for himself. He lives out a significant aspect of immaturity.
And he pays a very high price.

People who lack self-control may be inclined to overeat, drink too much, drive too fast, philander, waste money, ignore important matters, waste opportunities. Impulsive and demanding, they may explode with anger and indulge in the adult equivalent of childish temper tantrums when their impulses are thwarted and their demands not met. They often hurt other people and may be astonished to find that other people, in fact, are hurt by their outbursts and lack of consideration because, basically, they are blindly unaware of the feelings of others.

Often they are exploitive of others. In love and marriage, they may assume the role of dictator, or try to, making their partners slaves, and may be unable to understand the need for and the desirability of mutuality.

They can be charming when they set out to be—to gain some end. But they can be fickle in their relationships. They can be creative in some areas but may fail to follow through if patient, persistent effort is needed.

Many find themselves bored, blasé, unable to take interest in activities around them. They may drift and have no recognizable or achievable goal. Yet they want something out of life that they realize they are not getting, but they cannot find what it is they want and progress toward it; and despite an outward show of boredom, they are acutely unhappy.

Forms

Whims, demands, temper, fears and phobias are common forms of self-control difficulties.

Whims

All of us have occasional whims. We would like, at some moment, to have or do this or that, and if the whim does not infringe on someone else or on our own goals, we may indulge it. This differs considerably from a chronic giving in to whims without regard for infringements.

A person who caters to himself, indulging his whims ad libitum, usually has had no limits set on self-indulgence in child-hood. When he wishes to eat, he eats—even though he may eat excessively and become obese. When he has a whim to drink, he drinks and may do so to excess even though it infringes on his own adult goals.

In some cases, the self-indulgent person is a product of a home where a parental attitude, expressed or implied, was: "My son, you are a genius; you have great potential; you will be great—and I cater to your wishes because you have sterling stuff and will go to the top."

Such a child, raised under the influence of parental perfec-tionistic goals and oversubmission, finds out, as an adult, that he may indeed be bright but is unable to discipline himself well and is not setting the world on fire as his mother predicted. As an adult, he is outraged by his impulsiveness and turns against the impulsive child of the past within him, saying, "Your impulsive-ness is not allowing me to express myself properly." He becomes self-critical, self-belittling, and this hurts. And now his whim to drink, for example, becomes even stronger, for drinking provides a chemical silencer of his painful self-criticism. But the silencing is only temporary. In between drinking bouts, he turns against himself even more because he is aware of drinking's interference with the satisfaction of his adult goals. He is miserable and goes on making himself increasingly miserable.

It doesn't matter what the whim or indulgence—excessive drinking, excessive eating, moving from job to job, place to place, relationship to relationship—the process involved is often similar and the end result the same: unhappiness, failure to achieve wanted goals and very often outright misery.

Demands

An example of an excessively demanding person is to be found in the husband in a recent movie. In bed, victim of a mild indisposition, he yells for his wife, who is busy preparing his lunch and cleaning up the house. His yell is insistent; she comes; he announces he wants a glass of lemonade; and she dutifully goes to get it.

But he yells after her: "I want it with lemon, real lemon. I'm thinking about the lemonade I used to have as a child and how it really satisfied me. Naturally, you'll get me real lemons because I want them so much." A bit doubtfully, she replies: "Well, I have to go four blocks to the grocery and I am very busy."

"Four blocks!" he exclaims. "Well, is there something wrong with your legs? You can go four blocks to get what will please me, can't you?" And, being a kind of beat-down, self-belittling person, she goes, making no protest, although the viewer can see the rising resentment and hopeless feeling she has. And when she returns, there are other demands: to fetch this and fetch that, adjust and readjust the window shade, fluff his pillow.

A fictitious character, the husband—but many real-life characters behave in the same fashion, concerned only with their own impulses. They are not intrinsically bad people. They simply have been allowed to be demanding in their growing-up years, in effect trained to be demanding, and they are stuck with the pattern. Demanding people can be subtle or blatant, but the net result is that people are used in one way or another in the service of their immature demands.

All of us have occasion to do things for others and occasions when we expect them to do things for us. That is normal. But what we are considering here is habitual demand, habitual using of people as servants to immature, self-indulgent demands.

In virtually every restaurant, there is to be found the haughty diner who makes mincemeat of a waiter, sending him back and forth because the meat isn't exactly right, the salad is too much this or that. In stores, there are the customers who insist that the sales clerk bring out every shoe or bolt of cloth and then end up announcing that, well, they don't think they are really interested.

People can demand in various ways. They can demand forcefully: "I want this and, by golly, you had better get it for me." They can play on other people's guilt feelings, saying, in effect: "Naturally, you see that I am in some way handicapped; you must feel sorry for me and if you don't you are a callused, unfeeling person. If you are not callused, then naturally you will do this for me." The latter are the invalided, sickly sweet, sweetly sick types.

Blackmail of one kind or another can be used. "I know

something about you and if you don't give in to my demands, I can and will make it rough for you." Or: "I am your boss. I can hire and fire, promote or not promote, make your job pleasant or uncomfortable. It is not enough that you do your job; you must accede to my eccentric demands because I have power over you."

The person on whom excessive demands are made reacts— inwardly, outwardly or both. If the demandee is a self-belittler, the excessive demands on him will accentuate his self-belittling problem and simultaneously make him hostile. If the demandee is self-respecting, he may not even become hostile but simply refuse to do the demander's bidding and, if the demander insists that he comply, may break off the relationship.

An excessively demanding person may be so because he was either neglected or oversubmitted to in childhood. If he was neglected, he may have had few or no satisfactory, warm interchanges with others and may have lost the capacity to form and obtain satisfaction from deep-seated relationships. Without that capacity, he has no incentive for self-control—because a major reason for exerting self-control is a liking for others, a wish not to hurt them, a desire for warm, respectful, fulfilling interchange. Unable to form such a relationship, a neglected person often uses others only for self-gratification and has no hesitation about breaking off relationships if others do not come through for him.

On the other hand, the oversubmitted-to person can form, is even adept at forming, relationships. While he is demanding and may use people without compunction, he has had practice in being accepted by others and expects acceptance. He may be very warm; others may like him because of his adeptness and lack of a self-belittling barrier. He can often reach people with self-belittling barriers and break down the barriers; and because he can do that, self-belittling people often become hooked up with him, grateful that he has broken through. The self-belittler may even make a kind of compact with the demander, saying, in effect: "You broke through my barrier and I am so grateful that I will accede to your demands if you will promise to keep breaking through and give me some of the interchange I need so badly." But the catch is that the oversubmitted-to, demanding person is fickle and liable to go off and leave the self-belittler.

However he came to be that way, through neglect or oversubmission, the demanding person victimizes not only others but himself. Inevitably, his relationships with others are flawed, and sooner or later he must suffer from the feeling that something important is missing. He must also suffer, sooner or later, from the realization that he remains immature and either has no well-formed goals or, if he has, is not advancing their cause.

Temper

To feel an impulse toward anger or irritation when one is balked is common and may even be natural. If cruel things are uttered, they may be regretted later and the damage may not be easily repaired.

Many of us manage to control impulsive anger or irritation, out of consideration for the feelings of others and recognition that we are likely to be sorry later if we do not exercise control. We may count to ten, get up and pace the room or leave it and walk around the block. Not the least of helpful measures is recognition that a temper outburst is a venting of temporary fury, not genuine deep anger. Some injustices are worth considered adult anger that spurs efforts toward correction. Sudden temporary fury is another matter.

But the person lacking self-control just lets go. What he feels, he expresses. It doesn't matter to him, certainly not at the moment, that he hurts somebody else, even somebody who may have tried hard to help and could not for reasons beyond his control. He gives no thought to circumstances and must blame someone for his irritation and frustration.

Usually, such a person has trouble controlling temper in adult life because he grew up unaccustomed to control. It was as if his parents had told him: "Bow down before your temper because there is nothing we can do about it and your temper is so strong that we must accept that it can whip both you and us around." The child gets the idea that his temper must be extremely powerful and if his parents bow before it, he must too.

There may also be some encouragement for venting temper in a "steam boiler" type of psychiatric approach that says, in effect: "You have feelings inside that should come out. Bottle them up and they harm you." But people don't function like steam boilers. It is not a matter of exploding with anger or exploding the boiler.

When we get angry or experience fear or any strong emotion, adrenalin pours into the bloodstream. And the large amounts of the hormone, as we have noted, produce the typical adrenalin reaction designed to prepare the body for fight or flight: your heart beats faster, your breath comes quicker, your hands tingle, your mouth becomes dry. You are equipped for a surging expenditure of energy.

I am not at all convinced that failure to expend that energy must lead inevitably, as some people think, to ulcers, high blood pressure or other body damage. And even if it were true that energy must be expended to avoid such harm, I am certainly not convinced that giving vent to temper is the most useful way to do it or even useful at all.

To blow your top and then scold yourself for having done so is not useful. The self-belittlement for lack of control does not help those you have hurt; it doesn't help your self-control; it may even exacerbate your lack of control. If you scratch at yourself critically inside because you have a hard time with temper, you will get angry at the scratching and become ripe for still another temper outburst at a later time.

On the other hand, to develop mastery over your temper, to avoid destructive and hurtful exchanges with others, gives a feeling of accepting adult responsibility. And if there are times when you feel you must expend energy and get rid of some of the accumulated adrenalin in your bloodstream, by all means do so by a vigorous walk, a cleaning spree or any other activity that will allow you to release the pent-up feelings and restore your balance. This is useful treatment.

Fears and Phobias

Just as whims, demands and temper outbursts are uncontrolled impulses, so are fears. Fears may develop in childhood and then continue to grow in adult life if they are belittled, ignored or submitted to.

All children have occasional fears. Theirs is a constantly expanding world and there are anxious periods when new situations are met and mastered. Children, too, are immature and must distort reality to try to make it conform to their limited knowledge.

A child may hear the rustling of leaves and interpret the sound as something dangerous to him; he has a fear. A four-year-old can really believe there is a bear in the closet since he hasn't the knowledge to realize that a bear couldn't possibly be there. His fear, which may seem totally unrealistic to an adult, is very real to him.

Children need reassurance from parents—not belittling and not catering to, just simple reassurance. They can master situations more easily if reassured and given approving parental support. If they are either belittled or catered to, their confidence weakens.

When a child wakes and exclaims that there is a bear in his closet, the well-advised parent can say quite simply: "I know you have fears, but there is no bear in the closet. I guarantee it. And so you can go back to sleep." Simple reassurance—no long explanations, no belittling, no remark such as "Obviously, there couldn't possibly be a bear in the closet."

When a child insists: "Hold my hand, lie down with me, let me come to bed with you"—and gets his way—his fears almost certainly will grow. It's as if the wild horses of the child's fears have no harness and they can pull both adult and child along behind them. A matter-of-fact response from a supportive adult helps the child neutralize fear-engendering experiences; he can talk or play out the fears in the close relationship until they are dissipated.

In adult life, the more we try to sidestep fears and to avoid situations that evoke fears, the more the fears increase. And we may develop phobias. While fears may be responses to real dangers, small or large, phobias are unreasonable fears that have no foundation in fact.

If, for example, we fear to be in some possibly dangerous high place and allow the fear to control us, the fear may grow and become an unreasoned fear, a phobia, of all high places, dangerous or not. The list of phobias—of high places, closed-in areas, riding in cars or planes or elevators—is extremely long and varied.

There are means for getting over fears and phobias. One, called deconditioning, may be likened to antiallergy treatment. If an allergic patient's sensitivity is to a pollen, for example, he may benefit from being given doses of the pollen, very small to begin with and gradually increasing in amount, until he builds up resistance to the pollen. Similarly, a skilled therapist, working with a patient with an intense fear or phobia, may build up the patient's resistance by a deconditioning process. To begin with, the patient may be asked simply to imagine himself in a situation that might arouse mild anxiety or he may be shown a picture of such a situation. At the same time, the patient is encouraged to relax, and he usually can do so. Gradually, the patient is asked to imagine or view situations that in the past have produced stronger anxiety. Before long, the patient is able to maintain relaxation while imagining or viewing—and then while actually confronting—the situations in real life.

In adult life, there is usually at least some realistic basis for fears. "If I go in to see my boss and ask for a raise, he is liable to get sore and fire me," we may say. And this is a possibility. We have to weigh how well we do our job, whether we merit a raise, the personality of the boss and other factors.

But we also have to consider that influencing us, too, may be self-belittlement that leads us to disparage our own worth—or difficulty with control. We may hesitate to ask for a raise because impulsively we want to take the easy path. Even though a raise is deserved, it is easier to maintain the status quo and let things go along as they are, rather than have a confrontation with the boss and take risks.

What to do? We must respect ourselves and our rights, and if we have a case we should state the case, even though it is difficult to bring ourselves to do so. If we feel we must have this particular job and that raising the issue with the boss may jeopardize our family's welfare, this is a realistic matter that must be taken into account. If we weigh everything and determine that we simply cannot bring up the matter of a raise, then we cannot do it. But if that is not really the situation and what is really influencing us is self-belittlement or submission to the easier course, or both, then we have to wrestle with ourselves and achieve the self-esteem or self-control, or both, that will allow us to do what needs to be done. Otherwise, we further sacrifice self-respect or self-control and, while taking the easy impulsive course, mire ourselves down in the problem.

Examples

Let's look in on several examples of self-control difficulties, beginning with the case of a boy who, at age ten, already had more than one kind of resultant problem.

Jay

Jay was born into a home where he was the adored child of parents, grandparents and older siblings and was almost literally stifled with their excessive loving service.

When he was brought in to see me by his mother, her complaints were numerous. They started with the fact that Jay was "too fat." And he was, indeed, obese. At ten, Jay was also a bedwetter. He was, his mother said, "a nice boy; he can get mad and stubborn, but he gets over it quickly." She worried that he didn't like to play with other children much. "He is easily bored," she told me. "The other family members tend to do things for him. I find myself doing for him too. Jay is casual about letting people do things for him. I want him to get going and keep after him to get him to do things." Jay's schoolwork was not impressive; he was in the fourth grade, read well, but did not like written work.

When I talked to Jay, he proved to be an affable, noncommital boy who answered my questions but without elaboration. He had, he told me, no worries, liked his family, liked school and didn't feel that either his obesity or his bedwetting really was a problem. He cooperated well on tests I administered, and the results showed him to be of above-average intelligence.

Here, then, was an intelligent boy brought up in an environment that had the effect of encouraging gratification of his childish impulses. He had no motivation to discipline himself at meals or in nighttime habits. He thought nothing of gratifying his impulses to show temper and to be stubborn in his demands. For him, writing required some discipline so he didn't like written schoolwork. So far as he was concerned, he had no problems: overindulged, he indulged himself, doing and getting what he wanted at the moment.

Left to grow up that way, his problems would grow with him. With the cornucopia of his childhood days no longer there for him, he would have difficulty coping consistently with the demands of reality. He would tend to blame others for his being deprived of earlier gratifications and would be disappointed in those who did not indulge him. He would search restlessly for some job that would pay well without requiring him to accept responsibility. He might indulge himself in physical symptoms to avoid reality demands, might use alcohol for the same purpose. Left to grow up without self-control, he could never hope for real fulfillment and happiness in adulthood.

Vincent

Vincent, age twenty-nine, had a marital problem—and much more. I saw both him and his wife. And here again let them tell the story in brief in their own words and provide the diagnostic clues.

"Vincent and I," his wife told me, "are always arguing. He expects me to give in on every difference of opinion. I don't like his drinking. He doesn't take his job very seriously. Often he just sleeps in the morning rather than go to work. When he is home and not doing anything I sometimes want him to help me, but he resents this. His mother was easygoing and always doing for him. Vincent wants to live way beyond his means. He says I'm not cooperating when I don't agree with his spendthrift ways. Sometimes I do get angry and nag him, especially when he is drinking too much."

As Vincent told it: "I've been nervous for the last year and a half. Eight months ago I had an auto accident and the doctor said I had a mild concussion. Since the accident I have times when I feel weak and shake all over. Sometimes I get pains in my head and ringing in my ears. The doctors say there is nothing wrong physically. Sometimes I get nervous and can do nothing but pace up and down. I'm a salesman and have to travel. I have two small children; I've been married four years. My wife is easy to get along with, but she doesn't take too much interest in my work. It's hard for me to get going in the mornings. I get nervous but my wife doesn't understand that. I drink quite a bit."

Vincent provided some revealing facts in answering questions about his background. "I was considered a daydreamer in school. I never studied much or liked school. I quit after my junior year in high school and joined the Navy. My mother was always easygoing. She was always doing things for me. She would let me get away with things. My father was proper, quiet and dignified, but he was often nervous. I wasn't very close to him. I've held a number of jobs but I get restless and have changed jobs several times. I have had this present job for about a year."

The clues, of course, were: "He doesn't take his job very seriously . . . His mother was . . . always doing for him. Vincent wants to live way beyond his means. . . . I feel weak and shake all over. . . . I drink quite a bit. . . . I never studied much or liked school. . . . My mother was always easygoing . . . always doing things for me. She would let me get away with things. . . . I have changed jobs several times."

With a home life characterized by his mother's oversubmissiveness and overindulgence, Vincent grew up to become an adult lacking in initiative and with a tendency to indulge every whim and to capitalize on physical symptoms to avoid reality demands.

chapter 9

Family Sources of Self-control Difficulties

If you have difficulties with self-control, the family in which you grew up is the most probable major source. Of the parental pathogens largely responsible for self-control difficulties, two—oversubmission and neglect—may also lead to self-belittlement. The other two—overindulgence and excessive responsibility—have their effects almost entirely in the self-control area.

We've already had, in the preceding chapter, several examples of how parental pathogens lead to self-control problems. Let's consider a few more.

Fred

Fred was age six when he was brought in by parents who had reached a point of desperation because of his temper and belligerence, the belligerence often being directed against a four-year-old brother, to the latter's physical harm. Fred also dawdled and daydreamed. In school, he did poorly and was a problem to his first-grade teacher because he persisted in talking out of turn and pestering other children. "I try to find out why Fred does these things," his mother told me. "He often is in a nasty mean mood; he calls me an ass-head. There is constant upheaval in our household."

Fred was just one more case of an oversubmitted-to child running roughshod over parents, teachers and peers, calling his mother names, retorting "Make me" when asked to do anything. His father was angered by the boy's conduct but had been restrained from disciplining him by the mother, who had read extensively about child discipline and had tried to substitute reason and understanding for firmness. She was trying to avoid treating her children as she had been treated by a harsh, inconsiderate father. The net result was that both parents were oversubmissive and their attitudes allowed Fred, with all his immaturity, to dominate the home.

It was not too late then, although not easy, to do something constructive about Fred and to spare him the problems he could otherwise expect to result from his lack of self-control when he reached adulthood or even adolescence.

Paul

In adolescence, a child begins to assume for himself the parental function and in becoming a parent to himself tends to treat himself as his parents have treated him. If he lacks self-control, he is impulsive, finds it difficult to say "no" to himself, is disrespectful and has a hard time holding to long-range goals. He usually has trouble in school because he is undisciplined and fails to complete school tasks. He is often impulsive in sexual behavior. He usually has the ability to form close personal relationships but will often be excessively demanding and will use temper outbursts as a weapon to force others to do his bidding, leading to their hurt, resentment and often retaliation. And he may become openly defiant of his parents.

Paul, at fourteen, was an impulsive, demanding, resistive boy in a prolonged sulk over his family's move from another state to Ohio.

He had been happy until recently. As his parents put it: "He has gotten everything he wanted all his life. He didn't talk until age two because his sister talked for him. She also did his fighting for him. Many times when we should have punished him we didn't. We very much wanted a boy. He was very dear to us. In the last few years, he has been openly demanding things, nagging for what he wants and usually getting it. He rarely gets angry but when he does it is a cold anger. If he doesn't get his way, he makes us feel guilty until we relent. He does chores reluctantly and in his own time."

When his father, a plant manager, was transferred and the family had to move to Ohio, Paul withdrew into his room and had to be ordered out of it. After moving, the family joined a swim club, mainly to help the boy socialize, but he seldom chose to go to the club. He failed the seventh grade, was put in a private school and just barely managed to pass although he is normally intelligent.

Paul's impulsive behavior never really disturbed his parents until the family moved. Until then, the problem of his excessive demands was solved by giving in to him. But when his father got orders to move, they could not be modified by Paul's impulsive whims. For once in his life, he had to comply with something he did not like. But he reacted by spending much time in his room and refusing to adjust to his new surroundings—and, finally, impulsively stole his father's car and, in defiance, drove back to his former home.

Dianne

The reactions of Dianne, another teenager, to her oversubmissive upbringing, though less precipitous, had gradually become increasingly violent. A few months before I saw her, she had had "this fight with my parents. It was a kind of fist fight. I don't remember how it started. Since then I just don't talk to them very much."

She went on to tell me: "I like to go to dances and talk on the phone to boys. I have a couple of them that I like. I have some girlfriends too. I won't go to bed until my boyfriend calls. I worry about my report cards. If I get a bunch of bad grades, my folks yell and threaten me. I ran away a couple of weeks ago. Then I got grounded. I've run away before. I'm in the ninth grade. I don't like it. My teachers yell at me.

"I'm not hungry at mealtime. I eat between meals and that

gets me into trouble. I have a temper if I don't get what I want. I don't like school and want to quit as soon as I can. I would wish for lots of money and to be good-looking."

That was Dianne's side of the story. The family's side came to this: "Dianne has a violent temper. Usually little things throw her. She just blows up. She has no interest in anything except talking on the phone. She enjoys going to dances. Her temper has been more violent in the last two years. It makes for difficulties in living with her. She is discourteous in school and lacks self-control. She cannot seem to relax. She seems to isolate herself from the family but makes friends easily. We walk softly because she has a temper. We try not to aggravate her. We had a big blow-up in November. She kicked and screamed. She has no initiative and is given no chores. She doesn't converse with us."

If parents realize that a teenager lacks self-control, they can begin to hold the child within certain limits. It is useless to try to impose limits that cannot be enforced. But there are two types of limits parents can always place on an impulsive adolescent. They can walk away from him or her whenever they feel infringed on, and they can control the purse strings.

The impulsive teenager should receive no money without earning it. Use of the family car, for example, should be predicated on earning money for gasoline. If parents continue to bend to the adolescent whims and demands, they only increase the child's problem. Scolding, urging and criticism are wasted efforts that limit nothing. But the practical limits just mentioned often do help.

In late adolescence, the undisciplined teenager is usually more aware that he has a problem. His impulsiveness and lack of discipline often begin to hurt now as he finds himself unable to achieve strongly desired goals or others retaliate for his infringements on them. The hurt can be used as a lever for change.

Michael

An oversubmitted-to child, upon becoming an adult, often has some attractive qualities. In an era sometimes referred to as that of the plodding, conformist "Organization Man," impulsiveness often seems exciting and many people may be drawn to it.

The impulsive person, doing and saying things others sometimes wish they could do and say at least occasionally, may win attention and even admiration—but not necessarily for long.

One of my oversubmitted-to and impulsive adult patients, Michael, could be remarkably poised, witty and charming in almost any gathering, and people quickly warmed to him. Often, however, just as quickly—sometimes before an evening was out—they saw his limitations when, as many impulsives do, he began to take sarcastic digs at anyone drawn to him.

Michael was a business executive by grace of inheritance of a company from his father. It had been a successful enterprise but now was in difficulties. Entwined much of the time in his impulsive distractions, he paid little consistent attention to day-to-day business details. He had lost customers and he had also lost employees because of his impulsively sharp tongue.

Michael's temper, quick blame of others and excessive drinking complicated not only his business affairs but his marital life, and his wife had threatened to leave him.

Michael is not unaware of his problems. He has become increasingly chagrined over the deterioration of his business and, to a lesser extent, the deterioration of his marriage. He is well aware that he should devote himself more to the business, to improving employee morale, to being more solicitous of present customers and to seeking new ones. He has made resolutions but never has seemed able to keep them. He has been easily distracted and has given in to his whims to have another drink, to drop everything for a game of tennis. As he has failed to follow through, he has become more anxious, more intemperate, nastier to his employees and his wife.

But now, finally, he has begun to work on his basic problem in earnest and is making progress. It has taken a long time for him to realize the need and to get to work.

We shall be looking further into the parental pathogens involved in self-control problems later. Meanwhile, let's examine the cultural influences that may contribute to those problems.

chapter 10

Cultural Sources of Self-control Difficulties

The adult who has grown up impulsive and lacking in self-discipline often has his problems compounded by prevailing cultural attitudes and customs. Presenting as they do temptations to even the healthily self-controlled and self-disciplined, they are all the more seductive to and all the more likely to take in those with an undisciplined heritage. I would like to consider them with you because, with an understanding of them, it is often possible to minimize their influence.

"Give Yourself a Break" Complex

Much of the advertising of goods and services has been and continues to be centered on the theme: "You deserve it . . . give yourself a break, a treat, a gratification." You have only to look about to notice how much of the advertising you see and hear deals not with any merits a particular product or service may have over competitive items but with the concept that "you deserve it, need and should have a break."

To encourage impulsive buying, too, we have stores carefully laid out with the aim of attracting you to buy not just what you need but what you may, on the spur of the moment, decide to indulge in. In supermarkets, department stores and other shops, much attention goes into directing customer traffic, channeling it past tempting displays of what might be called "frill" and "luxury" items before the staple necessities are reached.

Credit buying further encourages impulsiveness. Easy, easy terms—low down payments, extended repayment periods, low monthly installments—make the impulse to buy, the treat to have, quite reasonable to gratify and take. And many of us spend our incomes long in advance of earning them.

The Stimulation of Impulsiveness

We hardly need dwell at length here on the quite obvious: the stimulation, often calculated, of sexual impulsiveness by much of our mass media. Sexuality, if long a somewhat muted theme, is to be found with far less muting and often none at all in movies, books, magazines and even the broadcast media. Flagrant pornography has become so commonplace that there are indications now of a swing of the pendulum away from it in revulsion.

In much of our entertainment—movies, theater, TV drama and even some of our serious literature—there is emphasis on impulsiveness. The heroes are celebrated as daring characters, romantically impulsive, willing, eager and brave enough to take chances, to gamble with their lives. And somehow, whether the heroes' chance taking and thought processes are rational or not, the very fact that they are not coldly calculated has been made to seem romantic, larger than life and desirable. To be "quick on the draw" is admirable—and little matter, it would seem, such attributes as sensitivity, intelligence, thoughtfulness, consideration of others and, in the highest sense, of oneself and life goals and how they may be reached honorably and without harm to others.

To well-stimulated impulsiveness we can attribute at least some of the blame for our national propensity to overweight and outright obesity. For most of us, eating is no longer something indulged in for survival purposes. All about us are temptations to eat. In addition to regular meals, we have our impulse-encouraging custom of coffee breaks with doughnuts or Danish pastry; our candy counters and peanut, soft-drink and other types of vending machines in office buildings; our popcorn and soft-drink vendors in movie houses.

When we are entertained, the hostess feels it incumbent upon her to see that we stuff ourselves, that our hands are never empty of drinks and hors d'oeuvres at cocktail parties and that course follows stuffing course at dinner parties.

The Pull of Fashion

There has been some tendency to consider overindulgence largely a female trait. Not men but women were the ones supposed to be unable to resist buying clothes. A woman "simply cannot have too many clothes" was a general cultural conviction and, to a large extent, still is.

A huge fashion industry has worked, by and large successfully, to whet appetites and impulses, to encourage overindulgence, to keep fashions constantly changing and women convinced of the need to keep up with the latest and to feel deprived, out of date, something less than what a woman should be, if their clothes are not in fashion.

Lately, the fashion industry has spread its net to include men—not without some opposition but not without a considerable measure of success, too. To be dominated by fashion, led around by the nose by it, no longer can be considered—if it ever really was—an exclusively feminine trait.

"Having a Ball"

Perhaps the most purely impulsive custom in our society is an informal, often spontaneous, episodic kind of socializing in which almost every type of impulsive behavior—from excessive spending to overdrinking, overeating and philandering—is given free rein and admired and approved, not just condoned.

What was once labeled "binge" has now been more or less

dignified with the label "having a ball." Reckless impulsiveness frequently becomes a topic for social conversation, pride and envy. Because impulsive behavior involves not just individuals but groups, is socially approved and spills over into so many areas, the price many of us pay for it is often concealed from us.

part IV

How to Become a Good Parent to Yourself

chapter **11**

And Now Into Action

At this point, you may very well have some idea of where your problems seem to lie and what, generally, you must do if you are to surmount them and develop your full potential for happy living. But how? To find a practical, effective way may seem like an impossibility.

It is not an impossibility. There are clear guidelines I can offer and will be offering in the rest of this book. They are based on what, over the years, has become a considerable body of experience. You will find that they are all simple—but not easy. I urge you to follow them as literally as you possibly can since, if you fail to do so—if you try "doing it your way"—you run the risk of repeating old mistakes.

A most important basic suggestion to be followed, even if you do so in the beginning only on faith, is to keep a permanent record. Some of my patients, since they have me to depend upon, have some difficulty at the beginning in seeing any need for a record of their own, but many soon realize the value of being able to refer to their own notes or, preferably, to hear the record they have put into an inexpensive tape recorder. The process of writing or recording one's thoughts aids in recall and often prevents recalled and other material from being forgotten or over-

106   *Your Inner Conflicts—How to Solve Them*

looked. For the reader of this book who has nobody to keep any form of record, it is even more vital.

Although a notebook is acceptable, I urge you to invest in an inexpensive tape recorder if at all possible since it will have extended value. If you find it difficult, as some do at first, to dictate, practice writing out notes first, then recording them, until the recording comes naturally.

Your first use of note taking or recording will be in aiding you in self-identification, as you will see in the following chapter. But, all along, you will find it a most useful aid.

You can write or tape accounts of certain situations as they arise, situations in which you feel unduly hurt, fearful, angry or impulsive. It is in these situations that you can expect old child-of-the-past patterns to be operating and interfering with adult life.

After setting down an account of such a situation, you can record your reaction—how you feel in your gut someplace. "This was the situation," you note, and tell about it, and then note, too: "I was pretty sore about it . . ." Or: "This made me so scared that I wanted to run away and hide." Or: "I was so insensitive that it wasn't until too late that I realized that somebody was being hurt by what I did." Or: "I came home, felt hopeless, despairing, depressed, and stayed awake all night."

You can go further to record a parental attitude or an attitude of your own or a childhood occurrence that you tend to think of during or after such a situation. You may say: "What happened makes me feel like the time when . . ." Without overdoing, you simply try to draw as many correlations as you can between the present event and the past in terms of the event itself, your handling of it and the feelings you have as a result.

And then, going on, you can record the best evaluation you can make at the moment of the situation and your feelings—what you think the situation really called for and what the proper feelings might have been.

And having done all this, you can sit back then or later, play the tape back or review your notes and—trying to act as a good parent to yourself—you can seek to arrive at what the objective evaluation of it all by a good parent might be. And if you are still shaky, because of your past conditioning, about imagining how a good parent might evaluate the account, you can imagine how a good friend might do the evaluating.

You can follow the same procedure with each situation in which you feel unduly hurt, fearful, angry or impulsive. And, as you do so, you will begin to notice a pattern and get a feel for the true dimensions of your child-of-the-past conditioning and how it operates.

From time to time, too, in periods of quiet meditation, you can think of and note or record accounts of other situations that may have occurred sometime in the past that show much the same pattern.

And there can—and should—be a positive side to your recording. You can note any situations in which you seem to have made a gain, situations similar to those in which in the past you did not do well and had disturbed feelings about but in which now you had less disturbed feelings and perhaps even some slight glow of acceptability. You can note what the situations were, how you handled them, what you did, how you felt immediately and how you felt later. For it is important for you to get a feel for even the smallest successes, an appreciation of them and of yourself for achieving them.

These note-taking or recording sessions are no exercises in foolishness, no babyish endeavors, no waste of time. In recording your feelings and reactions, in analyzing them, in detecting patterns of difficulties and patterns of successes, you are doing substantially what a therapist would do for you if you went to see one.

The therapist would be recorder and playback machine. He might provide some interpretation now and then, but his interpretation in itself would have little or no value; to be valuable, it would have to become your interpretation.

There is great likelihood that you can function effectively as your own therapist by following a planned procedure such as making notes on tape or in a notebook so patterns become clearer and you can begin to make interpretations and act on them.

Nor need you be hesitant—you would still remain your own therapist—if from time to time, feeling you are still not able to see the picture clearly and to interpret as objectively as you would like, to ask for help. You can approach someone you respect—minister, physician, good friend—and say, "Look, I recognize that I have a problem in self-control or in self-respect, in handling some situations as well as I should handle and want to handle them, and I am playing a little game with myself. I hope it is going to be a constructive game. I think I need your help for just a bit as a kind of umpire."

There is no shame in this at all. You can almost certainly get help. People like to help if they can. You can note another person's interpretation and consider it. It may be sound, as given. Or it may be valuable in allowing you to put it alongside your own and arrive at a more valid interpretation than the other person's or your own was originally.

In the chapters that follow in this section, I have set forth all the techniques that have worked for my patients over the years. With their aid, I believe you can be equally successful if you truly want to change. Rarely have I seen anyone fail who has thoroughly and conscientiously taken the steps outlined, and as helpful as I like to feel my role as therapist has been, I realize that without the willingness and determination of my patients, I could have accomplished nothing.

And so . . . to work. I know you can succeed.

chapter 12

Identifying Yourself

It is likely that you have already begun to identify from the earlier discussion a parental pathogenic attitude, or perhaps more than one, that influenced you in your childhood and may be doing so now.

Possibly your impression is valid. You can determine whether it is. Without great difficulty, you can recover an insightful knowledge of what you were like as a child, what the prevailing attitudes of your parents were toward you and what reactions you had to those attitudes. Both the prevailing parental attitudes and your own reactions to them are significant.

Offhand Memories

You can begin the identification process by letting any memories you have of your early home life emerge. Do you recall your moods as a child? Perhaps you can remember times when you made demands, whined, felt sorry for yourself, felt lonely; times when you had tantrums; times when you sought to win approval and praise from your parents and how you went about doing so; times when you were punished and how you were punished; times when you were afraid.

While such memories can be helpful, a word of caution: All of us can remember occasions when we were angry or lonely or were punished or felt abused. But isolated instances are not necessarily significant. For our purposes now, what is significant lies in prevailing parental attitudes, those that were more or less constant, that largely determined the parent-child relationship in themselves and also in the reactions they aroused in you.

Let all memories emerge as they come to you. But your cardinal interest will not be in an isolated punishment or a disappointment you may have had in not being able to do something at a particular time in childhood when it was what you most wanted to do. Instead, what you want to determine is, for example, what were your mother's overall, steady, day-by-day, week-by-week attitudes toward you? Was she, time after time, excessively strict, moralistic, determined that you be perfect? Or very much indulgent, catering, eager to do for you, slow to impose discipline?

What you also want to know is how you reacted to her. Were you polite? Respectful? Or did you show disrespect and possibly fly into temper tantrums? How did she react when you became angry with her? Did she try to make you follow many rules—anxious rules—that seemed to you then, and perhaps still seem to you, to have had no real usefulness? When you hurt yourself as a child and went to your mother, what was her response?

What, on all of these points, are your memories of your father? Was he home a lot of the time or gone much of the time? Did he have time for you? Could you approach him with your problems? And how did he react? And how did you react to his reaction?

What was the dinner-table atmosphere like? Pleasant? Full of happy conversation? Silent? Tense?

What do you recall of relationships with your brothers and sisters? These are important but usually not nearly as much so as relationships with parents. A certain amount of misunderstanding and bickering is to be expected among immature people, and children are immature. But a child usually can tolerate well considerable amounts of such misunderstanding and bickering if his relationship with his parents is healthy. It would be important, however, to consider the attitudes of brothers and sisters if they affected parental attitudes toward you—for example, if a brother teased you and you fought back and your parents consistently took your brother's part.

Because your main purpose is to get an overall view of your old home life and parental attitudes toward you and yours toward them, it can be helpful to recall as much as you can about your school days and your relationships with your peers—because these may reflect the home atmosphere, generally suggesting a fairly good home atmosphere if they were good and a disturbance in the home balance if they were poor.

We have pointed out that it is useless to assign blame to parents, that almost always any hurtful attitudes they may have had were not deliberately intended to be hurtful.

It is all to easy to block off memories of childhood if we assign blame. None of us really likes the idea of finding serious fault with a parent and many of us shut out memories if there is any likelihood that they may arouse old feelings of blame and resentment.

So approach recall with the recognition that almost certainly your parents had problems and were human, and their attitudes toward you arose out of their problems and humanness and not their lack of love or lack of desire to be kind, considerate and helpful toward you. If you do this, you are likely to recall much more readily.

Nor is it necessary to try to force recall—to make a big task of it, to consider that it must be done in a few minutes or a day or a week. Make a start. Let come what comes. Go on with other things. Once you have determined that you do want to recall, want to do so without rancor, and have become relaxed about it, more memories will come.

It is most helpful, as we have emphasized, if you keep a record of what you recall. Try to find some time of day when it is convenient for you to sit down quietly and in relaxed fashion let your mind go back home again. At that time, jot down what you recall or use your tape recorder. And jot down what you recall at other times as well—in your notebook if you have it with you or, if not, on a scrap of paper to be transferred later to the notebook or to be recorded on tape.

Sooner or later, as you continue this procedure, an increasingly clear picture of the emotional atmosphere in which you grew up will emerge. It will do so sooner if you avoid a common pitfall. In seeking to understand yourself and your background, you may sometimes wander a bit aimlessly and if you hit upon some painful memory, you may find yourself returning to it repeatedly, almost as if you were stuck there, because you find yourself trying to prove to yourself even now that you were innocent and wronged. Avoid that. The avoidance is not unduly difficult if you insistently remind yourself that one incident makes no real difference, that you don't have to prove anything, that any efforts to do so are of no real avail and in fact are wasteful now and keep you from getting on with what you want to accomplish.

Again, what you want to accomplish is to arrive at a clear, true, broad picture of your childhood home life—a picture in which you can see whether one parent or the other, or perhaps both, were stern toward you or indulgent and perhaps even over-indulgent; or whether they had a largely punitive attitude toward you; or were coercive; or were unduly anxious and concerned over you, your health, your safety; or whether they oversubmitted to you; or whether they loaded you, even if unknowingly, with excessive responsibilities.

And again too what you want to know is how you responded—when they expressed approval or disapproval, when they punished you, when they rewarded you, when they indulged you if they did, when they coerced you if they did that, when they expected you to be perfect, to do better than you were doing even if you were already doing well, if that is what they did.

Relating Past and Present

You may be tempted to approach the process of recalling your early home life with some directiveness; that is, you may have reason to suspect a particular parental pathogen that was present and seek to recall instances to buttress the suspicion. There is some danger in that, for more than one pathogen may have been operative. So let the memories come freely, unrestricted.

One of your prime purposes will be to relate past and present, to see how present difficulties—whether in marriage, in business, in relationships with friends or in other areas—may stem from use of old attitudes and methods from the past that are incongruous now.

A vital part of the identification process lies in considering any present difficulties and asking yourself how you got into them, in seeing whether you got into them because of the use of old home methods. Important in itself, this can also be helpful in recalling and clarifying memories of childhood, sometimes serving as memory releasers.

You can ask yourself such questions as these:

Where is it that I tend to get into difficulty most commonly? Where is it that I feel most uncomfortable? What types of situations seem to embarrass me, make me feel inadequate, irritate me? Are most of my difficulties in marriage? In business? Or are they across-the-board?

Do I, in some situations, develop feelings that are excessive or inappropriate? Do I get angry in situations that, viewed objectively, should not call for anger or any great emotion? Do I feel fearful in situations that really do not call for fear? Do I feel alone in situations where, objectively, I am not alone and people are not ostracizing me? Do I feel depressed when, in actuality, the situation around me is not all that depressing?

Whatever they may be, when feelings are inappropriate or excessive, the likelihood is that they arise because of the child of the past. This is *his* area, where *he* dominates, where *he* takes over automatically.

You can look back into your childhood, examine the emotional attitudes that prevailed, recall how they were expressed and your reactions to them. You can try to recall how your child of the past acted back in childhood when you faced situations somewhat analogous to those you face today. You can stimulate memories that way. As the memories return, you can come back to the present, place the remembered child of the past in present situations that arouse excessive or inappropriate feelings. And you can get a good idea about whether such feelings can be explained, in part or in whole, on the basis that if, indeed, the child of the past took over in such situations automatically and dominated you, those would, inevitably, have to be the feelings you experience.

In effect, then, you can work back from present difficulties to try to illuminate the past and work forward from the past to try to illuminate the present, and your difficulties can begin to make more sense to you.

If, for example, you had a domineering, critical father and you now get shaky every time you go in to talk to your boss, it is possible that the shakiness has much to do with the child of the past, that you are reacting in the present as if you were a small child being called on the carpet by a domineering father.

Frequently, patients who come to see me do so to explore a series of incidents that have bothered them. One woman, for example, complained of having difficulty accepting herself and mentioned specifics. She berated herself for being unable somehow to keep her home as tidy as she wished it to be. She sometimes forgot items when she shopped and was critical of herself for her forgetfulness. She was often uncomfortable at dinner parties and in other social situations and would find herself going over the situations repeatedly when she got home, with a great amount of self-belittlement.

It was not difficult to see the thread of childhood conditioning. I asked her to make a list of situations that induced in her any feeling of anxiety or depression. I also suggested that she think back to her past home life and try to recall in particular how it was when she had been given a chore such as sweeping a room or doing any kind of cleaning around the house, what her parents' reactions were to the job she did and how she reacted to the job itself and to their reactions, and how it was when she was sent to the grocery store and failed to bring back all she was supposed to, and how it was when she went to her first party as a child and what were her reactions and those of others and of her parents.

As she recalled, she could begin to get an idea of what was making things difficult for her in the present. And she could begin to differentiate between her evaluations of present situations so largely based, as she could begin to see, on an outlook carried over from the past and the situations as they might be viewed objectively.

Once you identify pathogens from the past still operating now—helped to do so by spontaneous memories and by memories you arouse by working back from present difficulties—you have a start. You have some insight from previous discussions of how such pathogens, operative in the past, can operate in the present and the discussions will be extended in later chapters.

And from the start you have, you can go on to the process of differentiation. You can begin to approach problems and difficulties knowingly, aware of how, if allowed, your child of the past can take over; you can differentiate between what your adult self tells you is proper action and feeling and what the child of the past would have the action and feeling be; and you can move on to begin to control the child of the past in specific situations and let your adult self, rightfully, take over.

Misdiagnosis?

The question might well be asked if it is possible to make a misdiagnosis of one's self, to dream up fictitious pathogenic parental attitudes or possibly to miss some that were actually present. And the answer is yes, that is possible. It is possible, for example, to miss a pathogen if, on the one hand, it was very weak or, on the other hand, was so strong that it is difficult to face.

Yet, there are checks.

You can observe how you react, how you treat yourself and treat others particularly in situations that hurt you or hurt others. You can reasonably figure that old borrowed attitudes are likely to be at work in those situations. You can ask yourself what those attitudes are. Are they attitudes that impose undue standards on you and never allow self-acceptance? Are they attitudes that provoke unmitigated self-criticism and belittlement? Are they attitudes that make it difficult for you to control yourself even though, for lack of control, you are hurting others, infringing on their rights or hurting yourself because the lack of control interferes with your important long-term goals?

You can reasonably assume that there is to be found in your past home life the prototype for your present self-belittlement or lack of self-control. You can look back, try to encourage the memories to come. If you still cannot see the prototype, you can fairly safely assume that is is nevertheless there, blocked out for now, but not necessarily blocked out permanently. Sometimes, you may be able to see clearly enough how you were treated in your growing-up years and yet be unable to see clearly how the treatment then relates to what you are doing to yourself now. Even so, you can proceed on the assumption, very likely valid, that the treatment back then, coupled with your reactions to it, has much to do with what is going on now.

Very likely, you now have or soon will have a reasonably definitive idea of the pathogen or pathogens active in your case. But even if you do not have, there is no need to wait until you do have such an idea before going on.

In terms of what we do to ourselves that hurts or hinders us, most of our problems fall into three broad areas, as we saw earlier: problems of self-belittlement or of self-control or combinations of both. We shall be dealing in Part V with certain other problems—such as hypochondriasis and excessive sexual stimulation—that can be considered special problems.

As we have seen, certain parental pathogens tend to be involved in problems of self-belittlement, others in problems of self-control and some in both types of problems. If you have any doubts about the parental pathogen or pathogens operative for you, you can settle immediately for deciding that you have problems of self-belittlement or of self-control or of both, and those are what you are going to work on.

You are not hamstrung by a need to first arrive at what, unmistakably, the parental pathogens were in your case before you proceed. Almost certainly, they will become clear as you start proceeding on the basis of attacking your broad problems of self-esteem or self-control or both. And as you do this, you will be very much involved with self-to-self transactions, with recognizing them as they take place, with learning how to influence them for the better, with how to let your child of the past have his way when it is a good way and how to curb the child when curbing is needed so that your adult self can come into control.

Pathogen Combinations

It is quite possible that you will discover that you have been affected by two or more parental pathogens. One parent may have one primary attitude toward a child while the other parent has another attitude, and often a single parent may combine several attitudes.

Overcoercion and perfectionism, for example, often go together. And it is not uncommon for overcoercion and oversubmission to be associated. In effect, the parent may make a pact with a child that comes to this: "I will twist your arm to push you to achievement but, at the same time, I will give in to your whims and demands."

Perfectionism and oversubmission are commonly found in the same parent and the pact then is: "I can't accept you and your performance as is, at the current level, and I will promise acceptance if you achieve a higher level—and, at the same time, I will be your slave, indulging you and doing your bidding."

Punitiveness and overcoercion may be combined: "I will twist your arm, twist it critically, twist it punishingly." Neglect and overindulgence may be combined; a parent may spend little time with a child but when he does may give the child an excess of goods and privileges to make up for his neglect.

A common combination to which a child may be exposed and which may turn him into an impulsive, resisting, self-critical person is that of a critical, moralistic father and a self-critical, submissive mother. The critical husband, in choosing his wife, has sought somebody he can use as a pounding board. The self-belittling woman, although not comfortable, feels at home with somebody who beats on her. And she is pounded down sufficiently so the child's natural impulsiveness runs roughshod over her and his impulsiveness is amplified. At the same time, the father's moralistic arm twisting makes the child resistive. But the child also feels guilty because of the belittling from the father and possibly, too, because of somewhat martyred belittling from the mother ("You hurt me; why must you do this to me?").

In examining your past background, you will want to be aware of the possibilities of these and other combinations. And you can also take into account the fact that the pathogenic influence of one parent on a child sometimes may become the triggering factor for a baleful influence of the other.

The Total Picture

You will want to consider, too, that some influences you may have carried over from your childhood could have had nothing to do with parental pathogens.

I can think, for example, of one couple, John and Joyce, who could not get up in the morning without having the two children of their past come into conflict. John's father had worked in the evening and had slept to noon daily. When John married, he reestablished the old home situation and slept to noon every day. On the other hand, Joyce grew up under the influence of a father who might be called by some a "health nut." It was his custom to leap out of bed at six in the morning, throw open his windows, exercise vigorously, take a cold shower, then rush through the house zipping the bedclothes off everybody and announcing: "Time to get up." And his daughter's inclination was to follow suit in her own home.

Conflict, of course. Child-of-the-past conditioning, yes. But parental pathogens involved? Not really. Was there a possibility for compromise? Yes. John and Joyce had other problems more difficult to solve, problems resulting from parental pathogens, and they had to work at those. But the up-in-the-morning conflict was handled quite well when he agreed to modify his habit a bit and get up at nine-thirty instead of noon and she allowed that, if he did that, she really didn't have to run a sweeper in front of his bed to get him up.

We are concerned with major parental pathogens and their effects, and those pathogens can be classified clearly. But not all human behavior and conditioning can be readily classified, nor is classification necessary. Differences in past conditioning that are not the results of parental pathogenic influences can be recognized, and when approached respectfully and cooperatively, the differences can be compromised to reach mutually satisfactory solutions. And such solutions are no small help in allowing attention to be focused on and efforts made to handle the major internalized parental pathogens.

It can be important to recognize nonpathogenic past influences as a way of avoiding needless self-belittlement. You may need to modify cultural influences to solve problems and avoid self-criticism. Obesity, for example, has many possible roots and one lies in tradition. The traditional foods of some peoples are rich and, if used routinely, will lead to overweight in people who are not very active physically. Self-criticism and belittlement will not get rid of excess weight and may in fact help to increase it. But modification of a cultural tradition may help solve the problem.

Similarly, somebody coming from a warm climate and a way of life that is more leisurely, deliberate and easygoing may have difficulty adjusting to the brisk pace usually found in an area where the climate is colder. And if you were raised in a rural area where everybody knew everybody else, all rallied around the church or the store, and there was friendly talk and give-and-take, you may find it difficult to adjust to life in a city, where people tend to be somewhat isolated from each other and where, if you stop for a friendly chat with a neighbor, he may respond in an uninterested, offhand manner that would have been considered a rebuff back home.

To be a good parent to yourself, you need to recognize any nonpathogenic influences and conditioning that may be working in your life—and to recognize, too, that they are no cause for self-belittlement. You may wish to make modifications in them or you may prefer to leave them unchanged and possibly go where you can maintain and be happy with them. That is a choice you should have—are entitled to—and there should be no self-belittlement about it.

chapter 13

What to Be Wary of if Overcoerced

You were directed and redirected, ordered to do this and then that. The characteristic response of any human being to such overcoercion is to develop resistance. And it is very much as if you have a fierce allergy to have-tos. Resistance very probably has become a critical barrier in the way of accomplishing many of your adult goals.

You often find it difficult to "get started." You determine, earnestly, that you are going to accomplish something, then somehow fail to do so, fail even to get around to making the effort. You tend to daydream much, achieve relatively little, and you may have a sense of chronic fatigue, enough to make you think that something must be physically wrong.

You may find yourself blaming others for your problems. You may develop a whole complex of reasons, of explanations to yourself, why it is simply "impossible" for you to get done what you want to do.

Perhaps your resistance in childhood was active, involving outright defiance, clear verbalized refusal. Perhaps it was passive, taking the form of delay and dawdling. In either case, it may have led, if not to punishment, to more nagging commands. And the added commands—or the punishment—led to more resistance.

It could have been that, if coercive control started early in your life and was maintained consistently, you obeyed docilely without resistance. In that case, as so often happens, all through your growing-up years and later in adult life you may have needed direction from others. Without such direction, you may be unable to function well or sometimes even to function at all. In your case, then, you have resistance, too—resistance to initiative.

As a victim of overcoerciveness, you can do much to help yourself. When you understand the command-resistance cycle as it operated in childhood, you can begin to see it at work in your adult life. It may not be operative in all areas; you can analyze to see where it is at work. You can then proceed to transmute the have-tos in those areas into want-tos, thus removing a critical element and so interrupting the vicious command-resistance cycle.

Resistance and Your Job

Resistance can operate in many areas and very frequently does so in work situations.

When you find each new work day that you have difficulty getting up and getting to the job on time, almost certainly resistance is accountable.

No matter how much you, as an adult, may see the need for getting to the job on time and doing it well, your child of the past doesn't see it that way. He is ruled by his long-nurtured resistance to what he sees as have-tos. And as long as he is uncontrolled within you, his clamor produces inner conflict and inhibition.

And the inhibition—whether it takes the form of difficulty in getting started or even getting up in the morning, or of submission to distractions that prevent getting down to work—may be made even worse by the barking of harsh self-commands.

If you take an honest look at this anxiety and these self-commands you can recognize their source in your resistance. This recognition makes your problem definite and as a result you can try to cope with it.

The best way to cope with it is by putting an arm around yourself kindly, by encouraging yourself. You can say to yourself: "I begin to understand now what the real problem is. I'm no longer groping in the dark. It's going to take time and effort but I can get control of the inner child I now recognize as the source of the conflict within. However, I am not going to control him by incessantly and disrespectfully barking orders at him."

Does your work situation accentuate your problem? That sometimes needs to be taken into account.

One of my patients, a young accountant named Jim, had had several jobs since graduation and had been happy in none. He had arrived at the point of being almost totally confused, uncertain of what he wanted to do, where he wanted to go.

Brought up in an achievement-oriented family, full of hard workers, Jim had had much expected of him and had been pushed to be an achiever. He had managed to achieve well enough in his growing-up years by pushing himself, and although he had developed resistances he had managed to overcome them.

Starting out in adult work, he had followed the same pattern, twisting his own arm and managing to overcome his resistances. But the arm twisting had made work unpleasant for him. He had changed jobs several times but none was any more pleasant for him than its predecessor.

Then he had landed a job with a firm of accountants where, if anything, overcoercion was a matter of policy. It was a firm of work addicts; the company principals and the employees worked hard and long, overtime and weekends, and took pride in the excessive work. And as Jim tried to keep up, barking commands at himself, his resistance kept mounting and he became increasingly self-critical as well.

The self-criticism helped only to make the job and every aspect of life seem entirely lackluster. Beat on yourself and, sooner or later, you begin to feel dull and find life dull.

Jim finally became aware of how the command-resistance cycle was operating in him. Although this is not always the case, it was necessary for him to leave that particular job and find one where the atmosphere was less coercive.

Varied Aspects of Overcoercion

Do you have trouble with ordinary social conventions? For example, do you feel awkward when it comes even to such a seemingly simple procedure as introducing people to each other? You may be puzzled by your awkwardness, upset by it, and perhaps you've castigated yourself for it as being stupid, gauche. And yet it could be—and often is—a reflection of resistance carried over from childhood to a parent who insisted, "Now, dear, remember you must introduce your little friend to everyone in the room, and you must do so properly."

Do you have money problems? Do you find yourself careless in your spending, with tendencies to "impulse buying" and perhaps to spending beyond your means? Here, again, as an overcoerced person, look for the resistance factor. It's important for you to understand that adults who were overly coerced in childhood about money matters—constantly directed to count every penny, to save and save some more, to not spend for this or that—often carry over a resistance that leads them unaccountably, or seemingly so, to spend unwisely.

If you're given to excesses in one or several kinds of activities—for example, partygoing, entertaining, TV watching, card playing—these too may be traced sometimes to resistance carried over from childhood to overly strict, coercive parental attitudes about recreational activities.

Excessive drinking sometimes may be a reaction to parental coercion against either such indulgence in particular or indulgences in general. Food likes and dislikes may reflect childhood resistances to parental badgering at the table. It often turns out that people who are unable to enjoy reading turned against it because, during a period of slowness or difficulty in reading in childhood, they were subjected by parents and teachers to insistent drilling and overcoercion.

Sexual promiscuity, too, may arise from the warnings and prohibitions of overcoercive parents. Reacting to constant cautionings about kissing, necking and petting, the adolescent, and later the adult, may, in effect, answer resistantly: "I won't follow your prohibitions. I am going to live my own life." To be dictated to by a resistant inner child is not to live one's own adult life.

Fears and Stuttering

If you have a fear that seems inexplicable, you may find the explanation in resistance. Such fears may be dramatic in children who have been overcoerced but adults may have them as well.

I recall the case of Janice R., a twelve-year-old, who was brought to see me by her mother because the child had confessed that she couldn't sleep at night and was fearful of getting up and killing somebody.

Janice, Mrs. R. told me, was a well-behaved child, and Mrs. R. also added: "I am an exacting mother." She was certainly that. Janice had to follow a rigid schedule, which began at 6 A.M. with an hour of piano practice. And, when she arrived home from school at 4 P.M., there was an hour of compulsory book reading, followed by dinner at 5, then dishes, and from then until 8, lessons, bath and a bit of TV, then bed. Janice did well in schoolwork. Janice played dutifully in the school band. And on weekends, Janice dutifully went with the family to their country place, there to spend much of her time clearing out brush, planting trees and doing other chores.

Janice had dreams—often about a witch, she told me. She didn't know what dreaming about a witch meant, but it was obvious to me as she described her dreams that the witch represented her coercive mother. When I asked the child about her fear that she might hurt people, her eyes filled with tears; she felt guilty and uncomfortable talking about the fear. Here, again, the meaning was obvious: the child resented very much being pushed and coerced but was fearful of her feelings of resentment and longings to retaliate.

In the case of a child like Janice, there is usually a gratifying response when the coercive parent can be convinced that coercion is hurtful, that the pressure should be eased, that a child needs to have time for recreation, time to be carefree.

In the case of an adult with such a fear, it is necessary to understand that the problem lies with the inner child and the inner child's dominance. It may not be possible to eliminate the inner child's fear, but it is possible to understand it and to deal with it. An adult with such an inner child can acknowledge the basis for the fear, and he can treat the child kindly, saying in effect: "If you, my child, are fearful, I understand why and don't blame you, but there is no longer need for fear, and as an adult I cannot and will not let your fear distract me from my adult pursuits."

Overcoercion can sometimes be a major factor in speech difficulties, as it was for Floyd, twenty-one, a personable, somewhat shy young man with a severe stutter. Floyd came to see me when he was a college senior soon to start job interviews and felt he had to get to the bottom of his speech trouble.

The clues to the source of the trouble came when he told me: "I keep telling myself that I ought to speak better than I do . . . I tend to make mountains out of molehills . . . My dad is all business. He was impatient with my speech."

Anxious attempts by parents to make a young child speak more fluently can actually initiate stuttering. And the stuttering may be perpetuated in adulthood when the stutterer gives himself the same anxious instructions and commands he had from his parents: "Go slow," "Be careful," "Don't stutter like that."

Floyd had to see that he was directing himself, particularly when he spoke, with his father's busy, rushing methods. He would tell himself: "Hurry up now. Do it better. You *can* do it better. Don't be such a dummy. Get the word out." His father's words.

He had to see that he didn't have to apply to himself his father's mistaken attitudes, that he himself could be in charge now and could treat himself in his own way, more tolerantly and more respectfully.

He was asked to imagine having beside him the nine-year-old boy he once was—hurt by pressure to speak correctly and by criticism of his efforts. How would *he* treat this boy? Wouldn't he put his arm around him and comfort him rather than badger him? Wouldn't he be patient with the boy's efforts to speak?

Able to consider that his speaking self was this nine-year-old boy, Floyd could practice tolerant friendship with this part of himself. As his self-badgering and self-criticism lessened, his speech improved. In five months, he competently took interviews for jobs, landed a good one and is productive in his work. He still has some difficulty with his speech but he can see that the more he accepts his manner of speaking exactly as it is, without inner badgering, the more fluent and expressive he becomes.

Overcoercion and Marriage

If, as an overcoerced person, you have encountered difficulties in your marriage, it is not surprising.

Even when two people free of overcoercive backgrounds marry, they have expectations, romantically colored, about each other. And it is the rare marriage that is entirely free of demands and resistances. A demand may develop when an expectation is not satisfied. The demand may lead to some resentment and resistance that, if minor, do no real harm.

But marriage can be a fertile ground for the sprouting of demands, coerciveness and resistance—and when one of the partners brings into the marriage a background of overcoercion, problems may multiply. In the extreme, there may be bitter resentment, even chaos. More often there are chronic feelings of distress and futility.

Resistant as the overcoerced person is to demands and requirements, he or she may nevertheless maneuver the spouse into being coercive and demanding, thus reestablishing the old home atmosphere in order to obtain the security of the familiar.

If you think you may be doing this be alert for such maneuvers on your part. For example, not uncommonly a wife with an overcoercive background, who feels resistant about doing household chores, forces her husband to become demanding. She may then do the chores resentfully and with much foot dragging, just as she did as a child.

There are many possible variations. Many a wife has been turned into a nagger because a husband with an overcoerced background dawdles and delays when it comes to undertaking minor but necessary repairs around the home. Sometimes one spouse who resists responsibility finally forces the other spouse to take the responsibility and then resents the other for doing so.

There may be repercussions in raising children. Overcoerced in childhood and somewhat anxious over your adequacy as a parent, you may turn to the same methods your parents used on you because they are familiar and you know no other methods. But these are not the methods familiar to your spouse. Quarrels ensue and may be detrimental not only to the happiness of you and your spouse but to the welfare of your children.

You may have sexual difficulties in your marriage that can be traced to overcoercion. Perhaps more so in the past than now, women often were taught to regard sexual intercourse as a "duty." A woman who looks upon sex in this way may carry out her "duty" resentfully and without satisfaction. Some women, concealing this resentment from themselves because of their wish to be good wives, develop headaches or other ailments to postpone or avert sex.

A Visual Image of Yourself

Productiveness is a natural human goal. It hurts to do less than you reasonably can do. Your adult self-esteem and inner confidence depend strongly on feelings of being productive, needed, useful, loving and loved. But the command-resistance cycle is a barrier.

Picking out some simple visual image on which you can focus, an image of what goes on within you, can be a most useful tool. You may choose an image of a donkey within you. You have a rope on the animal and you pull, but the harder you pull, the more stubbornly the animal plants its feet.

The donkey represents the command-resistance cycle that is your problem. The animal can be a sharp reminder of what your problem is and a help in remembering that more coercion is not the answer.

Transmuting the Have-tos

How can you learn to substitute want-tos for have-tos? To some extent, this is a matter of recognizing that many of the things you were commanded to do in childhood, and which you did resentfully or delayed or dawdled about doing, were things you might well have come to do on your own without commands. They were things you might well have wanted to do as you matured and realized the need for and desirability of doing them.

And if you examine your present have-tos, you will undoubtedly find that, considered in terms of your adult goals, of what you want to accomplish, most of them are really want-tos if you only allow them to become so.

You will need to be patient with the resistant child within you, saying to him, in effect, whenever you find him at work and do not wish him to dominate: "Look, this is something you don't want to do and you will be resisting. But I wish to do it. It fits in with my mature goals even if not with your immature desires. It is a want-to for me."

To take a simple example, you will say: "I know you don't like to vacuum the living room. I understand that and I understand the why from childhood. But the room needs cleaning. Come on, let's do it." You will use firmness—but with understanding and without criticism and deprecation.

The child of the past will scream: "You are forcing me." And you will say: "No, I am not forcing. But I find I, the adult, am happier when I achieve my goals."

You will tell yourself: "I know it is going to take me longer to do the living room because I have a reluctant child of the past to deal with. I realize that is my conditioning. I am not going to scold or criticize. I will take myself, conditioning and all, and do this thing. Because if I don't my resistant child of the past will have won again and my past orientation will only grow stronger."

To go on a little longer with that simple yet representative example, you may find your child of the past saying such things as "You know, there is much more of value in life than a clean living room. It is much more worthwhile and uplifting to listen to a symphony or read a good book than to vacuum a rug and furniture. You don't really want to clean the room." This is to be expected. Change takes time.

It's important to remember that lapses are likely to occur, since you cannot change a lifelong pattern on just the basis of deciding to do so. Work and patience are needed. You may need to sit back fairly frequently and go over in your mind the things you want to do because you want the results of doing them; you will not aim at perfection but do what you can, giving yourself time and encouragement.

You can expect to find help in many of the later chapters of the book. With each bit of progress, you will find satisfaction in your ability to accomplish something, no matter how small, without coercive self-threats. And with each little minor triumph, the resistance offered by your child of the past will diminish just a bit more and your confidence and ability to act without inner struggle will be enhanced.

chapter 14

What to Be Wary of if Oversubmitted To

Because one or both of your parents submitted to you much or most of the time, placing few or no limits on you, giving in to your whims and immature demands, you now tend to treat yourself in the same manner. You have difficulty saying no to yourself and your impulses even though you may recognize that they are harmful, hurting others or keeping you from what you really want to be and do.

Parents who are oversubmissive behave that way for a variety of reasons. It may have been because you were a desperately wanted, long-sought child, and there was great anxiety about keeping your love and giving you "everything your little heart desired." It may have been because a parent had been brought up subservient to her own parents' demands and was so used to serving them that she automatically served you because, with her upbringing, this was the only way she knew how to respond to any demanding person in the family. Or it may have been because a parent was so persistently self-belittling that she placed your whims above any needs of her own in importance, and even when she recognized a need to limit your impulsiveness, she could not respect herself and her own rights enough to be firm in the face of your temper and demands.

Whatever the reason, a pattern was laid down. A child, being immature, tends naturally to be impulsive and demanding. As he finds he can get what he wants, he becomes increasingly assertive. Whatever the motivation for the parent's oversubmissiveness, he or she must, being human, become irritated at times with the child's demands since they infringe on the parent's feelings and rights. However, commonly the parent does not act on the irritation. In fact, the presence of the irritation may even arouse guilt feelings, a sense of not being a good parent because of the irritation, whereupon there are greater efforts to give the child love and security—through even greater submission. And even if the child senses the parent's irritation and lack of basic approval, he increases his demands since he knows no other way to get approval.

As the cycle repeats itself, there may come a time when the parent's irritation and resentment build to a point where he or she blows up and gives vent to anger. The blow-up may come over some trifling matter, just one matter too many. And, having blown up, the parent is often appalled, feels guilty, and all the more so because of recognition that the blow-up was over a minor matter and, from that standpoint, was not fair. The child, too, usually reinforces the parental feeling of guilt by accusations of meanness and unfairness. And the parent then remorsefully makes even more concessions and becomes still more oversubmissive.

Now, as an adult, you carry within you the child of the past who was oversubmitted to and who dominates some or many aspects of your life. The child has always made demands and has been used to getting his way. And as you grew into adulthood, you may have let the inner child have his way as long as satisfying his whims and demands caused you no suffering. But, as you began to sense how much your impulsiveness—really, his impulsiveness—infringed on the rights and dignity of others and interfered with the achievement of your adult goals, you became concerned.

And perhaps you also became self-belittling.

There may have been self-belittling earlier—in fact, throughout childhood. In some cases, a parent may be oversubmissive and may go right on being so but may express resentment in the form of frequent but ineffective criticism. In essence, the parental attitude may be: "Shame on you for doing this to me, but I am not strong enough to say no to you." Thus, you got your way, but you were subjected to criticism and felt some twinges of belittlement. And, while you internalized the parental difficulty in setting limits on you, you also internalized the parental berating.

With or without such self-belittling internalized from childhood, you may have become self-belittling later in life as you recognized that the impulsive, undisciplined child of the past was running your life. And, outraged, you may have begun to belittle yourself with increasing harshness. The self-belittlement adds to your problem. It does not make the problem unsolvable but it must be considered and combatted.

Types of Difficulties

As an oversubmitted-to person, you may have encountered varied difficulties. Perhaps you've alienated your wife with your excessive demands, your expectations that she wait upon you as your mother did, or your temper tantrums over every minor frustration. Or perhaps you have difficulty saying no to extramarital affairs, to alcohol or to doing whatever strikes your fancy at the moment even though you regret it later.

If you are like the usual oversubmitted-to, impulsive person, you have two broad kinds of difficulties.

Without doing so intentionally, you trample down the feelings and rights of others. You may be astonished to find that others have been hurt by you. All your life, in doing or getting what you wanted, you had no particular awareness of the feelings and rights of others. Never having been required in childhood to learn to consider how your demands and tantrums might impinge on others, you indulge yourself in adulthood without consideration of the effects on others.

Your other area of difficulty lies in trying to achieve adult goals. Even when you have decided what you want to accomplish on a long-range basis, diversions and distractions interfere.

The goal is there; you want it; but from one moment to the next you impulsively want to do other things, and you give in to the impulses, failing to recognize how such distractions keep you from the long-term goal. An oversubmitted-to inner child of the past is in control, not an adult of the present.

It is helpful to recognize the power over you that the inner child has exercised, his responsibility for your difficulties in the two broad areas. It is still more helpful to understand the child's workings in specific areas of difficulty you have.

Temper Tantrums

Almost everyone who is frustrated experiences some anger and an impulse to express it. More often than not, however, an adult controls the impulse because he recognizes that a temper tantrum would not be justified and could be hurtful to others. Many people make use of simple aids such as taking a walk around the block or counting to ten to hold their tempers in check.

For you, as an oversubmitted-to person, such checkrein methods have little usefulness until you recognize the source of your emotion and the consequences it can have. In a temper outburst, cruel things may be said, another person may be deeply hurt and the damage, however much regretted later, may not be readily remediable. In addition, a temper tantrum needs to be recognized for what it is: an outburst of fury rather than a deep and genuine anger over a prolonged wrong, an automatic outburst coming not from the adult of the present but from the oversubmitted-to child of the past.

And if you have made use of the excuse that emotions must be released, that "I just had to get this off my chest, not bottle it up, not repress it, because that would be harmful"—you can discard that concept. As we noted earlier, people are not steam boilers and they can suppress impulses to temper outbursts coming from an impulse-ridden child of the past. Every emotion does not *have* to be expressed.

Extravagant Spending

While extravagant spending can be an occasional problem for most people, it may be a chronic problem for you. Having been granted almost anything you impulsively demanded as a child, you may almost habitually and automatically give in to impulses to buy things, needed or not, even if this leads to financial problems and sometimes leaves you unable to buy actual necessities.

Extravagant impulse spending may be simply a matter of self-aggrandizement. "I am used to having my wishes granted. Here is something I wish and I will have it. Because I wish it, I rate it." But sometimes it can be retaliative. For example, a woman may feel that her rights have been infringed on by her husband. She has the impulse to get back at him, to hurt him, and she proceeds to hurt him in his pocketbook.

If you have the problem of extravagant spending, ask yourself whether it is your inner child who is really doing the spending.

And as you become increasingly attentive to the child-of-the-past influence, you can make use of some relatively simple, even mechanistic, aids to help you establish realistic adult spending habits.

I often advise my extravagant patients to avoid charge accounts and credit cards—and give them up if they have them—so that it becomes less easy for them to indulge in impulse buying. This does not necessarily have to be a permanent measure but it is helpful at the beginning. I also advise patients to avoid "going shopping" on their lunch hours, to go into stores only when there is a real and clear-cut need for something. And I suggest that, before they do any shopping, they write down exactly what they need and stick to the list, taking along only enough money to pay for what is on the list.

It is often helpful, I have found, for the person prone to spend extravagantly to consult with another about actual needs before shopping—husband with wife, for example. If you talk over needs, what *you* consider to be needs, with another person whom you respect as being more objective, the other person can be a valuable guide in making sure that you buy only what is *really* necessary.

Obesity

Excess weight is a rampant problem. In the United States alone, almost 25 million have this problem and worry about it, some for cosmetic reasons alone, some out of recognition that it is a health hazard. And while reducing diets abound, the success rate is abysmally low. Efforts to cut food intake are often of the same impulsive nature as overeating, and almost invariably they fail.

This is particularly likely to be the case for the impulsive, oversubmitted-to person. If you've made repeated efforts to reduce, have tried one fad diet after another, you will do best to consider the kind of parent you are being to yourself rather than go on looking for the latest panacea diet.

As long as the child of your past controls your eating habits, you are likely to have trouble with your weight. However much the public in general likes to fancy that reducing is simply a matter of going on a diet for nine days or a month or whatever and getting rid of a lot of pounds fast even at the expense of some temporary misery, that isn't the case at all.

The only sound way to take off excess weight and keep it off is to reeducate oneself in eating habits and, very often, in activity patterns as well. After you have found a good, healthy, balanced diet you can live with for the rest of your life, you will need to reeducate your inner child. To get rid of excess weight requires less caloric intake than caloric outgo. It will take time—no nine-day crash diets. And once the excess is off, proper weight maintenance requires keeping intake and outgo in balance. It's logical but, in the face of the natural human proclivity to seek quick and easy panaceas, sound weight reduction can be something less than tempting to many people. If weight control is to be achieved, the adult must take over from the child.

Excessive Drinking

Many factors enter into alcoholism and into the social drinking that borders on alcoholism. While many family pathogens can result in an individual's having a drinking problem (perfectionism, neglect, rejection, excessive moralizing or the example of excessive parental drinking), there is sometimes an impulsive aspect to excessive drinking.

If you tend to drink to excess, the problem may lie with your child of the past and the lack of limits on him rather than what is in the bottle. And if you do drink to excess, an effort to control drinking deserves first priority, for drinking can inhibit other control efforts. It encourages the child of the past to dominate, tends to remove whatever limits you may have succeeded in imposing on him.

Here, as in other areas, it is essential to recognize that control can be achieved only in a respectful atmosphere that takes cognizance of the struggle and is not full of self-criticism and self-belittlement. A prime reason for the success of some groups in helping alcoholics lies not only in the group support given the individual until internal controls are strong enough to function well but also in the group atmosphere which is one not of criticism but of deep respect.

Just Getting up in the Morning

Getting up in the morning may be a serious problem for you, even a threat to job and career. If this seems amazing, it isn't really; it is part and parcel of the whole package of impulsiveness carried over from childhood. While few people relish that moment when they have to throw off the covers and get up and going, they recognize that they have to do it and, as a matter of course, proceed to do it. But the impulse to go on sleeping is a strong one for many of the oversubmitted-to.

Yet many of my patients have, quite quickly, been able to control the impulse. I often suggest that when they go to bed at night they tell themselves firmly, without scolding or self-criticism, that they want to get up at a certain hour in the morning because they don't want to jeopardize their job or because there is something they consider important to do and to do it requires getting up at that hour. Their child of the past has no right to dictate whether or not they will hold the job or do what they wish; that is their right.

I also suggest that they place an electric alarm clock with a loud buzz beyond immediate reach so they must get up to shut it off—and, when they get up to do that, they are simply to stand there for a while, then say kindly but firmly to themselves: "Now I will take a shower." Some people find that clock-radios work well. If you give yourself a favorable mind set without scolding or criticism the night before, it tends to filter through in the morning long enough for you to realize that you really want to get up.

When this solves the problem of getting up in the morning, or when any other measure does, it has additional value because once an impulsive person makes an inroad, even a partial one, on any problem of self-control, he has automatically strengthened his ability to make inroads on others.

Work

You may have encountered many problems in your work and career. Perhaps you keep changing jobs on impulse, attracted to new offers and to what seem to be greener fields without ever really sitting down and trying to evaluate them as objectively as possible. This tendency may work to your detriment, for often what appear, superficially, to be better opportunities turn out otherwise.

You may have difficulties because you are quick to lose your temper, even with superiors. You may have difficulties with subordinates who are made to bear the brunt of your impatience, whims, demands and temper outbursts—and if, up to a point, you may seem to get by nevertheless, you may lose the loyalty and complete cooperation of those who work for you and this may be reflected in the performance of your department.

An awareness of how your impulsiveness contributes to your

work difficulties, a refusal to automatically assign the difficulties to the stupidity or intransigence of others, a recognition of the need to set limits on yourself, can be a major step forward. In dealing with those working under you, you can ask yourself: "Am I treating my subordinates in ways that respect their rights and dignity? True, there are certain things I must ask of them and I may do so without need for apology. But over and above those, do I as boss try to maintain their self-respect or do I let my impulsiveness make me insensitive to their rights?"

Marriage and Sex

Whatever problems there may be outside the home because of impulsiveness and an oversubmitted-to background, the likelihood is that they will be multiplied within the home. Outside, some restraints may be imposed by conventions. But in the home, you may expect to be waited upon as your due and may feel hurt and unloved if not catered to, for in childhood being loved was equated with being catered to.

Rarely does an oversubmitted-to person marry another oversubmitted-to person. Both would make demands and each would refuse to accede to the other's. If they are attracted to each other, impulsive people usually learn quickly during courtship that each is expected to serve the other and forgo his or her own whims and demands; rather than do this, they often agree to forgo the relationship and marriage.

As an impulsive person you may have married someone who would cater to you and help to re-create the old home atmosphere. This is often the case. Aided by his spontaneity and ready ability for forming relationships, an impulsive person may marry a more restrained, even inhibited person who frequently enters into the relationship and tries to sustain it with some hope of eventually being able to acquire the impulsive person's spontaneity. Rarely does this happen. Instead, the more restrained spouse is swept along by the impulsive person's moods and sooner or later feels used, abused and resentful. I have been told many times by a husband or wife that living with the impulsive spouse is "like living on an emotional roller coaster. It's only his (or her) wants that matter and I am expected to go along for the ride and be satisfied with that."

Often a definite pattern of unhappiness develops in the marriage. While the more inhibited spouse has need for a close, warm relationship, the impulsive spouse, brought up able to depend upon submissive parental love and more facile than the inhibited spouse at forming relationships, has no such urgent need. He attaches much less importance to what seems vital to the inhibited spouse. The latter, after being puzzled and hurt by the inconsiderateness of the impulsive person, may then try to make demands that arouse only temper tantrums or a turning away, and the more inhibited spouse then submits but not without great resentment that may lead to frequent wrangling.

Do you recognize this pattern—and another in the area of sex?

Sex to an impulsive person often is only a sensuous experience and the partner only a vehicle. Because the impulsive person tends to be spontaneous and to show enjoyment, there may be some gratification for the partner who wishes to serve. But rarely can the impulsive person sustain the intimacy and closeness, and the partner comes to feel used and resentful.

Women often say of impulsive husbands: "He has no consideration of my feelings, bruises them much of the time he is at home, then expects me to make love with him enthusiastically at night."

Men often say of impulsive wives: "She pouts any time I don't gratify a whim of hers. She wants me to do this or that and if I don't, she wants nothing to do with me, particularly in bed. It's as if she uses sex for leverage to get what she wants."

A Cardinal Point

As we've noted, you may, as an impulsive person, have difficulty not only in saying no to yourself but also in recognizing when you infringe on the rights and dignity of others. If you are to set limits for yourself, you need to know where to set them. Because you tend to be most demanding at home, you may, if you try, get valuable cues from your spouse's reactions. And they may be valuable for determining the limits you should and would want to set for yourself not only at home but outside as well.

You may, if you approach it sensitively, as many of my patients have done, benefit from a long talk with your spouse. You may approach it by saying that you recognize now that you grew up in a home situation where you were submitted to, that you may be carrying your childhood pattern of behavior—whims, demands, temper—over into your adult life and into your home. Such openness on your part will usually be met with an honest attempt to help you. If you are met with hostility or bitterness you may have to do some changing on your own to prove your sincerity.

You may say: "I'm sure I transgress unintentionally in many areas. I don't know that I can do everything at once but I can make a beginning. What troubles you most?"

At least in the beginning, if you make the effort, you can get some feeling for the rights of others by intellect. You can begin by using your own ideas of the rights an adult should have in a relationship. You can try to sense the feelings your behavior arouses in others by asking your spouse to tell you when you transgress. As you learn it this way and make the effort to set limits, you will gradually develop the "gut" feeling that will tend to make suitable behavior somewhat automatic.

Developing Satisfaction

While many people gain satisfaction out of being helpful to others, rarely is the oversubmitted-to person one of these. Even when you succeed in setting reasonable limits on yourself and in behaving with more consideration for others, you don't automatically find satisfaction in doing so.

In fact, you must be wary of expecting others to be profusely appreciative of your efforts. As you substitute thoughtfulness and consideration for others for your excessive demands, you can usually expect to sense a positive response. But if you expect others to be full of awe and admiration you will be frustrated, and unless you discard the expectation, the frustration may only make it easy for you to slide back into the child-of-the-past pattern.

Yet, in time, if you keep making quiet, continuing efforts to be kindly, thoughtful, understanding, patient, warm and considerate, you may well be surprised to discover that you are gaining increasing satisfaction out of your efforts and out of helping others. I have had many patients who have felt much as did one formerly impulsive patient who remarked: "I have to confess to having been astonished today. I went a bit out of my way to do something for someone I hardly know. There was nothing in it for me, nothing to be expected in the way of a reward. Yet I felt, and still do, very good about it."

Fears and Demands

When an oversubmitted-to child becomes aware of how much he is pulled along by his impulsiveness, he may become fearful because he feels he has no control. Because of his fears, he may make demands for loving comfort. If the demands are excessive and the parents give in to them, the child's demanding pattern and fears are reinforced and may become even more extreme.

Sometimes a painful or shocking incident in a child's life may be handled by the parents in such a way that parental oversubmission begins, along with the reinforcement of fear and the establishment of a demand pattern.

I recall the case of Rita, an eleven-year-old, who had undergone what her parents thought must have been a terrifying experience one Sunday in church, when a woman seated beside her dropped dead. Six months after the incident, when the child was brought to see me, she was no longer able to sit in church, had developed a phobia against school and insisted on staying home and not even going to a store.

It turned out that her parents, anxious over the possible effect of the church incident, had showered the child with attention and concern. Responding, she had become demanding. As her parents submitted to the demands, the demands increased. If she had actually had a fearful reaction to the church incident, it would probably have been fleeting. But the fear fed upon the parental concern, the parental concern and oversubmission gave the fear a demanding quality, and as her fearful demands increased, Rita's parents redoubled their efforts at appeasement and a vicious cycle of fear intensification and demandingness was established.

Actually, all children have times of fear. If a child encounters a fear-producing experience, a matter-of-fact response from a supportive parent helps neutralize the experience. The child can play out the fear in a close, calm relationship until it is dissipated. But if the parents overreact—either by belittlement or by anxious concern and oversubmission—the fear is encouraged and grows and so do the excessive demands and other characteristics of the oversubmitted-to.

It is worth noting that another characteristic often found in the oversubmitted-to child is bed wetting. Certainly there are other causes of bed wetting, but oversubmission is a common one. Gratifying his impulses by day, the child sees no reason not to gratify the impulse to empty his bladder in bed at night. If treatment is directed solely at the bed wetting, it may not be enough. The child's whims, demands and temper during the day have to be limited—if necessary, by temporary isolation in his room. He has to be made to do normal chores, with no catering to him in anything he can do for himself. There must be no scolding or criticism. What counts is the parental firming up, the determination not to wait upon the child but to limit him gently and firmly and require him to do normal chores. Learning such discipline by day, the child often is able to respond quickly to habit training to avoid bed wetting at night.

The Essential Process

If you are to get your adult self into ascendancy over your over-submitted-to child of the past, you may find it helps you to isolate yourself temporarily when your whims, demands and temper infringe on others.

Another important step is to assign yourself chores and carry them out whether you want to or not. The chores can be the ordinary things you know you should do to function well day by day as an adult. You can assign them to yourself in a deliberately formal way each day and be firm with yourself about doing them even if it means staying after hours at work or staying up late at home to get them done.

Over weekends you can assign yourself projects around the house. These should be things that really need doing that are also practice in self-discipline, especially in the home situation, where you are likely to be most demanding and expect the most catering to.

You can remember that any time you flex your muscles in the service of preventing yourself from oversubmitting to yourself as you were oversubmitted to in childhood, you are flexing adult muscles and weakening the grip of the child of the past over your life.

None of this is easy; some of it can be very difficult; but none of it is impossible.

If there is a particular critical problem for the oversubmitted-to it is that they go along for many years largely unmindful of anything beyond their impulses of the moment. It usually takes a dramatic incident at work or a spouse who threatens to leave before they recognize the consequences of their behavior. They then come to recognize that they should have mature adult goals but are making no appreciable progress toward achieving them.

When they are ready to consider the why of all this, to trace it back to the parental pathogen of oversubmission and to try to do something that is constructive, they are often confused and their beginning efforts may be negated by the self-belittlement that may develop as they realize their "shortcomings." Self-belittlement is out of place here. Respect and control go together.

It is helpful to have a visual image to represent what goes on within you. And yours can be that of a child on a throne, placed there by your parents, who bowed low before you when you were a child. And there the child of the past within you still sits imperiously, and up to now, in the absence of your parents, it is you, the adult of the present, who has bowed low before the child. But no more. He will still try to command you to be impulsive, to satisfy his whims and demands, but recognizing him for what he is, you will learn to limit his childishness, not without some shrieking from him and considerable effort on your part, but limit it you will.

Many of the chapters that follow, including "Want Power Versus Will Power," "Just for Today," "Practice Times and Techniques" and "Acting 'as Though,' " will be helpful in setting those limits and in increasing both your self-control and your self-esteem.

chapter 15

What to Be Wary of if Perfectionistic

Your family standards were high. You had a difficult time pleasing one or both parents. Your standards for yourself now are unduly high and you have a very difficult time pleasing yourself.

People around you may say you have done a good job, even an outstanding job, but you have the feeling that you should have done better and could have done better. This is your old perfectionistic programming at work. Beyond robbing you of deserved satisfactions, it takes the fun and sparkle out of life, makes everything a tedious chore, even makes you depressed at times.

In the past, trying to win the prize of parental approval, you worked hard but no matter how hard you worked, the prize never came or if it did come the approval was fleeting.

Nobody's worth should be, or ever really is, dependent on what he or she does hour by hour. But for the perfectionist, the old tapes keep playing and say something like this: "That isn't good enough. If you do it better and do it faster, then I may approve of you. But the way you are going now is too slow and too incompetent and I can't possibly give you approval for this current performance."

You must see yourself in a true light. It is helpful to have a visual image of yourself—as, for example, a runner, a perpetual runner, always running rapidly and trying to run more rapidly, exhausting yourself but running, and no matter how hard you run you can never reach a prize, never finish the race, which keeps going on and on. You might even think of yourself as being on an automated treadmill, running automatically, and running harder and harder as the grade or incline of the treadmill automatically angles upward so the running becomes ever more difficult, and the pace of the treadmill automatically keeps increasing so you have to run faster and faster just to stay in the same place.

You will have to, and can, remove yourself from that race, that treadmill, that whole arena. Nothing about the race, treadmill or arena is valid. You will have to say to yourself repeatedly and learn to mean it and act on it: "I am valuable as I am. I don't have to run this no-prize, wasteful race. I don't have to be in a race atmosphere any more. There are certain things I want to do, goals I want to achieve—not because I have to but because I wish to. I am not going to be endlessly, uselessly, needlessly goaded. No one need be or ever can be perfect."

Social Wariness

When you prepare for some social event—a dinner party, dance, date—you must determine that whatever you do or don't do there, whatever you say or fail to say, you are not going to turn on yourself disapprovingly. For this occasion, you will keep your arm around yourself kindly. You will remember that you made no promise to give a good performance; you simply promised to be there. And whatever happens, you don't label yourself silly, bungling or incompetent or use any of your other favorite belittling terms to attach to your performance.

While you are there, if your arm is around yourself kindly, you can relate to others. You can take pleasure in their achievements without unfavorable mental comparisons between them and you. You can be sympathetic to any difficulties or problems they may recount. In the process of such interchange, they will be nourished, and so will you. But all this depends upon not putting up perfectionistic disappointment in your own performance as a barrier between you and others.

I don't mean to imply that simple determination will enable you to overcome your perfectionistic drives. But you can use each new social occasion for practice. Each time, you will say: "For this event, right now, I will practice *not* to do better, not to give thought to doing better, not to belittle my own performance, but simply to be kindly with myself and to be with other people."

Study and Work

When you sit down to study, you can promise yourself that for this particular study period, you will treat yourself with respect. You will not, for this hour or two or three, tell yourself what a poor student you are, how you fail to comprehend things that other people seemingly find easy to understand, how poorly you do in comparison with what you think you should do. You will promise yourself that, as long as the book is open, your arm is going to be around yourself kindly—and, whenever you catch yourself turning on yourself, you will immediately close the book and wrestle to regain kindliness, then open the book again.

When you are given a work assignment, you can tell yourself that your worth does not depend upon carrying out the assignment to perfection. You ask yourself to do the job as you see it, to complete it and to do no belittling of yourself along the way.

I know a first-rate scientist who is respected by all his colleagues but is unable to respect himself. He does a thorough, insightful job of research but then manages to turn in his report only with difficulty and foreboding. When the report is accepted enthusiastically by his colleagues and superiors and he is showered with compliments, he is unable to accept them and to believe in the sincerity of those offering them. He does beautiful work but he always gets to thinking about some little corner of the job that conceivably could have been done better. And he uses that to berate himself, to heap abuse on himself for failing to do an absolutely complete and perfect job. His life is full of a totally unwarranted feeling of inadequacy that often makes him depressed, constantly robs him of satisfactions and sometimes even interferes with, prolongs and makes his research more difficult.

Everything in life cannot and need not be done perfectly. Carl Hubbell, the great baseball pitcher, was once asked how he managed to be so near-perfect, how he managed such seemingly superhuman feats, how he could pitch so many innings without becoming exhausted. Carl pointed out that actually he threw the ball only a few minutes in each game and much of the rest of the time he didn't have to perform well or even be responsible; in fact, he observed, a lot of his time went into hitching up his trousers, adjusting his cap, dusting off his glove and slouching about.

Excellence Versus Perfection

One can pursue excellence without being perfectionistic, but if excellence is sought in order to prove one's worth, it has an unhealthy basis in perfectionism. If one likes to produce an excellent product and enjoys working toward that goal without having a do-or-die attitude toward the product as though it were oneself, there is no perfectionism involved.

Modifying perfectionism does not necessarily mean lowering standards. It does mean taking an adult view of performance without the old motivation from the past of striving to please reluctantly accepting parents.

As a perfectionistic person, you have to be wary of feeling that ordinary standards do not apply to you, of feeling superior to others in the sense of considering less-driven people inferior. You have to consider how much, if you take a realistic view, you actually yearn within for the satisfactions that you see so-called ordinary people enjoying, for the pleasures they find in life and for the enhancement of self-esteem they obtain through their achievements.

Perfectionists tend to see life as a joyless business. They feel that only by relentless striving are great things achieved. However, true masters of any art or craft attain their mastery by patient, persistent work. They know that it takes time to learn a skill and are able to enjoy the striving as well as the results. As they grow in mastery they grow in self-esteem. The perfectionist is never satisfied.

Other Areas of Perfectionism

Because perfectionism can manifest itself in many areas but more obviously in some than in others, it is often necessary for the perfectionistic person to take full stock, to make a thorough assessment, before arriving at the total picture of harm.

I remember a man I knew whose mother, all through his childhood years, had drilled him constantly in perfect speech and grammar. "Ordinarily," he told me, "I get along fine but if, in talking with anyone, I use a wrong word or make an error in grammar, I am ready to die. I turn as red as a beet, my heart pounds, I get so mad at myself that I can't sleep."

He could readily admit that he expected more of himself in that respect than other people do. "Why shouldn't I use perfect English," he observed. "It's been drilled into me since I could talk." He could also note: "When I make an error, especially if I'm talking to a stranger, I feel I've made a hopeless, irremediable error because first impressions are everything. Consequently, I am especially afraid of making an error. Therefore, I train myself, prepare myself for such a meeting if I have the chance. The result is that I generally make a good impression and whatever I say comes out perfectly."

But there is a strain and it becomes particularly pronounced when he is taken along by his boss to help sell a contract to an important client. He can't sleep the night before and "if I know the people we are going to be meeting are really well educated, I am hardly able to talk when we get there. Everything I might say—and it is important in selling and negotiation to be able to talk freely—becomes dangerous. I just dry up. I have to go over everything two or three times in my mind to make certain I am going to say it in perfect English."

While this man recognizes the perfectionism he demands of himself in English grammar, he does not realize the extent of the

child-of-the-past takeover of his speech. Good speech demands
that the adult be in charge.

Work is an area in which perfectionism frequently becomes
especially acute. A perfectionist may drive himself to the point of
exhaustion, overly concerned with every tiny detail, never satisfied with himself or those who work with or for him.

If you're perfectionistic, you have to be wary of the trap of
looking upon yourself as simply a keen competitor. You may, in
fact, have little real interest in competition per se. You are
basically concerned not so much with trying to outdo others as
trying to outdo yourself. If you want the approval of others, you
want far more the approval of yourself, which is never given,
only promised—always for "something more, something better,
something faster, something something" and invariably unattain-
able.

If you have managed to move into some field of work or
some job where you can work alone rather than as a team or
group member, that is not surprising. Because their excessive
demands alienate others sooner or later, perfectionists often
gravitate into situations where they can compete—never satisfied
and always driving—with themselves.

Sex and Marriage

Because of never-satisfied drive, you may, like many perfectionists, have difficulty not only in business and social relationships but also, and especially, in close relationships. Some perfectionists, in fact, are able to manage reasonably well their less
intimate relationships but not those involving love and affection.

However much you may feel a need for human love, for
warmth and for sexual fulfillment, your perfectionism may get in
the way. For you may quickly come to resent a sexual or marital
relationship: it is too time-consuming; it takes you away from the
race; it makes you anxious that you may lose the race. You may
fight a constant battle and be torn between your need for love
and warmth and your need to keep running.

You may take time out to develop a loving relationship only
to discover that whatever else it may do, it does nothing to satisfy
the inner compulsion to strive unceasingly.

Because of perfectionism, too, you may be overconcerned about your performance in sexual relationships. Since you must ever seek to excel in all areas, the need is not excluded from bed. Here, too, you may feel you must work to do better, to outdo yourself, to reach perfection, to achieve the perfect, explosive orgasm for you and your spouse simultaneously every time. Even if you should wish to do so, you would find it impossible to quantify warmth, affection, closeness. But physical aspects of the sexual relationship lend themselves more readily to quantification, and you can mark yourself down if you fall short of some fanciful goal. If you should feel a lack of sexual potency or feel that your partner is not responding "perfectly," you may devaluate yourself and the relationship, may become anxious and depressed and, out of fear of failure, may curtail sexual activity. All of this is true for both women and men perfectionists; women, too, may focus on performance, with no less hurtful results.

Perfectionists often delay marriage as they keep looking for the theoretically perfect mate; some never do marry. When they do marry, they move toward reestablishing in their own homes the perfectionistic atmosphere of childhood. Anything less than what they consider ideal—a bit of dust here, a burned piece of toast, a little excessive noise from a playful child—may arouse anxiety. They may make many demands, set up many arbitrary rules; they are difficult to live with.

The Case of Robert and Mary

When perfectionists encounter difficulties in marriage, they often fail to appreciate the source and to have any insight into what needs to be done if there is to be a chance for a happy outcome. Their pattern of continual striving is so much a part of their inner world that they do not see how it may cause serious difficulties in close relationships.

One of my patients, Mary, an intelligent, somewhat matronly gray-haired woman, told a story that from her viewpoint was entirely honest and yet could be misleading.

All her married life, as she saw it, she had made every effort to conform to what she was supposed to do—"to the point that I wish I hadn't." She and her husband, Robert, had raised two children, who were now married and doing well. Robert is a professional man involved in research and very much wrapped up in it. "He is not easy to talk to; you can't get into a conversation with him; all you get are monologues," Mary told me.

For years, she had busied herself—and had done so increasingly since the children had grown up—with church and civic activities and had enjoyed them, but she was bothered by her husband's complete lack of interest in anything she did.

"He," she characterized him, "is precise, clean, neat. He is unaffectionate, always right, and has a way of making me feel guilty. He came from a home where his father was remote from him while his mother catered to him but also was very moralistic and taught him responsibility. There was little laughing interchange in that home."

Mary herself came from a farm background. Her father was a lenient man. Her mother, she said, was strict, expected her to do things for herself and to carry out her chores and was often critical. There had been a tragedy. Before Mary was born, there had been a much-beloved baby who had died in infancy.

Mary had always been a hard worker and remained so in marriage. She also told me: "I am a self-belittling person. I tend to turn against and blame myself; this is one of my great problems. I am easily hurt. I get depressed. I am affectionate but that has been thwarted in my marriage."

Her husband, Robert, who also came to see me, was a distinguished-looking man. He had this to say: "I don't want to go ahead with things the way they are. My wife and I have very little we do together. There seem to be coldness and hostility in our marriage. She doesn't talk to me much and it has been this way through much of our married life but it seems to have gotten worse through the years. We seem to be in different worlds. She used to be affectionate but not any more. She is a hard worker and an excellent mother."

About his childhood, Robert said: "My father was a businessman who wasn't particularly happy in his work. He was somewhat remote from me and I was close to my mother, perhaps too close. She enjoyed doing things for me. She was a woman who was very strict about right and wrong. I didn't have many responsibilities at home. I am an orderly person, not self-critical."

Interestingly enough, Robert is not the perfectionistic one. He is neat, orderly, but quite comfortable with himself. He is used to being catered to and having his way in childhood and in adult life. He is opinionated and self-righteous and tends to monopolize conversations, which makes him difficult to live with. But his problem is not perfectionism. Perfectionism is the non-acceptance of current performance with a promise of acceptance if performance is better.

The person who cannot accept herself at her current level is Mary. She grew up under the influence of a mother who was critical and, in fact, refused to accept Mary no matter how great an effort the child made to please her. The mother's attitude was colored by her tragic experience with the beloved child before Mary who died in infancy. Without blaming her for an attitude of "I'll not get as involved with this second child; involvement is too painful," which she was unable to help, we have to note the harmful effects on Mary of her mother's nonacceptance and criticism, which Mary borrows and applies to herself in adult life. She cannot please herself no matter how much she tries and criticizes herself devastatingly. She also married a man conditioned to be self-serving, too much so to even begin to give her the acceptance she cannot give herself. So she lives in an atmosphere, both within herself and in her marriage, of acceptance starvation.

So Mary has two problems. There is the marital one, which is not hers alone. If her husband refuses to change, if he cannot accommodate to the needs of a close relationship and a happy interchange, then at some point after she has faced and solved her other problem and is able to more objectively evaluate the situation, she may wish to determine whether she can or cannot, wants or does not want to continue the marriage.

But first she must tackle her other problem—fully understanding her perfectionism and the role it is playing in her life and working to overcome it.

The Driving Force

The driving force for the perfectionist is not a need to win over competition; rather, it is a never-ending need to try to escape the awful feeling within that he or she could "do better." Anyone faced with grave misfortune or a failure may experience an emotional crisis, but in the face of neither misfortune nor failure, the perfectionist is self-belittling and driven.

You will need to make efforts to keep identifying the belittling phases in your life and, armed in each case with awareness, you will need to make efforts to remove the self-defeating self-belittlement.

You will need to establish a valid basic philosophy. If, for example, you happen to feel that you are unattractive, you will have to let go of perfectionist standards of beauty in order to make the most of your looks. You have to come to the point of saying to yourself: "I am what I am and I may not be able to change my physical features. But I will do the best I can with my appearance—my grooming, clothing, and so on—and then assume that I am acceptable. If someone then does not accept me because of my appearance, it is his problem, not mine. If I continue to devaluate myself because of my appearance, I will put a wall around myself and will not be able to have a friendly or loving give-and-take interchange with others. If I give undue importance to appearance—which, in reality, is important only to the child of the past within me—then I cut myself off from my adult goals in life."

You may have a hard time making decisions. This is not uncommon with perfectionists. One of my patients told me: "I never take the initiative. When I am hit from several directions to do something, I do nothing. I become immobilized. I feel that any decision I make will be the wrong one anyway. I don't feel I am a good, wise, perceptive person. I feel depressed but no one knows this because I am good at acting. But I am getting so I cannot keep up the smiles any more."

And no longer is he merely trying to keep up the smiles. He

has had to recognize that he came from a home where the mother was cold, efficient, unaffectionate, hard to please no matter how great the effort he made. His father was passive and remote, tried to appease the mother and did little to counteract the critical home atmosphere. And so he has carried over the old home atmosphere into his adult life. Recognizing that and determined to do something about it, he has set himself the task of making decisions and promising himself that no matter what he decides and how it comes out he is not going to turn against himself critically.

When it comes to work or any other kind of performance, you need to take the position that you never will be happy—and, indeed, you never will do as well as you otherwise could—as long as you keep telling yourself, "I am not doing well and should do better." You need to take the position that, in reality, your worth is not in question and you don't have to prove your worth every time you have a job to do, a situation to face, an interchange to make.

A Special Need of Perfectionists

Perhaps more than any other person, you, as a perfectionist, need to learn to take time out from the routine of daily responsibilities to look into and encourage your "other-centeredness" (see Chapter 27). Routine performance can be the will-of-the-wisp that leads the perfectionist into his child-of-the-past dominance. All of us have and must fulfill routine responsibilities, but the perfectionist overdoes and becomes lost in them.

I often recall a prayer (I wish I could recall the author) that, it seems to me, could have been written with the perfectionist in mind.

> Slow me down, Lord! Ease the pounding of my heart by the quieting of my mind.

> Steady my hurried pace with a vision of the eternal reach of time.

Give me amidst the confusion of my day the calmness of the everlasting hills.

Break the tension of my nerves and muscles with the soothing music of the singing streams that live in my memory.

Help me to know the magical, restorative powers of sleep.

Teach me the art of taking minute vacations, of slowing down to look at a flower, to chat with a friend, to pat a dog, to read a few lines of a good book.

Remind me each day of the fable of the Hare and the Tortoise that I may know that the race is not always to the swift, that there is more to life than increasing its speed.

Let me look upward into the branches of a towering oak and know that it grew because it grew slowly and well.

Slow me down, Lord, and inspire me to send my roots deep into the soil of life's eternal values that I may grow toward the stars of my greater destiny.

Amen.

chapter 16

What to Be Wary of if Overindulged

You know when you are under the domination of your child of the past: there are the feelings of listlessness and boredom, and what seems satisfying for others provides no satisfaction for you. You may be completely unaware of any clear adult goals or you may think sometimes that you have goals but at other times find they glimmer feebly. Quite probably, you tend to drift, to lack powerful initiative, to be short on persistence. You feel a passive discontent. You may restlessly seek to be the recipient of enjoyment and entertainment of one kind or another but you are rarely if ever thoroughly entertained or capable of thorough enjoyment. You often feel—and may disconsolately wonder why you feel—that life lacks all sparkle.

These are some of the broad, general characteristics of the overindulged. Where oversubmission produces an active, demanding individual, overindulgence, in contrast, produces a passive, bored, discontented one. Where the oversubmissive parent bows to a child's demands, the overindulgent parent anticipates them, showering the child with goods and services before the child calls for or may even have thought of them.

Why shouldn't the overindulged person, unless he gains insight, think there is something wrong with life? In effect, he is a spectator of, rather than participant in, it. The recipient in childhood of a flow from a parental cornucopia, without need even to make a demand, he has been deprived of opportunity to learn to take satisfaction in his own efforts, to take initiative, to develop persistence. His childhood learning experience has endowed him with a passive expectation that somebody will lay a little satisfaction on him without any effort on his part. He has no idea that effort is related in any way to satisfaction.

And that is where the rub comes in. Even in a game, the enjoyment derives in no small part from effort. You haven't really played and enjoyed a tennis game, for example, until you are sweating profusely and huffing and puffing and come off the court saying, "Boy, that was a hard game." The enjoyment may have nothing whatever to do with winning, with satisfying any competitive urge, but it does have much to do with the huffing and puffing, the excitement of the activity and the relaxation afterward.

Upon being asked to put on paper how he felt about life, a young man who was a patient of mine wrote this revealing statement:

"The goal of an individual's life is happiness for that individual. One therefore must decide what it is that will give him or help him to achieve happiness. Happiness to my way of thinking is impossible in this century. Complete happiness cannot be achieved in this century; only compensatory partial contentment.

"Why am I paralyzed? It has to be because I know that it is impossible to achieve my goals. Paralysis might be alleviated therefore if the end goals are changed. To achieve any of my goals regardless of how they are constantly modified, education plays a prominent role. I have decided that self-education for me is impossible and the mechanics of receiving guidance in learning from public institutions makes this method impossible, also.

"At this point the activity that should be in programs to achieve my end goals is one of employment. This to me is impossible.

"I am apathetic. My life is empty, hollow. I don't feel like typing any more so I will stop. There's no reason to, really."

This was a young man who had been subjected to extreme overindulgence all his life, and his is almost a classic statement of how the extremely overindulged view life. Anything calling for effort on his part is to him "impossible" and yet only such personal effort could change life for him, give him feelings of participation, provide satisfaction and open the way for him to achieve valid goals.

Major Characteristics

As an overindulged person, you probably possess—and should be aware of—two prime characteristics.

You feel lonely, restless, discontented, unable to take interest in most activities around you, and you may even be puzzled over how others can enjoy such activities. You feel bored and jaded and yet you feel that way not because of any sophisticated knowledge or great experience.

Second, if you make any effort at times, it is relatively feeble and not long persistent; you may know that you want something but cannot determine what it is; and, underneath, you have the hope that somehow, sometime, someone will come along to rescue you from your boredom, loneliness and discontent.

Areas of Overindulgence

Overindulged, although you didn't seek to be, throughout childhood, you are overindulgent to yourself and the self-indulgence may take many forms.

You may be given to eating or drinking to excess, or to both. Finding a job may be difficult for you because of lack of initiative and you may depend upon others to find one for you. Once on the job, you may do poorly, get little satisfaction and complain frequently about assignments.

Because your parents anticipated what they thought might be your wishes, you may expect those about you in adult life to be as anticipatory. You may expect them not merely to fulfill any demands you make; in fact, you may make few or no demands because you never had need to do so and are not accustomed to doing so. Rather, you may expect others to know what it is you want, to read your mind. "My wife," you may think, "ought to surprise me with something different for dinner." Or, "My husband ought to know how tired and bored I get with housework and ought to send me on vacations without my even asking."

However illogical it may appear when presented in black and white on a printed page, the thought nevertheless may be often in the back of your mind that if spouse or friend fails to anticipate your desires, to read your mind, that means lack of love or real friendship. Yet, up against your background of having parents for whom the anticipation of your desires was a way of showing love, the thought, if illogical, is quite understandable.

Because of your overindulgence, you may find yourself drifting in many ways—from job to job, career to career, event to event, person to person, never quite able to actively make choices, pursue reasoned-out goals or persist for long at any endeavor.

The Case of Vance

Of the many people suffering from overindulgence whom I have seen, Vance presents perhaps one of the most all-inclusive examples of the manifestations of the problem.

He had once been physically attractive but overeating and excessive drinking had made him paunchy. He worked at an insignificant job in a large company and one day, at a company party where he was sitting off by himself trying to appear blasé but looking very lonely, he drew the attention of Ellen, an effervescent young woman who held a responsible job with the company. She sat down with him, chatted for a while, then lightly suggested that they might dance. With a jaded air, he announced that he could see no point to dancing and proceeded, with fulsome quotes from philosophers, to give her a lecture on how civilization had managed to ruin dancing.

At once amused and impressed, the woman chatted some more and, when she learned of his almost-menial job, was startled. But he dismissed that with a blasé air. After all, the significant jobs in the company were controlled by "you know whom" and he didn't care to deal with them or even know them. Intrigued by his air and somewhat challenged by his indifference to her, Ellen invited him to dinner at her apartment and managed to get him talking about his childhood as the only son of a well-to-do widow. When she urged him to look for a better job, he just shook his head. But, being a determined woman, Ellen looked around, found one for him and gently but firmly pushed him into taking it, even getting a car for him when he protested that the lack of one would stand in his way.

And Ellen went right on taking the initiative with his problems and finally married him. She got him thinking about going beyond his present job and preparing for a professional career. He decided that he might want to be a chiropodist, and they decided that in due time, after he had finished his training, opened his office and developed a practice, she would quit her job. Largely because of her continued encouragement and gentle prodding, he did actually finish his training and open an office, but his practice failed to develop. He blamed it on physicians. No M.D., he claimed, would consider sending him patients since he was not an M.D. And one day he announced that he was giving up his office and had decided to take up flying. There, he told Ellen, was where the big future was; before long everything, including freight, would move by air.

Ellen carried on with her job while he got his pilot's training. But soon after he got his license, he complained about rules and regulations and about his age being held against him. Next he decided to study heating and air conditioning, and did, but never went into business because, as he said, "You need capital and the big fellows never give a little guy a chance."

When Ellen consulted me and urged me to see Vance, she was all too aware now that he could not take any real initiative and could not persist in carrying out any plans. She felt bitter over being used by him, wanted to leave him, but couldn't see how he could get along without her. He stayed at home by day, eating and drinking; by night, he went to a tavern; he now had excuses for everything, was indifferent to her, had even told her he wished she would "just disappear," but, as he later told me, he didn't really mean that because he couldn't live without her support and sympathy.

He still had almost no concept of what was wrong; we had to begin with that.

Very Common Areas

Even if we have had no background of overindulgence, any of us, if we have always wanted something and have felt deprived for not having it, may finally indulge ourselves in adulthood when there is a chance to get what we have wanted, even if it means giving up other things. It may be a special kind of car, a fur coat, almost anything, including rich foods.

While obesity on the one hand or finicky eating on the other may have many possible causes, a feeling of deprivation may be a reason for either in the overindulged. Any effort to take responsibility or to work at something persistently is, for the indulged, not "natural"; he wasn't brought up to think that way. With his background, effort may represent deprivation in the sense that he is deprived of having something done *for* him.

As a result, as a kind of compensatory maneuver, he may then overindulge himself in some way, and it may be in eating. He may pick and choose, loading himself only with "treats" to the exclusion of a balanced diet. Or he may load the "treats" on top. And until he can see that it is his feeling of deprivation that is not natural and that he bears burdens no different from or greater than those others bear, he may have little chance of controlling his obesity or the finicky eating habits which may undermine his health.

Excessive drinking, too, can be a form of overindulgence, a seeking in the bottle for a refuge from boredom, loneliness, dissatisfaction. If he comes to depend upon drinking for feeling at least occasionally even if only temporarily "alive," the price may be heavy and yet he may be able to do little or nothing about the drinking problem until he recognizes the reason for it and takes more positive refuge in doing something constructive about it.

If, like many of the overindulged, you are given to extravagance and cannot handle money realistically, the reason may be that you fritter away money to buy things that you hope will somehow satisfy your discontent. They never do. They never did in childhood.

The Man Who Went on a Sit-down Strike

Many of the overindulged manage to do their jobs in adult life, but in routine fashion. They hang on without real interest. They lived life in childhood in a featherbed but find no featherbed in adulthood. No goodies come in automatically. Adult life is full of responsibilities and it may be just barely tolerable—and sometimes not.

One of my overindulged patients at one point in his life went on a sit-down strike. He was a brilliant professional man who did his job and did it fairly well but got no kick out of it. So he drank—heavily—almost every night. His wife took an increasingly dim view of this and kept protesting that it wasn't fair to her or the children. Finally, she announced that if he didn't stop the drinking, she was prepared to get a divorce.

So he did stop the drinking. And he went on with his work for a time. But the only "fun" in his life—his refuge from dissatisfaction—had been drinking, and now, with that gone, he had no "fun" at all and life didn't seem worthwhile.

He developed depression, or so it appeared to several physicians. He said openly: "I might as well end this life because it simply is not giving me any satisfaction." Hearing that complaint, the physicians understandably diagnosed depression. They were all the more convinced that he was depressed because now he had stopped working and sat around the house, and when questioned about why he was doing that, he replied that life wasn't worth getting up and doing anything about.

He was sent to a mental hospital for treatment for his depression. But it wasn't depression. He wasn't self-critical, as depressed people usually are. He just felt that life wasn't worth living—period.

When he came out of the hospital, not benefited at all by the well-intentioned treatment there, he did finally begin to improve. A brilliant man, he had no great difficulty, once it was called to his attention, in recognizing his overindulgence and the seeds of it in his childhood. He decided that he had better go back to work because if work hadn't been fun, there was also no fun sitting around at home waiting for something to come along from the outside to fulfill him. At first, he could give only lip service to the idea that he had to actively pursue satisfaction. But he went on and gradually developed a feeling for being active and persistent and an ability to get a kick out of challenges on the job and in family relationships at home.

Hypochondriasis

An overindulgent person may develop hypochondriasis, an often disabling preoccupation with aches, pains and even body sensations. And although he may have been examined repeatedly without anything being found organically wrong, the overindulgent person with hypochondriasis may persist here, as in no other area of his life, and keep going from physician to physician, ever hoping to have some cure laid on him. He is seeking a magic pill to free him of all complaints and concerns. To be told the truth—that nothing is physically wrong but that one's indulged inner child cannot face adult responsibilities—is a tough pill to swallow.

The Case of Arnold

Arnold was a slim man in his late forties who looked much older. Ten years earlier, he had had some mysterious fainting spells and, after a year of them, had had a medication prescribed for "brain arrhythmia." Even before that, he had suffered from what had seemed to be thrombophlebitis, with severe leg pain. Not long after the period of the fainting spells, he had spent a week at a renowned clinic because of great weakness and had been told that his problem was one of tension and that he must take three vacations a year.

About two years before he had come to see me, he had developed a pain in one foot. His family physician had diagnosed the problem as foot strain and had prescribed for it, but when there was no improvement, Arnold had gone to a hospital where, for thirty days, he had been put through elaborate tests. The hospitalization, he told me, demoralized him, made him feel depressed and even suicidal. A month before coming to see me, he had traveled again to the famed clinic where he had been told that all his problems were really psychosomatic in nature.

Arnold was a lawyer. He made a fair living, he told me, and to some extent liked his work but had no great love for it. He had been married for twenty-five years, and his wife was sympathetic and solicitous. "I just have to hint," he told me, "and my wife is eager to do things for me." He has three children, all now grown and doing well.

Here is a man whose problems, on the surface, seem to make little if any sense. He is a reasonably successful professional, without financial strains, with a loving wife and successful children. But he has one physical complaint after another, never traced to anything organic despite repeated x-rays, assorted tests and multitudinous physical examinations. He is a man who, to no small extent, has become an emotional cripple because he has spent so much of his energy worrying about his ailments and so much of his time in hospitals, clinics and physicians' offices.

His problems couldn't make sense to him, or to anyone else, without consideration of his child of the past. Arnold did, indeed, grow up in an emotional featherbed: everybody liked him; his father was kind and considerate and loved to do for him; his mother was solicitous, eager to cater to him. And he went from one featherbed into another when he married a kindly, solicitous, catering wife.

Overindulged and tending to overindulge himself, Arnold centers his self-indulgence on his body feelings. He caters to them. The more he caters to them, the more they clamor; the more they clamor, the more he caters to them; he goes from doctor to doctor, further catering to himself and his body feelings.

No one can focus on any particular area of the body without becoming aware of what could seem to be symptoms. If you go to bed and happen to lie in a position in which you feel the beat of your heart and if you focus on and become concerned about it, before long the beat will seem to be erratic or abnormal. And, in fact, concern about it can actually produce some temporary off-rhythm. Wake in the morning and search with concern for a minor ache or bit of stiffness and chances are you'll find it. It's often there fleetingly for many and even most of us. But focus on it and it becomes magnified and what is essentially normal seems abnormal.

If you happen to be intolerant of anything that doesn't feel comfortable and cozy because you have lived all your life in a comfortable and cozy atmosphere—compliments of your parents to start with and then of your spouse—anything even fleetingly uncomfortable can be alarming.

After exploring his past with him I could tell Arnold something about the source of his overconcern with physical ailments. "It is essential to live in the present and to forget the featherbed of the past. You are going to have to say to yourself: 'I am going to bear some aches and pains and go on and do what I want to do. I am going to keep the aches and pains in perspective, realizing that everybody has some on occasion and they may be somewhat more common in the forties. This is adult-of-the-present reality; it has nothing to do with the emotional coddling I'm accustomed to and that makes me set up a great big cry every time I feel an ache or pain.'"

Being an intelligent man, he could blink and say, "Yes, I guess I have been coddling myself."

I could go on to add: "You can either go along with your child of the past and take your aches and pains seriously and forget about carrying on your affairs in the present and be a dependent child going to every clinic in the country. Or you can take them as a matter of course, recognizing that they may be uncomfortable but not so uncomfortable that you can't live with them and go on to do what you want to do. And the less attention you pay to them, the more effective you will be and, actually, the less discomforting the aches and pains will be."

I could tell him all this and he could see it—but acting on it is another matter, not achieved instantaneously. Practice is involved and failures and relapses. But there must be no self-criticism.

Often it is helpful in cases like Arnold's to have in mind a picture ready for the next time some concern with an ache develops—a picture of literally getting out of a featherbed and walking around on a good hard floor and getting a bit of pain in the soles of the feet, which need toughening.

Sex and Marriage

In nearly all marriages and in more-than-casual sexual relationships, there is some tendency to seek indulgence. The popular expression "the honeymoon is over" may be related to the realization that there comes a time when indulgence must end and adult responsibility be accepted.

For the overindulged, however, many of the difficulties in marriages and sex relationships may stem from the attitude of passive expectancy that others will pour out love, affection and services and there is no need to do anything to get and retain them.

In fact, the intimacy and emotional character of marriage and sex underline, more strongly than do any other relationships, the overindulged person's needs and expectations.

It is all too easy for the overindulged to be disappointed in his marital or sex partner for not providing the same cornucopia of goods, affection and services as his parents, to feel disappointed if the partner expects anything in return and to wave aside the partner's disappointments. As childhood was, sex or marriage often becomes a one-way emotional street for the overindulged.

Ironically, the partner of an overindulged spouse, after repeated disappointments and rebuffs, feeling cheated and used, may wish to end the relationship—and yet may not do so, may feel guilt at the thought of doing so, because of awareness of how dependent the overindulged has become. And the relationship may go on although neither party is happy.

Sometimes, however, the relationship may be broken. Occasionally, the partner may do the breaking. More often, however, it is the overindulged who, in effect, passively withdraws in order to get into a mainstream where he hopes that somehow, someone will come along and pursue and win him and provide for him as his parents did. But the parent-figure mate rarely if ever turns up.

A Woman and Her Three Husbands

Drifting into a lonely, empty existence, watching in some puzzlement while others find enjoyment and satisfaction in life, many of the overindulged never recognize what their problem really is. Yet some do get fleeting insights.

Sylvia is an exquisitely beautiful woman. She has always been pursued by men and has been married three times. In her childhood and adolescence her well-to-do parents provided everything they could think of for her. In school and college, she never liked to work; boys did her homework for her and let her crib from their examination answers. She had no desire to go to college except for the social life. In everything, she has always been obliged, waited upon, catered to; she has relied on her beauty and also on pretending to be much weaker than she is in order to avoid doing anything herself and to get others to do virtually everything for her.

All three of her marriages have been unhappy. All three husbands indulged her. The first two marriages were short-lived. The men involved rather quickly tired of being required to admire her, cater to her, excuse her from all duties and "make her happy" without the slightest consideration in return. The third has become self-contemptuous because he has indulged her so long.

Because her third husband threatened to leave her and because she is now getting along in years and her beauty inevitably is beginning to fade a bit, she sought help. When she did so, she had no real idea of what her problem was. But she did remark that she sometimes wished she had met a man "who would absolutely make me do everything he wants and beat me if I didn't." And she could even recall having wishes as a child to be made to do things.

No one made her do them then; no one could make her do them now. With her firmly ingrained overindulgent passivity, any effort of someone else to make her do things would only reinforce the passivity.

In childhood, it would have been different.

I see many overindulged children as patients—or, rather, it is their parents who must be the patients. There is no sudden bit of insight or enlightenment of which I am aware that can be given to a child to make him over. It is the parents who must firmly, kindly limit him, give him chores to do whether he wants to do them or not and refrain from being his money pump, his handmaiden, his short-order cook, his chauffeur or chairman of his entertainment committee.

If you have an overindulged child of the past, there is no point in trying to change him. Overindulged he was and remains, but overindulged *you* need not continue to be. What you need to and can do is bring the adult of the present into ascendancy, limiting the child of the past.

Just as the parent of any child currently being overindulged needs to stop catering to him, so you will have to stop catering to the child within you. You need to recognize the influence of that child wherever that influence is to be found. And, recognizing it, you need to set out to limit it by exercising your adult muscles. You can learn to become active rather than passive, persistent rather than fickle, considerate of others rather than insensitive, and aggressively interested in work, games, hobbies.

A Helpful Visual Image

It's very useful to have a visual image for your inner child. You can visualize him as a surfeited child at the receiving end of a cornucopia, with goods and services endlessly pouring out.

That image can be a reminder to you of what your real problem is when the problem only seems to be unaccountable drifting, or fatigue, or boredom, or a tendency to view everything that would require any effort from you as impossible or beyond you.

Other Aids

Learning to assert your adult self and limit the child of the past
is not easy. It requires effort and repeated practice, and there will
be off days and setbacks. All learning takes time.

I must warn you that you will find the effort somewhat
painful at times. You will be using a new parental attitude
toward the inner child. You will feel some loss of inner security,
of the old "at home" feeling inherent in following the pattern of
childhood days. You will be asking yourself to undertake responsibilities and tasks you have long thought of as unnecessary,
tiresome. The rewards come but not all at once.

You will find many helpful aids in the chapters "Acting 'as
Though,'" "Just for Today" and "Practice Times and Techniques."
And perhaps even more than others who have parental pathogens
to overcome, you are likely to find the chapter "Other-Centeredness" of great importance.

chapter 17

What to Be Wary of if Punished

Even when those who were punitively treated in childhood are able to identify themselves, they may not be aware of the diverse ways in which, as a result, they are punishing themselves in adulthood and by such self-punishment are destroying their ability to be happy and productive.

Few of us escaped entirely the punitive atmosphere that was prevalent in the past in both homes and schools—an atmosphere created by a widely held axiom: to spare the rod is to spoil the child. Perhaps there is less adherence to that idea today but it is not entirely gone.

It is not a matter only of physical punitiveness. Harsh scoldings, repeated solemn moralizings and ridicule can have equally detrimental effects.

If you often feel that you are "bad," if you punish yourself and even put yourself into situations that cause others to punish you, if your work is rough and tough calling for unusual ability to "take it," if you often find yourself filled with a desire for getting even, you have strong indications of a child of the past within you who was raised in a punitive atmosphere.

A child raised in this way may get so he requires punishment in order to maintain the childhood pattern that, however hurtful, has some security in it, some feeling of "at homeness." Without thorough self-study, it is difficult to recognize all the ways this need may show itself and how they rule his life. As an adult, he may be well enough aware of and may complain about punitive treatment in childhood. And he may complain about how hard he must work, about his discomfort in social situations, about his great difficulty in giving or receiving love and affection, about his inability to relax, about his bouts of depression—and yet he may not relate any of these to the basic fact that he is treating himself as his punitive parent or parents treated him in childhood.

If you were punitively treated, you can do most to help yourself if you understand clearly the major characteristics of the punitively treated, the cycle that may be set up in their lives and the diverse areas in which the effects may be felt.

Three Major Characteristics

The emotional aftermaths for the punitively raised child are guilt, revenge and fear.

Guilt feelings arise because a child who is repeatedly punished, either physically or verbally, comes to think of himself as "bad," as someone who must deserve that punishment.

Do you wonder why you often find yourself feeling vaguely guilty without, to your knowledge, having done anything to warrant guilt? Do you think sometimes that you must have done something wrong but possibly are too insensitive or stupid to recognize the wrongdoing? Do you tend to feel especially guilty when you try to relax or to engage in something pleasurable? These could well be indications that your child of the past is at work, calling upon you to treat yourself as you were treated long ago.

So long as you feel this gnawing, underlying sense of guilt, you can punish yourself and reestablish the old pattern. You can do it by never allowing yourself relaxed free time, by never feeling that your job is done, by working almost to exhaustion or even by choosing difficult, punishing types of work.

Because the guilt feelings can deprive you of self-esteem,

you may downgrade everything you do even though you do things well. You cannot accept well-meant and deserved compliments and congratulations from others; they do not jibe with your feelings of guilt and self-deprecation.

If you find that you tend to enjoy something—sex, for example—guilt rears up and you cannot tolerate the enjoyment; you become inhibited. Any enjoyment may make you feel guilty and anxious.

Because of your punitive background, you find yourself often full of great anger at even minor irritations. You tend to overload small irritations with far more meaning than they really have. You long for retaliation, which you may or may not express. You feel keenly any injustices done to you and sometimes see injustices where there are none. You are quick to feel wronged and long to right any wrongs.

Your burning inner hatred, easily aroused, may express itself as criticism, as protest, as furious complaint, as a great desire to "get even" with the world or sometimes as envy or jealousy. "It's as if," one punitively treated patient once remarked, "I have a fire going within and must keep looking around for fuel to toss on the flames, as if I can't be 'happy' without being angry and feeling guilty about the anger. Ridiculous!"

Ridiculous, yes and no.

Rarely does a child have any difficulty in accepting justified and loving punishment. In fact, children feel safer when there are clearly defined rules and when reasonable limits are placed on impulsiveness. But when punished excessively, a child can come to have hatred for the punitive parent. The parent is bigger, stronger; the child can't stop the punitiveness; but he can vow to retaliate later. At the same time, he can have self-contempt because he cannot, somehow, retaliate immediately—and he may use lies to avoid at least some of the punitiveness and deprecate himself for lying.

Later, in adulthood, with his punitive parent or parents removed from his immediate scene, he still has a desire to retaliate and now may give vent to it in various ways. He may punish those who are smaller and weaker than he is, as he was punished. He may get back at his parents by doing, now, what they forbade—anything from promiscuity to stealing or other crime. He may be excessively critical, impudent, self-righteous.

In addition to growing up with a desire for revenge and with guilt feelings, a punitively treated person may be fearful that his dreams of revenge will be discovered and he will be punished. He may also fear that he will not be able to keep his retaliatory longings under control and, as a result, will suffer more punishment. He may recognize, too, that his angry, retaliatory feelings are not reasonable and feel remorse, guilt and self-deprecation.

However much he may try to appear confidently defiant, internally he may be shaken by fear and by anxiety and tension. While he wants to punish because he has been punished excessively, he may, ironically, find that he does "best" to punish himself; it seems safer.

A Cycle

In adulthood, the person who was excessively punished in childhood continues the pattern by punishing himself. His self-punishment gives him an "at-home" feeling and stokes the fire of retaliatory desires still burning because of past punishment. Combining within himself the roles of child and parent, he both punishes himself and feels the burning desire to retaliate against the punishment. Feeling a deep sense of self-belittlement, he may find himself attracted to situations in which others punish him as well.

The cycle needs to—and can—be broken.

When you recognize the childhood sources of your driving retaliatory desires, you can begin to control lashing out at yourself and others. When you understand the origins of your guilt feelings and fears, and see, too, how they serve as a type of self-punishment, you can begin to allow esteem for yourself, built on your achievements and capacities, to develop. When self-esteem grows, your retaliatory drives diminish, as does the need to punish yourself both directly and through others.

Areas of Punitiveness

Work

Many of the punitively treated are attracted to work that is harsh and difficult for them or that allows them to retaliate against others. Some enjoy police jobs or careers in the armed forces, where they can carry out disciplinary functions. Some professional boxers and football players are attracted to their hit-and-be-hit professions because of punitive backgrounds.

A housewife needlessly exhausts herself with housekeeping routines and her activities seem unreasonable to herself and others until they are seen as means of self-punishment.

Some ruthlessly successful business people who are even more interested in crushing competition than in financial rewards are expressing retaliatory feelings. From a distance they may seem to be successful, happy human beings, achieving true self-fulfillment, but a closer look will reveal the truth.

The punitively bred encounter many difficulties in work and careers. For one thing, their tendency to react quickly to slight provocation, to what others might not consider provocation at all, may hamper them and even destroy opportunities. Commonly, for example, bosses have occasions to reprimand employees and it is hardly realistic to consider that all reprimands are undeserved. It is a legitimate function of a boss to say: "You didn't do this properly. I have to call it to your attention so you won't do it again the same way."

A punitively raised person, quick to feel injustice even where none may exist, may see even the mildest reprimand as unwarranted, provocative and unjust and may react with outright anger and retaliation or restrained but not entirely concealed fury. It doesn't necessarily take telling off the boss or walking off the job to end a job; a few incidents of restrained fury accompanied by recalcitrance can be enough to mark a man as unpromotable or undesirable.

If you recognize that you have a punitive background, you

will do well in any such situation to say to yourself kindly but
firmly: "Now, let's examine this. Is there some real justification
for what my boss is telling me? Am I letting the situation be
handled by my child of the past instead of my adult of the
present, who would be more objective and, if allowed to, could
handle the situation more maturely and wisely?"

Moralizing

When strict moralizing accompanies parental punitiveness,
the child may adopt the parental standards, hoping to secure
parental approval. The resulting self-righteousness often takes a
toll later, even beginning in adolescence. Denied by his parents
the pleasures his friends have he tends to make his peers feel
guilty as a retaliation for the unreasonable restrictions imposed
on him.

The hostile self-righteousness expressed by his parents and
adopted by the child sets him apart from normal intercourse with
others of his age. It may cause him to punish himself with excessive work. It may lead him to expect attention and honors as his
due because of his "goodness."

The pattern—to be found in many unhappy and bewildered
men and women—is typified by Betty, who was brought up by
parents whose punitiveness took the form of almost constant
moralizing. To them, movies, all entertainment, represented
wastefulness. Dating was "loose." Betty duly grew up a "good"
girl, did well in school but not in personal relationships. She
feared boys and drove them off by her prudery; she had no
friends among girls because of the self-righteousness that quickly
palled on them.

When she got a job as an office worker in a large financial
firm, she worked hard, won praise from her superiors and was at
first liked by her co-workers. But again her righteousness and
prudery alienated those around her. She felt hurt, lonely and
depressed, and her hurt and depression deepened as she saw
others win praise for less conscientious—but cheerful—work.

As she grew older, saw more and more clearly how her attitude drove people from her and became convinced that she was

being "punished" for being good, she finally rebelled against her parents, moved out of their home, tried to meet and socialize with others. But the self-righteous attitude remained and barred companionship. Even more lonely now than before because she had left home, she made even greater efforts to find companionship and affection but didn't.

Finally, in utter bewilderment and desperation, she sought help. Only when she could see that the chief obstacle for her, the barrier to the affection and friendship she longed for, was her self-righteous "goodness" forced upon her by her punitive, self-righteous parents was she able to begin to free herself.

Sex and Marriage

For some people, the punishment-retaliation cycle is very largely confined to the home. Often the reason for this is that by leaving home to attend college or share an apartment, they force themselves to establish new rules for themselves. They consider their own needs, likes and dislikes. They are able to seize the opportunities afforded by a new atmosphere and situation. The restrictive parents are not physically present. There is a chance for self-determination. It takes some daring and effort but the very recognition of the need for one's own new rules, for playing a parent-to-oneself role, tends to enhance self-respect. And with the enhancement of self-respect and the loosening of restrictions, the urge to retaliate diminishes.

The young adult who does seize such an opportunity may go on to do well, until he marries, establishes a home and suddenly finds old emotional echoes sounding out. This is "home" and the child of the past demands the reestablishment of all the old home attitudes, the old rules and old punitiveness and the cycle of punitiveness-retaliation.

It is not uncommon for the child of the past to feel acutely that something is missing in a warm, loving marriage. Although a person may welcome the warmth and loving, the absence of punitiveness and retaliatory feelings leaves the child feeling dissatisfied, not fully "at home."

The discontent shows up in many situations. As a child a

woman was punished by being made to scrub floors. Now, as a housewife, she neglects the housework. By keeping an untidy home, she can irritate her husband until he becomes enraged and may angrily, as her parents did, call her "no good." The cycle is begun. Furiously, then, she exhausts herself cleaning up the house, thus punishing herself, relieving some of her guilt feelings and increasingly resenting her husband's remarks. And quarrel may follow quarrel as the cycle of punishment and retaliation continues.

Some men, punitively treated in childhood, may physically abuse their wives, striking them violently. They are able now because of their physical strength to do in their new home situation what they could not do in the old one: physically give vent to their retaliatory feelings. After the physical abuse they mete out, they feel guilty, call themselves brutal and unfair, try to make up for their transgressions, punish themselves—until, in the old cycle, the self-punishment arouses retaliatory feelings and once more they strike out.

The problem is compounded when both spouses have had punitive childhoods. The physically abused wife may try and seem to succeed in forgiving and forgetting but then may give vent to little digs and cutting remarks. She, too, is caught up in the punishment-retaliation cycle. And her little retaliative remarks provoke retaliation in return, and on it goes.

Physical abuse is only one form of retaliation. Others include extravagant spending, reckless driving, excessive drinking, flirtations or sometimes infidelity.

Very often, however cruel and retributive they may have become toward each other, the two spouses unite against any outside interference with the marriage and against any thought of separation or divorce. They are conditioned to be together to retaliate, to re-create the old battlefield atmosphere.

Jealousy in marriage may be traceable to punitive upbringing. One patient, Erica, an attractive young housewife, was married to a man who was very much in love with her. But she was consumed by jealousy, convinced that her husband was interested in other women and strongly suspicious that he was unfaithful to her. She had left him twice and had left the children behind with him.

She was the product of a home in which the father, a physically big and powerful man and a heavy drinker, had physically abused both Erica and her mother whenever he was drunk and had sneered at them contemptuously when he was sober. As an adult, Erica punished herself with a sneering, contemptuous attitude borrowed from her father. Needing vengeance for her self-punishment, she found it in striking out verbally at her husband, in being suspicious of him. Although she longed for love and warmth from a man, she could not accept them at home from a man; she had never had any from the man in her past home life, her father. Able to view her husband only in the light of her experience with her father, to expect from him only contempt, she had to strike back at him. Until she could see the origins of her problem, she could not help herself and could not accept the love and warmth she wanted and were there for her to have.

Punitively treated people often tend to put themselves into punitive situations. I think of the young woman mentioned before who had been beaten almost every day of her life by her father with a rubber hose. In her teens, she eloped to escape the home situation but she married a man who beat her almost as relentlessly as her father.

Parental Distrust as a Special Form

A harmful form of punitiveness involves parental distrust of a child's adequacy, an anticipation of his failure and even an expectation that the child will be disobedient if left unobserved.

A child who senses the distrust may, in fact, do what is expected of him, including resorting to disobedience when he has the chance. He may be hurt in other ways. The natural growth and development of a child is retarded when he is repeatedly told, "You're too young for a bicycle; you'll only hurt yourself," or, "You shouldn't even think of having a chemistry set; that would be too dangerous for you," or, "No, you cannot have a pet; you wouldn't know how to take care of it properly."

The child brought up by distrustful parents becomes self-belittling in a special and potentially incapacitating way. Most self-belittlement is based upon past efforts. But distrustful self-belittlement is anticipatory; it may convince the child he is doomed to fail, licked before he starts, and he may not even start.

None of us is ever immune from an occasional feeling of foreboding that we may fail at something. But even if the failure comes to pass, we realize that perhaps we weren't prepared enough, needed more skill or more training. We don't let anticipation of failure become our way of life. But the victim of distrust suffers chronically from a feeling of being doomed to fail. He is likely to shun many or all efforts that could demonstrate that he has far more capacity than he has given himself, or been given, credit for having. Without confidence in himself, he is a poor competitor and may be able to make only fumbling, abortive efforts when he seeks a job or tries to enter into relationships.

Often, in rebellion against his borrowed distrustful attitude toward himself and the feelings of self-contempt and despondency it has produced, he may try to succeed at activities in which he actually most distrusts his abilities. His efforts are usually desperate, ill-considered, without adequate preparation and poorly timed. Almost always, they fail and create greater self-contempt and despondency and provide reason for not attempting anything at all in the future. Ironically, if he had not been so driven by his self-distrust to center his efforts in areas in which he was most self-distrustful, he might have taken advantage of opportunities for achievements within his capacities and, however small, they could have helped reduce his self-distrust and bolster his self-confidence.

Changing the Pattern

I see many punitively treated children and always the need is to change, if possible, the home atmosphere. It is not the children but rather the parental attitudes that need alteration. If it isn't possible to change parental attitudes, an effort is made to help the parents feel comfortable about transferring the child to a suitable relative, foster home or boarding school.

If the child can have a respite in his growing years, if he can be in an environment that may provide firm but not harsh discipline, the absence of the punitiveness pathogen often mitigates his need for retaliatory reactions and makes them seem out of place.

As an adult punitively treated in childhood, your need is similar. It is not your child of the past who must somehow be changed but rather the parent you have been to yourself. You need now, as a parent to yourself, to direct your life in your own way rather than in the way used by one or both of your parents in the old home atmosphere.

You have to recognize that you are an angrier person inside than the usual person because you carry within you a child of the past who was unfairly treated, is resentful, is quick to take offense, is insistent upon vengeance.

If you let this angry child have free rein, you will find that he leads you to run roughshod over other people's feelings and rights and gets in the way of your adult goals. You spend far too much time looking for slights and for opportunities for retaliation, which can only leave you lonely, unhappy, unfulfilled. You need to be a firm but kindly parent to the inner child, setting limits on him, saying no to his feelings of resentment and demands for retaliation.

Don't make the mistake of not respecting the feelings and demands. Respect them by all means. Under the circumstances in which they arose, there was nothing abnormal about *them;* it was the circumstances that were abnormal. The feelings and demands are understandable, should occasion no guilt, no self-belittlement. They do not mean at all that you are worthless, stupid, bad, childish.

A Visual Image

You might see your child of the past as a galley slave being mercilessly tormented by a galley master. Or as a small, light, very slender boxer, face bloodied, eyes blackened, down on one knee, in the ring with his opponent—a smug, satisfied giant of a figure. The little boxer, like the galley slave, feels the injustice of the situation, feels his helplessness and burns for revenge.

Such an image of your inner child can be useful in sharply

focusing your overall problem, in reminding you of what force within you may be at work in various situations and in helping you to be a good parent to yourself.

Your Adult Job

Your adult job is to respect your inner child and his feelings, to be aware of them, to uncover them in every area in which they are operative and then to set limits on them.

In effect, you must say to your inner child: "I understand how you feel, the reason for your feeling that way, the hurt you developed, the sensitivity you have, the urge to get revenge. But all that arose in the past; it wasn't right then that you were punitively treated; it wouldn't be right now for me to punish myself as I would be doing if I let you have full sway. So I must limit you."

You face two broad problems in acting as a good parent to yourself. Because of your excessive punishment in childhood, you developed feelings of unworthiness and came to belittle yourself. In adulthood, you have very probably gone on punishing yourself with the same feelings—particularly if you make a mistake, even a minor one, or do something that wasn't permissible when you were a child, or experience a disappointment or failure. Those feelings, created by abnormal influences in childhood, don't belong in your life today, have nothing to do with your present activities. If you make a mistake, you try to correct it. If you experience a disappointment or failure, you try again, perhaps under more suitable circumstances or with better information or more training. But you don't beat up on yourself. For to belittle yourself does no good; it is self-punishment calculated to drive you to vengeance and retaliation—often against someone you love.

The management of retaliatory feelings is your second broad problem, and if you reduce your tendency to punish yourself with belittlement, you simultaneously diminish your retaliatory impulses.

At the same time, going further, you must set to work on

limiting retaliatory impulses. You need to recognize that if you don't limit them, you will punish yourself afterward for having allowed them expression when you can calmly assess their excessiveness.

I often suggest to patients that, whenever they are in a situation where they feel, or even begin to sense, that the old patterns of the past are being called forth—the oversensitivity to slight irritation and the urge to retaliate—they can go through a series of steps in their mind.

They can determine first that they will not immediately rebel—not yet. Instead, they will—just for now—listen closely or otherwise give close attention. Second, they will weigh the situation very carefully. Third, they will think back quickly to their childhood and how they used to rebel under similar circumstances. And, fourth, they will say to themselves: "Look, I am bigger than this kind of thing, than my automatic child-of-the-past response. And even though I may end up unconvinced that it is 100 percent right to do so, I will react anyhow for now in the conventional way, just as any other polite, well-mannered, in-control person would do—at least until I have more time to think about it."

If, after calm consideration, you really feel that somebody is doing you in or jeopardizing you, you can then take reasonable steps either to get out of the situation or to bring the other person to justice. But you will not let an immediate child-of-the-past reaction jeopardize your adultness.

By setting kindly limits in this way on your inner child, refusing immediate automatic expression of his furious retaliative feelings, you can be more objective and can express your adult feelings more forcefully, avoiding excesses that later will make you punish yourself with guilt and self-belittling feelings.

It is no easy matter. Patience is needed. It is often helpful to have the support of a respected friend or loved one to buttress your self-esteem. You will find support, too, and helpful guidelines in the later chapters of this book.

chapter 18

What to Be Wary of if Neglected

If neglect was the pathogen in your childhood, you tend to idealize other people, to look hopefully to them as being capable of providing satisfactions you missed as a child. You want closeness—but you fear it. The closer you do get to another person, the more uncomfortable you feel and you may drift in and out of relationships. Although you may suffer intensely from loneliness, you tend to keep people at a distance and it may even seem to you that people mean little to you.

But the reality is that the closer you get to someone else, the more you feel the desire for mothering, for active caring, for the unlimited acceptance you missed in childhood. You long to fill the need but you also recognize that you are asking more of current relationships than they can provide. And you feel guilt and belittle yourself for having such expectations.

As a neglected person, too, you may have a feeling deep down that somehow you lack an identity of your own. In assessing his past life, one of my patients remarked wistfully: "It was as if I felt that I wasn't somebody."

From infancy through adolescence, every child needs a feeling, a conviction, that someone cares about him, is "on his side," stands behind his effort to develop an identity, to be someone. He needs to be made to feel he is a unique and worthy person.

Patterns of Deprivation

Almost all of us experienced at least isolated moments of neglect, times when, because of parental preoccupation elsewhere, we missed their attention and support. They were short-lived instances of neglect and did no lasting harm.

A few of us suffered from extreme parental neglect, virtual abandonment. Fortunately, this is rare. A fair number of us, however, did suffer from partial neglect, and that can have detrimental effects on development and personality, the extent of the effects dependent upon the degree of neglect.

In getting a perspective on the role of neglect in your life, you need to remember that it is most commonly experienced in emotional rather than physical form and so is a phantom kind of thing, elusive because it is the absence of something.

Usually, the neglect stems from parental preoccupation with work or duties and a lack of awareness that a child needs a continuing close relationship with an adult who can satisfy his vital emotional needs and to whom he can turn for support, sympathy, understanding and reassurance.

A father may be away for extended periods on business trips or he may come home every night bringing work to do or be fatigued and concerned only with relaxing. He may be or seem unapproachable to a child. He may be abrupt and superficial in attending to the child, not meaning any harm but unaware that he is depriving the child of anything important. Similarly, a mother, not aware of any serious deprivation in it for her child, may occupy herself with her own career or with her own physical or emotional problems or with useful civic, club and other activities.

A child may be emotionally neglected for other reasons— serious business difficulties, sickness or death of a parent—but more often the cause is a matter of parental preoccupation with other things and lack of awareness of the child's needs.

If you have been suffering because of neglect in childhood, particularly as you come to recognize the wide influence such deprivation has had in your life and how hampered you may have been by it, you will understand and feel compassion for your problems now. If you have imagined that conceivably your problems have stemmed from some great traumatic experience in childhood and have tried to search your memory for that experience, you probably have been frustrated. If your parents' pathogen was neglect, most likely it existed without there being any single great traumatic incident of it.

Basic Mechanisms

The neglected person usually erects a wall or barrier around himself and if you were neglected it is important for you to understand that mechanism thoroughly.

Although neglect is the absence of affectionate concern or loving attention, something the child has not experienced often, the child nevertheless realizes that something is missing from his life. At the same time, he feels that there must be something wrong with him or he would not have experienced the deprivation. The element of self-deprecation enters into his picture.

Lacking a close, warm, approving relationship with a parent who makes him feel unique and worthy, the child develops uncertain feelings about himself. Because of those uncertain feelings, he is unable to respond to others well and to be concerned about their feelings. As he grows, he may develop relationships with his peers but they are often superficial and unrewarding. He may go from relationship to relationship, in childhood and adolescence, seeking what he feels is missing in his life, trying always unsuccessfully to find someone who can supply it and constantly moving on.

In adulthood, he tends to become acutely aware that he has great longings for someone to care for him. Although he may try to inhibit those longings, they return. But even if he makes tentative approaches to others, he can never find what he is seeking: the good, caring, concerned parent missing from his childhood. And his feelings of self-deprecation are reinforced and, in turn, reinforce his longings.

But, as the longings intensify, he recognizes that if he allowed them to be expressed, he would be asking to be taken care of as a baby, and this intensifies his self-scorn. He works to hide the longings, to contain them and prevent their expression. He avoids relationships that could have deep emotional character. He is frightened at the thought that if he allowed any such relationship to blossom, he would reveal himself as infantile, would be ridiculed and possibly exploited.

He erects a barrier, making every effort to appear self-sufficient, independent of others, detached, aloof. The barrier may hide his needs but it cuts him off from many relationships that, while they could not make up for his deprived childhood, could contribute otherwise to more satisfactory adult life.

Neglect and Impulsiveness

If you were neglected, you may tend to be impulsive because of your difficulty in forming and maintaining close relationships, trying to fill your life with the gratification of impulses so that you are at least somewhat distracted from inner needs.

Often, a continuous, single-minded striving for success represents a desperate effort to deny the inner needs, to rebut the feelings of emptiness. Not always, of course; the success-focused may have other motivations, including past economic rather than emotional deprivation. But a striving after wealth or reputation or both, to the exclusion of other values in life, often represents a fruitless effort by the neglected to fill up the voids in their lives.

Some of those drawn into theatrical and movie work are victims of neglect, uncertain of themselves and their identities, trying to find satisfaction not only in seeking fame and fortune but also in creating fantasy identities. I remember well a patient who told me: "When you feel you're a nobody, maybe the only way you can find to be anybody is to be somebody else." Being somebody else doesn't solve the problem but it is often resorted to desperately by the neglected, even when they do not try to project a playwright's or screen writer's characters but only the image of self-sufficiency, independence and detachment.

Exploiting Others

Some of the neglected tend to exploit others, to use them, to whip up their sympathy and interest by one means or another, sometimes even by aloofness, and then to take from them emotional and even material support without giving anything in return.

A neglected person may form calculated relationships, still keeping his barrier up. In studying severe cases of childhood neglect, investigators have commented upon how often the severely neglected lack conscience and feel it normal and desirable to take and use what belongs to others.

Although most of the neglected are not victims of extreme deprivation and not totally without conscience and scruples, I have often noted a correlation between the amount of guilt an adult feels about doing something inconsiderate or wrong and the amount of neglect he did or didn't suffer in childhood. If he suffers acutely from guilt feelings, almost certainly he had someone close to him in childhood.

Retaliation

If your neglect stemmed from loss of a parent in childhood, perhaps you can recall to some extent your feelings of anger, rage, despair and yearning that were part of the process of mourning.

At first, tearfully, angrily, you may have demanded the return of the parent and hoped there would be a return. After several days, as your hopes faded, you began to despair, to whimper and perhaps to alternate between protest and despair. Then may have come a period of detachment during which you even seemed to forget the lost parent as you locked your anger and yearning inside. In each of these stages, you may have had tantrums and episodes of destructive behavior.

If you experienced the loss when you were old enough to

realize that the death of the parent was no deliberate blow at you, not something meant to hurt you deliberately, you may have felt ashamed and guilty about your angry feelings. In fact, you may still feel some shame and guilt even though the mourning process you went through was natural and no shame or guilt should attach to it.

Sometimes, the hurt from a loss is so great that a child is filled with retaliatory longings. He wants to strike back and he may carry the retaliatory longings with him into adulthood.

One of my patients who carried retaliatory longings with him for twenty years had lost his father not through death but through desertion. The father, a quiet and timid man, had finally reached the point where he could no longer stand up under the dominating, demanding mother. The patient, who had enjoyed the father's quiet affection, was the oldest son and had had thrust upon him many of the responsibilities and chores of the father. Encouraged to no small extent by the mother, who characterized the father as a "no-good bum," the son had become bitter and had vowed that some day he would catch up with his father.

Twenty years later, he happened to discover that his father was living in a nearby city, phoned him to announce he was coming, proceeded to visit him and had this unexpected reaction, which I think is significant enough to warrant letting him tell it in his own words:

"When I saw my father then, it was as though I were seeing him for the first time in my life. I saw he was a quiet, timid little man and the minute I saw him I knew why he had run away. He just couldn't stand my mother's demands, her bossy ways, her noise and the kids. He just wasn't built for it. I knew that because I had had to take it—and I couldn't take it, and this little man couldn't take it half as well as I could. And suddenly it seemed pointless, my dream of making him pay for the trouble we had seen. He had had his troubles. He had been hurt, too. I know he loved us when we were kids.

"So I just said I had wanted to see him for a long time and we stood there. Finally, he asked how everybody was and I said, okay, and for a moment I almost said, 'And no thanks to you.' But I didn't. He said, 'I am sorry about everything but that, I guess, is the way it had to be.' I said, 'I know, I know.' Then I realized he was going to tell me how sorry he was, and I didn't want to hear it but I let him say it and then I felt like a damned fool. I just kept saying, 'I know, I know.' So I grabbed my hat and said, 'Well, okay, I just wanted to see you,' and then I left. I hadn't said a single one of those bitter nasty things I had been saving up for years. I saw that I was a man now and he was a man, and I understood he couldn't have stayed with my mother and stayed alive. He just had to get out to save himself, and I don't blame him any more, but I had to see him to get it out of my system."

Often, people who have suffered from neglect never do get the retaliatory feelings of their inner child out of their systems as this man finally could. If you have such feelings and can recognize that they are really those of the child you once were and not of the adult you are now, you can make a major advance in managing your life. With such feelings, you are misdirecting much of your energy, wasting it nursing a hurt of the past.

There is another aspect of loss of a parent—by death, divorce or otherwise—that might possibly be having an effect in your life. An absent parent may be idealized by a child. The child may not have had time enough to see the parent not as an all-powerful giant figure, a superhuman, but rather as the human being he or she really was. Inevitably, with time and with daily involvement with the parent, the child comes to see him or her in a realistic light, as a human with the strengths and failings of a human. But if the parent is lost before such realistic appraisal can be made, the child may carry into adolescence and adulthood an idealized fantasy parent—and the repercussions may be many.

If the lost mother is seen as an idealized, saintly person, all other women may seem shallow, trivial, even sinful in comparison. Among other things, saints do not engage in sexual activities. A boy may thus be laden with unrealistic standards for all women. Similarly, a girl who has lost her father and idealizes him unrealistically may impose upon herself a set of unrealistic standards for men.

Was a father lost in combat? If the father is overidealized by a son as someone superbrave, the son may undertake reckless, misguided feats, driven by a feeling that he lacks the courage and bravery of his father. Was the father a self-employed businessman? Then the son who overidealizes him may look down upon himself if he finds himself working as an employee.

Idealization of a parent, leading as it so often does to the setting of impossible standards by which you measure yourself and others, may interfere seriously with your ability to enjoy life, to fulfill your own personal capacities, to relate to others who could have much to offer to enrich your life.

Sex and Marriage

You may need to be especially aware of how neglect may be affecting sexual and marital relations for you. Such relations, to be rewarding, require warmth, affection and closeness, all of which are likely to be difficult for you as a victim of neglect.

As we have seen, you may long for closeness yet try to deny the need and go to great lengths to avoid close emotional relationships. Many patients have told me that when they begin to feel close to another person and feel the other close to them, they feel panic-stricken and just want to run.

Many neglected people try to explore relationships tentatively to see if one might fulfill the gnawing need within. But they hide behind a pose of aloofness, make no effort, expect the other person to do all the work. Their aloofness and nongiving tend to inhibit the spontaneous warmth and interest of the other person and the relationship never develops fully or is quickly broken off. Some of the neglected, struggling against their past, try to make advances, but these are not wholehearted enough to have much chance for success, and often they begin to make the advances only after many real, potentially fruitful opportunities have slipped by.

I am aware of the story of a noted concert pianist, Gregory, who, because of neglect by both a busy mother and a father often away on business, had failed to marry and had long lived a painfully lonely, melancholy life. When he was quite young, Gregory, by chance, had met a musician in the neighborhood who believed he had musical talent and gave him lessons, encouragement, praise and friendship. There was no real closeness in the relationship because even then Gregory could not accept closeness.

Throughout his childhood and adolescent years, he had no friends, entered into no close relationships but turned entirely, aside from school, to music. He worked his way through college as a professional musician playing at social affairs. At the same time, he worked hard at preparing himself for the concert stage.

For some years now he has given concerts and has attained some recognition but not nearly as much as he had hoped for. He has been hurt repeatedly by critics who point out that while he has virtuoso technique, there is lack of color, feeling and depth in his playing. His old music teacher has tried to guide him for many years toward overcoming this lack, pointing out that music essentially is feeling and that while technique is needed to make it possible to express feeling, technique can't produce the feeling. "You have to live a little, Gregory," he has told him. "You have to get out and meet life and relate to people and get to know their feelings and your own." His inability to do this finally led him to seek help in finding out what was wrong in his life and how he might face up to his real problem.

Promiscuity

Some of the neglected tend to be promiscuous in their sex relationships. They manage to eroticize their dependent longings and by emphasizing the physical satisfactions of sex can exclude emotional interchange. But there is no lasting satisfaction since emotional interchange is an essential part of deep sexual fulfillment.

Unable to obtain the fulfillment, the neglected person may keep seeking endlessly, trying one new relationship after another. But such promiscuity solves nothing and may create an illusion of capacity for loving intimacy that stands in the way of recognition of the real problem.

Your Needs

Because of childhood neglect, you have within you a child with deep feelings of deprivation and with a tremendous ache for what was missing. While the child wants to get what is missing, you cannot tolerate the getting. You may go to extremes to avoid letting the child have what he yearns for and you may feel self-contempt because the yearnings exist.

Yet the self-contempt is unjustified. The child's yearnings are natural under the circumstances. They were imposed on him, are no fault of his and no fault of yours as an adult.

But it is a fact that the yearnings cannot be fulfilled. Everybody in the present is doomed to remain in the present and cannot live in the past except the inner child, who has never left it. Try as you may, you cannot find someone who can satisfy the child's yearnings, someone who can slide back into the past with the inner child and provide what was missing in the past. No one with whom you have an adult relationship can be your mother or father—or, more accurately, an ideal mother or father for your child of the past—and if they were to try, if you were to insist that they try, in order to quiet the inner child, the adult relationship would be destroyed.

The child of the past will ache. There is no satisfying the ache. But the influence of that ache on your whole life up to now—in however many ways it may have been influential—can be recognized. And, knowing that there is no way you can satisfy the child, you can begin to satisfy and encourage the adult to flourish.

If you can begin to accept the child's longings as being natural but impossible to fulfill, and if you can begin to proceed with your life without giving in to those longings, without allowing them to dominate you and without feeling guilty about them, you can begin to get satisfactions out of your daily life that could never appeal to the child but can be rewarding to the adult.

Helpful Visual Images

Having a visual image of what has been taking place within you can be helpful in keeping your focus on your basic problem, in recognizing when it is influencing your life and in helping you to become a good parent to yourself and to overcome the problem.

One such image might be that of a child, outdoors on a cold, blustery night, shivering, his nose pressed up against the window of a house where, inside, there is warmth, but this is the house of his parents, the house of neglect, from which he has been banished. Yet all his days and nights he spends there, nose pressed up against the window, longing, shivering, hungry—unable to see that there is a warm coat right by his side that would make him more comfortable if he noticed and put it on, and all around him there are other houses, with some of the occupants even standing at their doors trying to attract his attention and to invite him in, but he doesn't see them.

Or you can use another image, in which you see, immediately in front of you, a muddy little stream of current available satisfactions and, off in the distance, what seems to be a tremendous and exciting waterfall, one of great potential satisfaction. Actually, the waterfall is a mirage for your inner child, a representation of an all-giving, all-comforting parent. Because of his great yearnings, the child sees the waterfall as real and, influenced by his yearnings, you think you see it. And the more you think so and attend to it, the less attention you pay to the muddy little stream before you. But the muddy little stream can start you off with current satisfactions and lead you to others; the waterfall is all mirage.

As you come to accept the stream as reality, you can begin to try to put less distance between yourself and other people. You must expect that you will feel some anxiety and discomfort in doing so—but, if you recognize that such feelings are bound up with your inner child, not with you as an adult, you can work at reducing them gradually. In time, you will be able to feel more comfortable in your personal relationships.

In time, too, you will be able to evaluate the real worth of people in adult terms rather than in terms of how they appear to satisfy the demands of the inner child—and, by threatening to satisfy them, make you draw back for fear of revealing yourself. You may, in fact, arrive at the point where you wish to and can reveal yourself to a loved one. You may say, openly and productively, that you are a victim of neglect, that you are not entirely free of the problem yet, that you still tend to fear closeness and to want to reject it but this is a carryover, not what you want as an adult and are working to achieve.

If you are married and have been disappointed in your marriage, if your spouse has proved to be human rather than a saint and not possessed of all the idealized virtues you may have attributed to her before marriage, you may find that as you work at disregarding the yearnings of the inner child, you can settle for your spouse as a human being and give and receive love.

If you have tried in the past to obtain ersatz nourishment from busy-ness, promiscuity or narrow concern with material success, you may now begin to find real nourishment in a new and broader outlook on life, on the pleasures to be found in it, on the deepening of once-shallow relationships and the establishment of meaningful new ones.

It is not an easy process; it is a slow process, a day-by-day one, often an "Acting-as-Though" process. You should find help in many of the later chapters of this book.

chapter 19

What to Be Wary of if Rejected

It is difficult to feel at home in the world if you have never felt at home in your own home. If you were rejected as a child, you have an extreme emotional handicap; you are, in effect, the original person "without a country."

You may see yourself as an outlaw, unacceptable to yourself and to others. Your self-deprecation is bitter and you feel, almost automatically, bitterness toward others that leads you often to distort the attitudes of others, even those closest to you, and to flare into hostility against them.

You may suspect that you were rejected in childhood—and you may be right. But, as we have noted earlier, rejection is a relatively rare parental attitude. The term is sometimes used incorrectly in cases of neglect or punitive parental attitudes. True rejection is an extreme and infrequent pathogen.

Parents may be extremely punitive and abusive and yet, within their limitations, they try to make a place for the child in their affection. With true parental rejection, the child is quite literally rejected, denied any acceptance, treated as a nuisance and burden. The attitude of the parent who rejects is blatant and unmistakable—and often involves such exhortations as "go walk into the ocean and keep walking" and the repeated and obviously sincere comment "I wish you had never been born."

The Mechanics

Obviously the rejected child is terribly and deeply hurt and bitter and tends to remain through childhood, adolescence and adulthood very sensitive to rebuff or seeming slight and almost automatically hostile.

As a rejected person, you may often mistakenly sense slights to you in what everyone else considers ordinary give and take. You may be suspicious of even the most friendly overtures because you consider a friendly overture a possible trick, an invitation to another grueling rejection. To test those who want to be your friends, you may behave so hostilely, with such obnoxious behavior, that you force them to abandon their friendly efforts. In effect, you ask others to reject you.

You may have feelings of guilt, convinced that in some way, you don't know how, you must have been responsible for the parental rejection for, after all, even as a small child, you could not help noticing how unusual was your case, how greatly different was the attitude of your parents toward you from the attitude of other parents toward their children. You may also have feelings of complete worthlessness. With such feelings, how could you be other than suspicious of the friendly overtures of others. What, you ask, could they possibly see in you?

Like many rejected people, you may often think of yourself as not just worthless but horrible in some mysterious way—a creature from a black lagoon, a repulsive figure beyond the pale. And while you may have developed long spines of hostility to keep others off, to protect yourself from the possibility of further hurt, inside you may be tremulously dependent, full of dependency needs like the neglected person, but even more so.

Some of the rejected resort to excessive drinking. Drunk enough, they may find at least temporary surcease from their own self-hatred. Especially when in the company of others, they may feel when drunk at least for a moment that they are interesting, desirable. But even under the spell of alcoholic conviviality, they soon feel uncomfortable, anxious, distrusting—and often display their spines of hostility and become obnoxious to "test" others. And as rejection does indeed follow the testing, they may become caught up in excessive drinking as the only way they know to anesthetize the pain within.

Sex and Marriage

The rejected have difficulty in all relationships and, as a consequence, in work situations and, if they can bring themselves ever to try, in play situations. And they have great difficulty in maintaining a satisfying sexual and marital life.

Starved for love, they may finally bring themselves to the point of believing that someone may love and want them, and they may enter into a sexual or marital relationship. Once they have done so, their need for affection is so intense and their demands for it may be so insatiable that the partner, without the same intense need, may become satiated or exhausted. But the slightest slackening off by the partner is taken for rejection and that leads to hurt, bitterness and hostility.

Frequently, on entering a relationship, a rejected person does so with an attitude of "All right, you want me to believe you love me and want me. I want you and will go along. But I don't really believe you." His attitude, from the beginning, is full of challenge and he tests repeatedly, looking for slights or any indifference in order to find some ground for complaint. As long as he finds none, the relationship goes on but not without his having an expectation of rejection. And as the relationship goes on, the expectation drives him to test even harder—until finally the partner expresses irritation. And that is enough. Now, at last, the rejected person thinks—and says—"the truth is out." And he sincerely believes it, is convinced he has been rejected, feels deeply hurt, breaks off, becomes isolated, suffers a new and more intense assault of self-belittlement and becomes even more hostile to all around him.

Sometimes there is a whole series of incidents, of ups and downs, before the relationship breaks up. I once had a thoughtful and kindly man who had lavished love on his wife and had tried repeatedly to reassure her tell me that he couldn't go on living with her. She had a background of rejection and being married to her, he told me, was "like being a yo-yo. Either she is affectionate and I am going up or I am going down because she has taken offense at something and imagined I intended it as a dirty dig. If I tell her that her stocking seam is crooked or the soup could use a little salt, her feelings are hurt, she leaves the room silently, then returns with all guns firing. I can't live with her because I can't live with anybody to whom I can safely say only one thing: 'Honey, you are sent from Heaven and a dream.' Maybe somebody else can do that but I can't."

Not many people can or will. And yet the rejected person always has a fuse lit, a fuse of suspicion that leads to easy explosions and to destruction of chances for stable, continuing relationships.

Like some neglected, some of the rejected are attracted to people who are unkind to them, who treat them with contempt, who sneer and belittle and may even punish them physically. It is familiar territory and though they are hurt by such treatment, they find it difficult to withdraw. Just a single word of affection from a cruel, abusive partner means everything to them. But this is understandable, for what they have done is to reestablish virtually the whole atmosphere of their childhoods when they were cruelly rejected and yet could turn nowhere else for affection and approval.

Your Needs

There is a road away from the consequences of rejection but it is not an easy one. No parental pathogen allowed to exert its effects for long periods is ever easy to overcome and certainly not the particularly harsh one of rejection.

All children need parental acceptance, encouragement, support, approval and stimulation in order to develop a balanced personality, but you had none of this—only harsh rejection, indifference, possibly even outright contempt. You could hardly avoid feeling that the world is hostile, that you are no good, not worth acceptance and loving.

You are now an adult—but your inner child of the past who had that harsh, humiliating experience is still with you and always will be. He has never stopped reacting to that experience. He cannot stop reacting now. But where he lacked a kindly parent, you can be one to yourself; you must be; and you can be.

You can understand that you have tended all your life to treat yourself with the beyond-the-pale rejection with which your inner child was treated; the child and his hurt have been dominant in your life.

As an adult, you need recognition, acceptance, warmth, love. But you have to know that your child-of-the-past feeling of anger and hostility on the outside and self-belittling and longing on the inside keep you from getting what you need.

You must recognize, as part of the feelings of the inner child, the urge to hurt and reject others—and you will have to limit the expression of that urge. You can do this if you accept yourself as worthy and limit your own self-criticism and self-belittlement. Only in this way can you free yourself from the self-defeating pattern of rejection.

Does the self-belittlement you have carried into your adult life have any validity at all? A small child thought it did; but a small child would think so. In his immaturity, what else is he to think when the giants in his world not only turn away from him but abuse him! Yet, in reality, the parental rejection had nothing to do with your worth. The truth is that anyone born to your parents—anyone you admire, anyone the world admires—would, no less than you, have been rejected.

The rejection arose not from any problem with you but from problems your parents had. Studies of rejecting parents have shown varied reasons for their rejection of their children. Many themselves were rejected in childhood. They had hostile attitudes toward their parents and they had hostile attitudes toward their own children, particularly children of the same sex as the sex of the parent who was most rejecting of them. A woman who particularly hated her mother rejected most of all a daughter; a man who hated his father tended most to hate and reject a son.

The studies of rejecting parents showed that some were immature and not ready to become parents—and, solely because they had to sacrifice some social activities with the coming of a child, they immaturely turned against the child. Some mothers felt that they had been forced by pregnancy to marry men they didn't love; some feared, entirely without any basis in fact, the inheritance by the child of "bad blood." Clearly, the children of such parents were rejected not because the children lacked worth but because the parents had problems of ignorance, immaturity or worse.

Understanding the origins of your rejection in your parents' own problems rather than in your lack of worth, you can start to rebuild your self-esteem. You didn't *deserve* rejection; it was foisted upon you. If you doubt your worth and belittle yourself, it is because the hurt and still unable-to-understand inner-child victim of rejection is dominant. But as an adult, you can see the situation: Rejected because of parental problems, the inner child has rejected himself and, through his hurt, demeaned image of himself, has given you your image of yourself, a reflection of his.

Your task is to obliterate that false image by accepting yourself for what you are—a worthy human being. Start to do that with understanding. And go on to take a look at what it is that you are doing that is worthwhile. Make a list of even the little worthwhile things you do. Don't confine it to what you are absolutely convinced is worthwhile; you may still not be in a position to judge well, for you have had little if any practice in regarding anything you do as worthwhile. What things do you do or have you done that others have told you are worthwhile? Again, you have had no practice in accepting their judgment; until now, in fact, you may have automatically assumed that their judgment was not valid. But, for a start now, if you can do no more than grudgingly make the assumption of validity, do that.

Each item on the list is at least a small weapon you can use to fight your self-rejection. And the list will grow if you keep fighting.

Going Out to Others

You have stood off others with defensive spines. But that was because of your self-belittlement, your suspicion that you could only be unattractive to others, your fear that since you could only think of yourself as beyond the pale they must think so, and your fear that if you did go out to them or let them get close, you would only be inviting more rejection. But all the suspicion and fears had false premises. You are discovering the falsity. You are trying to reestablish your self-esteem.

You have to go out to others. You need them. You need the reinforcement of your self-esteem that only successful dealings with others and the establishment at least gradually of warm relationships can provide.

You have to start by going out to others whether you want to or not, even if you still feel, as you will at first, vulnerable. You have to take yourself kindly but firmly by the scruff of the neck and say, "Do it. Do it because I, the adult, have a right to adult interchange, a right to the confidence, strength, warmth and fulfillment I can get only in this way. I am not going to let the part of me that is focused on the past rule my life—not any more."

It will take effort to go out to people in respectful interchange, to differentiate between the rejecting attitude you have taken toward yourself automatically and the more adult attitude that says, "Look, I have a right to live here, too. I, too, am worthwhile."

You have a battle to fight, and although it is a tough battle it is not impossible to win. I have seen it won—but only after great effort.

It can be helpful for you to take a little time out each day for what might be called a daily strategy session or, more accurately, a meditation session. In such sessions, you can say over and over again the helpful sentences below until they become second nature:

1. I am not going to expect any human with whom I deal to be God-like.

2. I am going to expect that it is possible to make friends only by starting out to make acquaintances.

3. I will expect no more from my acquaintances than I can give in return.

4. I will expect that, little by little, as I succeed in being polite, warm and interested in others, others will be polite, warm and interested in me, and friendships will blossom.

5. I need practice. I will remember that in dealing with others warmly and comfortably I am trying to do something that, although easy and natural for many others, is as difficult for me as it would be for many others to play a violin. They would have to practice before they could play. I have to practice in establishing and maintaining relationships.

6. And I have to remember always in my practicing that the better one learns to draw a bow across a violin string, the more likely a beautiful tone. But if the string happens to be sour one day, the most practiced efforts to elicit a beautiful tone may fail—for that day. And, similarly, I must expect that there will be days when other people will not respond, when they for reasons of their own will be withdrawn and no more than merely polite or even perhaps rebuffing—and that when this happens I must remember that they do have problems that do not necessarily have anything to do with me and they are not necessarily rejecting me.

A Helpful Visual Image

To have a visual image of yourself is helpful in keeping your focus on your problem and in overcoming it. You may have one of your own choice. Always the one I see for the person who has been rejected is that of a human cactus plant, identifiable as human only by the face, with projecting spines everywhere, and yet, inside, a soft, dependent hidden center.

He has grown that armament of spines to fend off others, to "protect" himself from them, for fear, despite his tremendous inner need, that to come close to them is to risk almost certain hurt, almost inevitable rejection again.

If you keep such an image or any other suitable one in mind, if you call it up and see it in your mind's eye in the many situations in which your rejected inner child is trying to influence and direct your thoughts and behavior, it can help you to more effectively be a kind and good parent to the child and to yourself.

I would suggest, too, that you will find many of the later chapters of this book of value.

chapter 20

What to Be Wary of if Excessively Responsible

It is difficult to play if one has rarely if ever played, to enjoy moments of relaxation and freedom from responsibility if one has always been driven by a need to work and to be responsible. And this is no less true even when the need to work is no longer so overriding and when play, relaxation and moments of irresponsibility do not conflict with actual need.

As an overly responsible person, you may recognize that you have worked and continue to work to excess and have been dulled by your all-work regimen. You may realize that your work itself suffers because you give yourself no opportunity for refreshment. You may feel a staleness about your work and even have come to feel a staleness about life. You may recognize well enough that you are endangering your marriage, infringing on your children, cutting yourself off from so much of life that others value and that you suspect you might value if you could only allow yourself.

But you are seemingly caught in a tight grip, unable to extricate yourself, to give yourself a chance. You may even have made great efforts to learn to play and enjoy games and sports, only to find that you cannot really enjoy them, that you have turned any of those you have tried—golf, fishing, tennis—into work and you don't really play them, you work at them and they aren't fun and aren't relaxing.

The Mechanics

When a child assumes excessive responsibility for whatever reason—the death or illness of a parent, a great financial burden on the family or for other causes—the child's longing for childhood carefreeness, for normal play and for having parents take responsibility and provide protection and encouragement does not vanish.

Dependency is normal with immaturity, and however much the child may accomplish, however well he handles his responsibilities, the longing to be dependent persists. It gnaws even if there is profuse parental appreciation for his assumption of responsibility fully as much as when there is no such appreciation and the child also bears resentment.

And so the child carries on, bearing his load of excessive responsibility, possibly bearing resentment, smothering down the longing he has for carefree childhood. He acts with responsibility and he is responsible, and before very long the responsibility becomes habitual. There is no time for play, no practice at play, and absence of play becomes habitual.

The pattern is strengthened in adolescence—and, in adulthood, it is firm, seemingly bedrock, an integral part of the individual.

At some point, often during courtship, the overly responsible person may be asked to play, urged to relax. He tries, goes through the motions. He feels uncomfortable and even anxious, but in courtship he may be able to go on anyhow with his half-hearted efforts, encouraged by his fiancee, who sees a challenge in helping him learn to relax and play. Or it may be the woman who needs to learn how to play. In either case the couple may be encouraged by some small progress and both may hope and expect that with time there will be further progress toward achievement of relaxation and play.

But often there is very little progress after marriage. With

the establishment of a home, the old at-home pattern is reestablished more firmly. Also, there are now new responsibilities—marriage, home and usually children. It is even harder to let down.
Even more now than before, the overresponsible person feels that
to let down, to "waste" time, would be a threat; everything
would go to hell, the children would starve, the family would
disintegrate.

But is the threat real? Almost 100 percent of the time, it is
not. The threat does not lie in the real situation but in the anxiety
aroused by the feeling of strangeness associated with relaxation
and play, the feeling of not being "at home" unless one is working.

Almost always, too, there is additional anxiety. The inner
longing for play has not disappeared. What if it should take
over? Once out of control the urge to play all the time, to make
up for lost play in childhood might never be controlled again.

Although the superresponsible may give in at times to the
urgings and even demands of spouses or children to take time
off, inevitably they find themselves cutting into the time-out
periods; to see what they can do to make those periods constructive, to exercise responsibility even here when, purportedly, they
are trying to leave off responsibility. Because they are under
strain even when making the effort to play, there is no refreshment in it.

Yet, however difficult the predicament may seem, if it is
yours, you are not doomed to go on with it.

Your Needs

For just a moment, forget the adult problem. Consider the case
of Jan, a fourteen-year-old girl who was brought to me by her
alarmed parents when she threatened suicide.

Jan's story turned out to be this. Both parents were bread-
winners, who worked hard and had expected Jan to take care of
things in their absence—to go to school and do her homework, of
course, but also to watch over the other children, tidy up the
house, get meals ready. As a teenage daughter, Jan, in effect,
became mother surrogate and houseworker, with no time for any

recreational life and no time for any extracurricular activities at school.

She did what she was asked to do, bearing the burden of excessive responsibility, forgoing the normal life of a teenager. She went on with it as long as she could without complaint. But finally it became too much for her. She wasn't articulate about her feelings. All she knew was that she felt tired, that life seemed dull and that there didn't seem to be any point in going on living. And, in her inarticulateness, all she could do was to burst out one day and say, "I feel like I want to commit suicide."

She didn't really mean it. It was the only way of protesting that she could think of.

When she told me about the feelings that led her to make the threat, I discussed them with her parents. They were appalled. They were conscientious people, but they had been insensitive and unthinking about Jan. They told me: "We just didn't realize. We didn't mean to put this kind of burden and responsibility on Jan. It was just that it seemed a convenient way to do things—to ask her to look out for the younger children, to tidy up, to get things ready for meals. And she seemed to accept it and it seemed to work out; everything seemed to be going along well. We realize now that we just weren't close enough to the situation. It just didn't occur to us that we were overburdening the child."

They meant exactly what they said. They proceeded immediately to lighten the load on Jan, to get a neighbor in to do the housework and keep an eye on the younger children. Jan still worked a bit after school but only on routine adolescent chores. She was free to have a life of her own. She is getting along fine.

In this case, the parents could become what the child needed: understanding, caring, able to lighten the load for her, to give her the opportunity to be a normal teenager.

Can you, as an adult, achieve the same for yourself? You can, in largely the same fashion, but not so easily—for you have lived many years with the burden of excessive responsibility, first imposed on you in childhood and since imposed on yourself in adulthood.

You need to become a good parent to yourself, to set out

deliberately to treat yourself in a different way now. You need to say to yourself in effect: "I have adult rights and the privilege of assuming adult responsibilities. But I also have the right to have some fun and recreation, which I will deliberately take time for even though I don't feel like doing so. I will experiment until my fun skills are developed. I will not experiment compulsively, gritting my teeth and working at playing. The only thing I will ask of myself, in those times I deliberately cut out of my work schedule, is that I look about and see if I can find recreational activities that do not demand responsibility techniques. This will be irresponsible research in the appreciation of fun."

You can expect no fun at first. You may have to drive yourself to take time off to goof, to experiment to see what might eventually be fun for you. The question at the beginning will not be whether this or that activity offers fun for you. You can't expect that it will—immediately. Rather, the question should be, conceivably, if you went on with this, might it at some future point provide relaxation, enjoyment, a rewarding break in responsibility?

You will not feel at home at first. You will undoubtedly experience some anxiety. You will be tempted to minimize the time-outs, to take them infrequently, to cut them short.

A Helpful Visual Image

If you have a visual image of what is going on within you, it will be helpful. One that may be useful for you is an image of your child of the past as a giant, made bigger than normal in stature because of having to shoulder excessive responsibility. That child within you now is still a giant for work, blind to anything but work and responsibility, without experience and practice in anything but them. That single-focus giant of a child has a firm clutch on your adult of the present. In his clutch, you are always turned toward work and responsibility, cannot turn around and look at fun and relaxation. You are going to have to make continuous efforts to turn around, until finally the clutch of the child is weakened and broken. Once the grip is broken, it is not easy for the child to reestablish it except for brief periods.

Your Schedule

If you are going to be successful at this, you need to set up a
schedule for some goofing off daily—and a schedule for a vacation every month even if it is no more than a weekend totally
divorced from business chores, household chores, any chores.

Practice is what you need. Practice in just taking the time
off. Practice in experimenting with hobbies and other pleasures.
Practice in learning how to experiment without compulsiveness,
in finding out what it is you could come to enjoy. Practice in
letting your anxiety surface, in giving yourself opportunity to
analyze the anxiety, see its origins clearly and dampen it. Practice
in seeing that what you may have feared—that if you take time
off, you will become uncontrolledly irresponsible—does not come
to pass. I can guarantee that you, of all people, do not have in
you the makings of a playboy. But you have to give yourself a
chance to see this for yourself.

You need practice, too, in seeing that nobody blames you for
taking time off, that your affairs do not go to pot, that indeed you
come back to your work refreshed and accomplish more, more
easily and efficiently, and you haven't really sacrificed work
because of taking time off but rather have added to your capacity
for work.

I have seen some people fail to rid themselves of the pattern
and effects of excessive responsibility and others succeed bril-
liantly. And the difference has been that those who succeeded
undertook to practice, practice, practice; to recognize the
strangeness, the almost-alien nature, of relaxation for them; and
for a time, in some cases for quite a long time, they took it on
faith that they could learn to relax and enjoy it and it would be
worthwhile.

chapter 21

Some Blocks to Beware Of

Whatever the pathogen or combination of pathogens in your life, you are ready to begin a voyage in search of your true self and adult fulfillment. And, just as a sailor in unfamiliar waters uses a chart to avoid being shipwrecked by unknown reefs, you need an awareness of a certain few but potentially critical hazards you may encounter. Prepared for them, you can keep from foundering.

The Feeling of Uniqueness

All of us tend to look upon ourselves as unique. We may or may not use the word "unique" but we do view ourselves as that. When we have problems, we are inclined to think that nobody else has had such problems or so many of them. We are inclined to believe that we have taken a turn in the road nobody else has taken and, for example, that we are uniquely alienated and alone. As a result, we may feel that there is nothing we can do about the distress we suffer; perhaps other people can, yes, but we cannot.

The feeling of being unique, however, amounts to a reason—an excuse—we can use for maintaining the familiar atmosphere

of our past home lives. As we have pointed out repeatedly, we
are reluctant to go away from home however much we may
suffer there. Home is familiar to us and when we think of depart-
ing from it, we have much the same feeling a child has when he
thinks of going away from home. We will be in foreign territory;
we will not know our way around; it is risky out there. We resort
to any excuse we may think of, including the argument that our
problems are unique, in order to stay at home and remain, if
distressed, nevertheless secure.

You cannot make a frontal attack on the feeling of uniqueness and expect instant success. It is your child-of-the-past
feeling and that child will maintain it, stubbornly and fiercely, if
it is attacked directly.

You need to recognize that you do have within this feeling of
uniqueness and that it resides in only part of you—the child part.
As an adult, you know better than to believe it; you have only to
look around to know better. When you consider other people
objectively, you realize that all of us have problems and while we
don't necessarily have all the same problems, many of us share
problems in common, and no problem is unique to any one
individual.

This is not to deny that there is uniqueness in people. The
uniqueness, however resides not in their problems but in how
they approach life, work at their problems, free themselves for
creative explorations. It lies not in their child of the past but in
the adult of the present they have worked at letting themselves
become, the adult they have given precedence over the child of
the past.

It is the child of the past who fits into one stereotype or
another. Only if the adult of the present is freed from the child's
domination can you work out your individual self and discover
your true talents and desires, the job you want to do, the values
most important to you and who you really are. As long as you
take stock in the child's claim of having unique troubles and
unique causes for them, making them impossible to overcome
and even dangerous to try to overcome, you have less chance of
being the unique self you can be.

For virtually all people, however brave and self-assured they may seem, there is some anxiety in the unfamiliar. There is no shame in the anxiety, nor in the tendency to resort to excuses to avoid moving into unfamiliar territory. All of us have to "nerve" up at least a little in order to step into the unfamiliar. We have to tell ourselves that it may be a little less cold there than we imagine and we have to determine that we are going to try it.

No matter how difficult it may seem, no matter the excuses for not trying the child of the past may offer, you try. You figure out what comes naturally for you, what comes naturally but hurts—something you avoid doing or overdo—and then you do the opposite to see what happens, aware of your anxieties and aware that there is some risk, but, with anxieties and all, you try because you have a right to loosen the grip of past conditioning.

And you can expect that when you do try, when you take even just a small step into the unfamiliar, there will be some exhilaration in that bit of progress and you will begin to develop an impetus to keep moving forward.

False Humility

Some self-belittling people find a reason for avoiding taking any steps toward the development of self-esteem in the argument: "If I treated myself differently, I would probably become an egotist. I prefer to be humble."

But self-respect and self-esteem are not the same as egotism. When you respect yourself, you recognize your own worth; you also recognize the worth of people around you. To be self-respectful does not mean that you consider yourself better than others, which is the stance of the egotist, but that you are just as worthwhile as anyone else. You can learn to respect yourself without losing true humility.

There is a false humility that some people burden themselves with. They have belittled themselves so much and have come to regard themselves as so relatively worthless that they have decided that the only way they can get any of the acceptance they crave from others is to be servile. They thus buy acceptance with servility but hurt inside, feel like doormats and become increasingly angry with themselves and more and more self-belittling.

Yet their servility gains them, if anything, only an ersatz kind of acceptance. People don't usually want to relate to doormats. When they do, and accept servility, it is usually because they have a problem of their own. And when the servile person feeds and nourishes that problem by his servility, he does no real service for the recipient, who at some point may recognize the disservice and turn on him.

Guilt Feelings

Any of us may feel guilt when we break a law of society or rule of the particular group in which we live. Such guilt feelings serve a useful purpose when they lead us to make amends or restitution in order to regain group acceptance.

Guilt involves some self-deprecation. But self-deprecation does not necessarily involve guilt, though many people who are victims of parental pathogens confuse the two. They think they feel guilty when, in reality, they are experiencing self-deprecation.

In peculiar ways, we load ourselves with what we may mistakenly consider to be guilt feelings. If we fasten on the idea that, through our behavior, we have hurt someone, we are presuming that we are important enough and have power enough to do that. Yet rarely are other people as hurt by us as we think they are—and, to no small extent, when they are hurt, they may have made some contributions themselves to their hurt. Many of us eventually come to find out that no one, except possibly in extreme circumstances, can really hurt us in a lasting way unless we cooperate in permitting them to do so for reasons going back to our childhood. And rarely are we all-powerful in hurting others.

We may sometimes use guilt feelings to try to gain the sympathy of others and yet that solves no problems. Perhaps the most destructive thing we can do is to use excessive or misplaced guilt feelings to convince ourselves that we are too "bad" or too "weak" to change. Because of our "badness" or "weakness," we tell ourselves misguidedly, we can never hope to learn to be good parents to ourselves so we might as well stick with our familiar old patterns.

"Too Set to Change"

The notion that one is too set in his ways, too long accustomed to them, too firmly habituated, to make changes can be a stumbling block if we allow it to be.

But the fact is that living organisms are dynamic and constantly changing or they would not be living. Nothing ever stands still or stays the same inside you: cells wear out and are replaced; your blood is never the same today, with the same cells moving in it, as yesterday.

You are always developing in one way or another. It may be more difficult to modify firmly entrenched habits and patterns, but they have not become unchangeable because of the passage of time. Modifications are possible—and the need for them may be even greater in older people than in younger. If less remains of life, why should it not be a happier, more fulfilling life?—and it can be. Modifications to make it so can be achieved as long as any life remains, for dynamism is what life is all about. No one is ever "too set to change."

Anger, Resentment, Self-pity and Depression

Being human, no matter how insightful we become, we cannot expect to free ourselves from feeling negative emotions at times. But once we have come to know ourselves better, we will quickly recognize the emotions of anger, resentment, self-pity and depression and their effects, and we will be able to institute prompt measures to prevent ourselves from prolonging them and acting them out. We can free ourselves in this way from a great deal of our unhappiness.

In the beginning, as we attempt to review our past honestly we must be wary about being overwhelmed by these negative emotions, for this will delay or prevent our growth. We must recognize that to have such feelings occasionally is natural and that, in fact, once we gain control of them, they can be helpful warnings, alerts that something is amiss. Armed then with understanding of our childhood tapes and with positive techniques we can muster, we can search out and correct the causes of our lapse into old attitudes. Such feelings can serve as do the symptoms of a physical disease—fever or nausea, for example—which, while unpleasant, play a vital role in alerting us to an underlying condition that may threaten our health.

Often, anger, resentment, self-pity or depression may be a product of nothing specific although we may attribute the feelings to failure in work, unkindness of others and so on. They may stem, as may even physical symptoms, from a general anxiety that someone once described as "fright spread thin." We are often so disturbed by such anxiety that we seek to attach it to something specific we can put a name to. Unfortunately, while our anxiety may be decreased when we replace it with a specific emotion, we are still left immobilized.

Until we can learn more about controlling and overcoming our negative feelings, we need a handy first-aid kit. The major tool in that kit is the knowledge that rarely if ever can we as humans be occupied or preoccupied with two things simultaneously. So action is in order. Survey your problem and see if there is anything at all you can do right now, today, to ameliorate it.

If there is nothing you can really do or feel strong or ready enough to do about what is bothering you, you can get much relief by substituting some action. Concentrate on something you can do now—call a friend, finish some overdue work project or work on a hobby. Whatever you do, do not sit and brood and castigate yourself. Say gently, firmly: "Come on, now, this is probably only an overreaction of mine—and even if it is not, there is nothing I can do at this moment about it, so let's go on living. I won't permit anyone, or any situation, to spoil my life or even spoil my day. I will have faith that if I truly try to live in 'now,' I will, by some tomorrow, be able to resolve my problems and some may even resolve themselves."

chapter 22

Just for Today

It may seem to you at first view like a mountain of a task: to become a good parent to yourself, to identify the ways in which you have not been, to set limits on your inner child of the past, to stop belittling yourself or others, to stop yielding to long-entrenched habits of thought and behavior that only serve to limit you.

Yet it is not overwhelming, if you look at it in proper perspective and approach it in what is the only reasonable way.

Life in Day-tight Compartments

One of the greatest single tools you can make use of is the "twenty-four-hour" concept. Although centuries old, that concept was perhaps put best by the distinguished physician Sir William Osler in an address to the 1913 graduating class of Yale Medical School. Later, Osler's address was published in a very small but valuable book, *A Way of Life*. I recommend that you read it if you can—it is to be found in most libraries—for it will be helpful in grasping a principle that, like most great ones, is simple but not easy.

In his address, Osler spoke of "day-tight" compartments, comparing them to the watertight compartments on a great ocean liner that permit it to proceed with safety even if badly damaged in some areas. He spoke of the practice of living for the day only, and for the day's work—"life in day-tight compartments."

When the address was published in the book form, with it was included a poem from the Sanskrit that had been sent to Dr. Osler:

> Listen to the Exhortation of the Dawn!
>   Look to this Day!
> For it is Life, the very Life of Life.
> In its brief course lie all the
> Varieties and Realities of your Existence:
>   The Bliss of Growth,
>   The Glory of Action,
>   The Splendour of Beauty;
> For Yesterday is but a Dream,
> And To-morrow is only a Vision.
>   But To-day well lived makes
> Every Yesterday a Dream of Happiness,
> And every To-morrow a Vision of Hope.
> Look well, therefore, to this Day!
> Such is the Salutation of the Dawn.

If you have a large task ahead of you, it can be made manageable if approached day by day. If you have fifty letters to write or a dozen small jobs to do around the house you can do them if you do a few at a time. A fundamental truth is that there is *nothing* you cannot bear, or make a beginning about doing or refrain from doing for a short period only.

The validity of this is demonstrated in the experience of Alcoholics Anonymous, a worldwide organization of half a million people, which has had greater success in helping those with alcohol addiction than any other organization or treatment approach. Although total lifetime abstention from alcohol is a must for AA members, they work at it only on a daily basis. They never say, "I shall never take another drink"; they say only, "I will not drink for today." And this approach is used not only by the new member but by the member who has stayed sober for thirty years. If this works so well and so often for people "hooked" physically as well as mentally and emotionally, it can work for those of us who have no physical disease.

Only day-to-day effort, not some sweeping declaration of intent, can help us wrestle with our inner child of the past, with bringing under control his feelings as they keep welling up every day, with giving our adult of the present a chance to become dominant.

Twenty-four hours is a convenient, workable time period for most of us, but sometimes, when temptation is extreme or provocation great, we may have to break the period down into hours or even minutes. We can rely upon our strength for some brief period of time. We can say to ourselves: "OK, we may have to yield in the end, to give in finally—but not now, not right now. Tomorrow, perhaps. We'll wait until tomorrow to make a choice again."

Safe in Today

We can be safe in today. Yesterday is gone. All our remorse and self-belittlement will not bring it back and may give us only excuses for not trying to do any better. Similarly, if we peer ahead to tomorrow, we may become afraid, and our fears can reduce us to impotency. We forget that when tomorrow comes, we will be a little different than we are today, for each day we grow, and even if the situation we fear does actually materialize, our reactions to it may be different. "Ninety percent of the crises in my life have never occurred!" a patient once remarked.

It is fine to take some thought for tomorrow, to do some planning for it—but not to live in it.

If you are careful to stay with the "just for today" principle, you are likely to amaze yourself over a period of time. The process of approaching your problems from day to day—of trying to at least nibble a little at those problems today without riveting your attention on what may be necessary tomorrow or some time in the future—will strengthen your ability to make a little progress today and enhance your ability to make more progress tomorrow.

I have found it helpful to advise patients to try to have a quiet time, a few minutes with themselves in the morning, either immediately before or soon after getting out of bed. In this quiet time, they say to themselves: "Just for today, I am going to try to be a good parent to myself." And they remind themselves what this means.

A good parent does not belittle a child who is making an earnest effort. So you say to yourself: "For today, I will try to be patient with myself. No matter what I do or fail to do, I will not think of, or speak to, myself in any negative way."

Further, a good parent does not demand perfect performance from a child whose comprehension or coordination are not yet adequate. So you must say to yourself: "Just for today, I will not try to accomplish sudden great changes in my life or character. I will set myself small tasks and be content to know that I carry them out faithfully. I will be strengthening myself for larger ones later."

I also suggest to patients that they say to themselves: "Just for today, I will do three things: one that I have been putting off (it may be a very small thing and, in fact, should be to begin with); another for someone else (and this can be simply holding a door for someone or smiling at a sad face); and a third that is just for me because I would like it (and it may be simply buying a book you want, viewing a TV program you'd like to see or just indulging in a long, hot bath)."

As you go about your day, try to keep the feeling of the morning with you. If you feel it slipping away, if you find the child-of-the-past tapes sounding loud, if you have difficulty handling your resentments or fears, try to avoid reacting automatically, blindly. Stop yourself. Say: "Easy does it. I am not going to poke somebody in the nose just yet—or be frightened just yet." Don't blame yourself for having resentments or fears. Try to realize that you have already punished yourself by having such uncomfortable feelings. You may be surprised at how much relief this provides.

At night, many people find it helpful to take an inventory of their day. It should not be a "judgmental" inventory but a simple totting up of the successes you have had in doing what you set out to do for the day and the areas in which you have gone back to past conditioning. Like a good parent, you say "bravo" to the first and, to the other, "Never mind; tomorrow you will be a little older, wiser and stronger, and you will probably find all that a little easier."

After that, you can go over in your mind those things you can be grateful for. You can then go off to sleep in the proper frame of mind to earn true refreshment of body and spirit. Most of us have far more to be grateful for than we ever acknowledge to ourselves. Often, we count our blessings only in reverse. It is only after we have *lost* something that we value it. No wonder our lives seem grayer than they need be. To cultivate gratitude for what we do have is a powerful aid to self-esteem and self-control.

Staying Power

Sometimes, even though we have faithfully followed the one-day-at-a-time principle, serenity may evade us. We may feel that we have reached a plateau and are making no progress. In our disappointment, we may even feel that we are worse off than before. We are not.

This is the time when our "other-centeredness" is doing its work, but our minds are not yet registering it. Tomorrow or the day after, we may awake with new strength and courage, a sudden new view of things, and wonder where it all came from. Human progress is not a smooth, continuing line. We progress much in the fashion of a caterpillar, however unlovely that comparison may seem. If you have ever watched a caterpillar, you have noticed that it extends its long body upward, grasping a stem as far up as it can reach with its front legs, but it has not got anywhere until it pulls its very last legs up to where its head is. And then it must repeat the process.

In similar fashion, we can use our minds to select the spot

we wish to reach, use our minds and effort to reach it with part of us, but our progress often remains stationary for a time and then one day, without thought, we suddenly are there.

So be patient. If you have done the best you can each day—remembering that the best can vary widely from day to day—you need not worry about your hind legs; they will follow. If you put forth effort, you don't have to give thought to the details of the workings of the progress mechanism.

One of our major impediments to change is a doubt of our own staying power, and such doubt is almost inevitable if we think in terms of a lifetime. But we needn't, and shouldn't, think in those terms. We have the staying power for a day at a time; each day of staying provides a little growth; the growth is cumulative. Never forget that new ways of doing things can be as habit-forming as bad ways, and the new ways provide the additional carrot of self-esteem to nourish us and keep us going.

I like very much the perceptiveness of one of my patients, who remarked: "If I tell myself that I must do this or must not do that until the day I die, I will never know if I have succeeded or not. This way each day I have a triumph to celebrate!"

chapter 23

Want Power Versus Will Power

Most of us associate "will power" with taking ourselves by the scruff of the neck and forcing ourselves to do something part of us is not willing or ready to do. We also associate it with failure because so frequently will power does fail. It may fail for many of us, regardless of our particular parental pathogens and child-of-the-past conditioning, simply because of lack of willingness or readiness. And for some of us, the use of will power on ourselves, because we came from overcoercive or overperfectionistic home lives, reinforces the almost automatic reaction we have long had to barking commands. We then become more reluctant, and spinning our wheels in the old conditioning, we get nowhere.

Want power is another matter. It involves effort, as much effort as would be involved if will power were successful. But with want power, we don't tell ourselves that we must do this or have to do that; we don't push or force ourselves to do anything because we have decided, or somebody else has decided for us, that we *must*. We want something and, because we want it, we determine that we are going to do whatever is necessary to achieve it. We have a legitimate adult goal and we ask ourselves to go after it even though it takes some sweat.

And this is the approach you will find most helpful to use in your efforts to become a good parent to yourself.

What does it mean in practical terms? It means that when you find it necessary to say no to yourself, to limit an impulse, to ask for a halt to self-belittlement, you do so as much as possible on the basis of wanting to achieve something, to gain a specific goal, rather than because you are imposing an arbitrary limitation that has nothing to do with fulfillment.

It means thinking in terms of not trying to change yourself for the sake of change but rather to achieve a desired end, as specific an end as you can possibly formulate, because you wish to do what is necessary to reach that end. It means that whenever you ask yourself to give up something, it is not for the sake of simply imposing a prohibition but rather to free yourself from a hindrance to getting something you deem desirable and worthwhile.

"I thought at first," one man remarked, "that this was a kind of game, an exercise in semantics. Yet when I really gave it a fair trial and made an effort to think in those terms, I couldn't help but notice the difference it made. I got myself on my own side. I wasn't doing something for the boss or my wife or anybody but me."

This man was a mixture of oversubmitted-to and over-coerced and, as might be expected, had a terrible problem of getting to work on time and a resistance to any demands that he perceived because of his background as being "unfair." Although he was realistic enough to admit that being on time for work was hardly more than his employer could expect, his overcoerced child resisted firmly. He was convinced that he was "weak" and had no "will power" when, in fact, he had enormous will power wrongly directed. In order to satisfy his inner child he had to almost literally buck everyone around him. The only way he ever could "make himself" conform was out of fear of losing his job. And for most of us in the beginning, fear of the negative consequences of our actions is all that we know about because we have not yet experienced the rewards of proper behavior undertaken for ourselves alone. But the effort to control behavior through fear fails; it is exhausting; and soon the game doesn't seem worth it.

One woman talking of want power versus will power put it

another way: "It was all the difference between running *after* something I wanted instead of *away* from something I feared. When I was doing the latter, I felt anxious and tired all the time.

"And," she added after a moment's thought, "anyhow, it didn't work; my husband always criticized me for something—I could never really please him."

This woman also was overcoerced, but in her there were strong threads of perfectionism. She had been very dependent upon the approval of her mother, who made inordinate demands on her. In marriage, she transferred the dependence to her husband, who, unhappily, was a very critical person. He also tended to be moody, and what pleased him one day might not please him the next. It seemed to her, too, that he took for granted whatever she did that pleased him and rarely rewarded her with the praise she craved.

Eventually, her life had narrowed down to avoiding his active displeasure, with the results already noted. It began to change when she came to see that her husband's reactions were due to his own nature. He was overresponsible, worried, insecure. His apparent nitpicking stemmed from his anxieties. Good things were not to be relied upon; "bad" things must be corrected instantly or, he feared, the roof would fall in. Once she could see that his reactions overall were not due to anything she did or didn't do, she was free to begin to live positively according to her own lights. She could view her goals and then see the areas where she was acting in ways that prevented her from achieving those goals. She could want to change. "The most surprising thing I discovered," she reported, "was that in a funny way I had prevented myself from doing things I really wanted to do. I had looked upon them as unfair demands of my husband, and not doing them had represented a way of punishing him for not appreciating me. But the person who suffered was myself!"

A List of Goals

It can be helpful to draw up a list of goals, both broad and
specific, as a means of developing and sustaining want power.
Think of it as an open-ended list, to which you may wish to add
tomorrow, a month from now, a year from now. Quite likely, new
goals will occur to you as you move along, possibly as you give
consideration to "other-centeredness," about which we have more
to say in a later chapter.

The list of goals, always available for reference, can help
minimize or avoid slipbacks. The more goals you see on it—some
of which you may want to move toward immediately and others
you may want to progress toward later—the greater your want
power and the less likely you are to be constrained to drift back
into old past patterns.

A full list of goals helps, too, as a spur as you begin to feel
better. To a great extent, you want now to do something about
your life, your way of living, because it has been painful. Pain is
your stimulus for action to begin with. But as pain decreases, the
stimulus from that source decreases. It is easy for any of us, as
we make some progress and do feel better, to think: "Ah, now
that's fine; that's all I need; now I can rest on the oars."

The danger is that we are cut off from so much else we
would find valuable if we would only explore. Another danger is
that resting on the oars can lead to drifting, to being pulled back
downstream again, for the inner child is still there waiting to
impose old methods if given the chance.

No Rigidity

As we grow and discover who we really are, our goals are very
likely to change. We must not be rigid about them or we may
find ourselves putting our energies into something we used to
want rather than what we truly want now.

Such a discovery came late, most people would think, for a

very successful young advertising man. At twenty-nine, he was a richly rewarded account executive in a major agency and clearly was earmarked for great things. Already, he had many of the trappings of "big success": luxury foreign car, lavish apartment, wardrobe full of custom-tailored clothes. Luckily for him, the woman he wanted to marry turned him down. Brought up short by that, he began to do some thinking. The more he thought, the more he concluded that advertising was not really for him, that there was no fulfillment in it for him. Since he wasn't going to get married, he needed no money to support a wife. What he wanted most of all to do, he decided, was to study medicine, and abruptly he resigned from his job to do exactly that.

Twenty-nine is "old age" for beginning the study of medicine. He had to go back to college to take premedical courses. There were then the four years of medical school, followed by internship and residency. It was a long time before he could expect to earn money again. All his friends thought him insane. Oddly enough, the only one who didn't think so was the woman he loved, who then accepted him. They started a happy married life together in a cold-water flat while he went to school. Today he is a very successful physician, one of the country's leading internists.

His is an extreme example, but I have seen many less extreme examples of the recognition that an original goal was either mistaken or outgrown. When that recognition is combined with the flexibility and courage to act on it, it has made all the difference in work satisfaction and a rewarding life.

Sweat, Patience and Little Rewards Along the Way

Perhaps one of the most important things to keep in mind if we are to develop and implement want power is the need to have patience with ourselves. We have to realize that there will be times when, like a field, we must lie fallow or, like a seed, we need time to germinate.

We must also remember that the inner child is always there with his urgent demands and we must set limits on those that could be damaging. That takes sweat. The effort that goes into setting and holding to limits gradually does diminish in time as you concern yourself with your adult goals and efforts to achieve them and gain satisfaction in the achievements. What makes it easier to set limits is not the disappearance of the child of the past but less preoccupation with him as you enjoy and become more happily preoccupied with the present.

Even from the beginning, it should not be all toil, sweat and ceaseless struggle, with never any reward along the way. On the contrary, you should reward yourself often for each success, even those that seem trifling. No success is trifling; one follows and builds upon another; each is significant.

Reward yourself for successes without fear that to treat yourself to something you like when you have had a little triumph is an interruption, a resting on the oars, a self-indulgence that should not be allowed. Is it bubble baths that you like and consider to be treats? Fine, take a bubble bath. One woman who, fortunately, has no weight problem enjoys two things with a passion—ice cream sodas and bubble baths. So for her treat occasions she takes an ice cream soda into her bubble bath.

Far from being negative self-indulgence, rewards for your triumphs can convince you at least a little that you like yourself— and that is all to the good.

chapter 24

Acting "as Though"

You are encouraged by insights into your problems now to think that maybe you can do something constructive about them. You are also encouraged by the realization that, however mountainous they may seen in toto, you can handle them in small chunks, a little at a time. You may see, too, how you can help yourself by the use of want rather than will power. And you start to work.

But, at the very beginning, you may not have deep feelings about the whole process and its feasibility for you. You can't will those feelings into being; they come only when you have made a fair start. Once you've got going and they develop, they help mightily. If only they were present at the very beginning, they would help mightily to get you started.

Yet there is an effective substitute which you can use until those deep feelings develop. You can act "as though."

Indeed, you have been using this principle although it has not been previously discussed as such. When you get yourself into states of despair and hopelessness that, your mind and heart would have you believe, are irremediable and yet you reach out for help even insofar as you pick up this book, you are acting "as though" there could be help. You are nourishing the healthy person within you who is trying to escape your old attitudes.

Especially in the beginning, when you face the need to handle your old problems in a new way, you may not think and feel that the new way will be better and may, in fact, be inclined to think it could be dangerous because it is unfamiliar. You are like the proverbial man from Missouri who wants to be shown. Acting as though can do the showing.

Ordinarily, people use their minds and emotions as guides for behavior, but you can operate the other way around, too. By your behavior, you can demonstrate to the inner "man from Missouri" that a new way doesn't make the sky fall in, *is* a better way, and you can then bring your mind and emotions into line.

It isn't that you are too stupid, too lazy, too selfish, or any of the other deprecating things you have called yourself because of faulty techniques. What often has happened is that you have been blocked by fear. In little ways at first, acting as though can gradually remove the fear and enable you to move ahead even though you may not quite believe, from the start, in what you are doing.

Have you indicted yourself for being ungenerous? You will do best to act as though you are generous. Self-belittling? You will do best to act as though you are worthwhile.

Acting as Though Versus Pretending

There is a major difference between acting as though and pretending. Pretending involves an attempt to deceive others or oneself. Acting as though involves no deception. It is practice in fitting on a desired trait rather than wearing it as if owned.

For a time, if you cannot yet enjoy and get a feeling of achievement out of what you are trying to do, you will need to act as though such enjoyment and feeling will come. Your acting as though will not bring this about but will help you persist so you can bring it about.

You will need to act as though you are combination coach and cheerleader to yourself. When you make even the smallest gain—just a bit of self-respect beginning to peep through in a situation where before you have not been self-respecting, or a bit of self-control becoming evident in a situation where before you had no control—then you become your own cheerleader, saying to yourself: "This is great; we don't have it made; we will have to keep working at it tomorrow and the next day and the day after that, too; but it is a gain, and if we let ourselves, we can feel good about it because we did have to struggle to make that little gain and we deserve congratulations."

When you are thrown for a loss, as all of us are from time to time, you become your own coach and, going to the sidelines, you as coach ask yourself: "What went wrong? Why the loss?" And, as coach, you can analyze the situation, see how old patterns entered into your handling of it, so that the next time the situation arises, you will be less likely to be thrown for a loss.

If, however, you sometimes are repeatedly thrown for a loss when you have truly acted as though, this, too, is a valuable clue. It is one way, as we shall see in more detail later, you get to know who you really are and what your true values are. It suggests that your man from Missouri remains unconvinced because you are trying to be something you truly are not or have no wish to be. This may be due to superimposed parental or cultural ideas, an unrealistic appraisal of yourself or an outgrown goal.

But what is more common is a wide variation of behavior in given situations according to whether we are sick or well, under stress or calm, generally happy or despondent. We all know that we have a "best" self, which we wish were ever present. Acting as though that self were indeed present often can be helpful.

Max Beerbohm's "The Happy Hypocrite" helps to illustrate the importance of acting as though.

A Lovely Fable

There was once an English Lord, Beerbohm wrote, whose dissolute life and wicked ways had stamped his face with ugliness. He fell in love with a beautiful, pure young girl, who shrank from him in horror when he proposed to her. He went to a marvelous silversmith, who fashioned him a mask of Apollo, so fine that it could not be told from flesh. Thus disguised, the Lord wooed and won his love and carried her off to a beautiful estate in the country surrounded by a great wall to keep out all his former life. There he lived in great happiness with her for some years.

But one day one of his old drinking companions forced his way through the gate and in the ensuing struggle tore the mask from the Lord's face. In horror, the nobleman clapped his hands over his face and shrank away from his anxiously questioning wife. Gently, she pulled away his resisting hands and then, to his great joy, he saw reflected in her loving eyes twin images of Apollo!

I probably need not belabor the point, but this is what can happen to all of us. The love that inspired the making and wearing of the mask is our true desire for change and growth; and the mask is our acting as though, the practice on a daily basis and the persistence that remove the ugliness of years of distortion of our true selves to reveal the beauty of Apollo that really lies beneath.

chapter 25

Practice Times and Techniques

Although the lovely fable that closed the preceding chapter suggests how our transformed inner lives can change our outward selves as well, in real life we are not provided with a beautiful, cloistered estate to which we can retreat to work the change. In real life, the fable's protagonist might well have had to set to work carving out his retreat in the midst of the hurly-burly of everyday London. He would have had to proceed slowly, finding new ways to react to traffic, shops, markets and friends, so that the busy life about him would not be disruptive.

What to Practice ... When ... How

So, in a way, it is with us—and luckily. For if we are unable to change much in our outer lives in the beginning, as we get stronger we must try to resist the temptation to change too much too fast. It will take us time, and some trial and error, to find out not only what we are capable of but what we want. Any precipitous decision is almost certain to be a mistake.

And I urge that, for at least a year, unless drastic change is forced upon you, you stick to whatever situation you find yourself in, trying only for better ways of handling the situation.

Actually, although much of our growth is achieved by displacing faulty attitudes and techniques with new ones developed through purposeful action and practice, almost as important, at least in the beginning, is what we do not do. To *not* act out, to not do as we are used to doing—that, too, is a form of action even though, superficially, it may seem like the reverse. To paraphrase a well-known saying, "To have the good prevail, it is often necessary only that the evil do nothing." We come to see that we cannot have two things in the same place at once. By not acting upon all our old impulses, we leave room in which the better ones can operate.

We need not—and should not attempt to—bite off more than we can chew. We can go into action but only by making lightning raids to begin with on terrain of our own choosing, and we can make strategic retreats when indicated without feeling in danger of losing the war.

We can work within manageable time periods, twenty-four hours or less. We can make it a major concern to refrain from what we have been doing that we know we don't want to do. We can try to stop and think before we do anything impulsive or before we deprecate ourselves. Then we are ready for tasks we don't like to even think of doing or think of doing only with great reluctance. Some of these, quite naturally, will be tasks that reality demands we do. But often we can construct practice situations for ourselves that strengthen us for the bigger things later. Hopefully, we will confine our practice in the beginning to little things or structured situations.

If you have been shy, self-critical and uncomfortable in social situations, you need to consider social events of any kind to be situations for practice in developing self-respect. If there are certain types of situations that, in the past, have made you lose control, such situations need to become practice arenas for the development of self-control.

I have asked easily irritated people—people who became exasperated to the point of explosiveness when, in driving, they encountered stoplights—to undertake to practice becoming philosophical about stoplights. Not without some headshaking on their part about the seeming foolishness of it, they did as I asked them to do, seeking out routes with many stoplights. Arriving at each light, they practiced telling themselves: "Now this has always irritated me, but why should it? The irritation solves nothing. And the light is not here to irritate me—only to prevent accidents and snarls that might otherwise occur." Silly practice? But not any sillier, if you want to put it that way, than the previous habitual irritation. And, with some practice, they lost their irritability about stoplights. That in itself represented no tremendous stride but it was an exercise to build up adult muscles and made its contribution to strengthening those muscles for handling other problems as well.

Desensitizing Yourself

If you are uncomfortable in various types of social situations—if you dislike or worry about entering rooms, meeting strangers or making speeches, for example—you have fairly obvious fears about such situations. To help overcome those fears, you can use the same approach that is being applied successfully to the treatment of phobias, or persistent abnormal and sometimes incapacitating fears such as those of high places, open spaces, enclosed spaces, darkness and crossing streets.

In the modern approach to treating phobias, the first effort is to achieve relaxation. You do this yourself but a therapist helps. The relaxation technique can be simple—a matter of sitting down quietly, breathing deeply and imagining a pleasant situation. As mental relaxation follows, you then gradually relax the muscles of your body.

Once you have achieved a state of relative mental and physical relaxation, the next step is to imagine a situation of a type that under ordinary circumstances makes you uncomfortable—to begin with, a situation that would ordinarily be only mildly, not severely, discomforting for you. And that is all for the first day.

On another day, you repeat the steps for achieving mental and physical relaxation and then imagine a situation that ordinarily would make you just a little more uncomfortable than the previously imagined situation.

236 Your Inner Conflicts—How to Solve Them

As you continue this, little by little imagining situations that previously would have made you more and more uncomfortable until finally you arrive at some that before would have sent you into full-blown terror, what you are doing is desensitizing yourself.

The process is much like the desensitization or hyposensitization treatment often employed to help sufferers from hay fever and other allergies. In such treatment, once an allergy-provoking material is pinpointed, it is injected over a period of time in small, gradually increasing doses, until resistance to the culprit material is built up. Thereafter, exposure to that material under normal circumstances—for example, to a hay fever–producing pollen during the pollen season—may produce minimal or no allergic symptoms.

You can use the antiphobia, antiallergy technique to desensitize yourself to situations you fear. To avoid such situations is to solve nothing. You must seek them out and practice in them if the fear is to be overcome. And you can help encourage yourself to seek out the practice and help to make the practice less discomforting by first going through the mental practice.

If, for example, you dislike and have stayed away from high places, you relax yourself and imagine putting yourself in the least frightening high place and then go on to imagine yourself in more and more "dangerous" and higher places. After that, you go out into the real world, beginning easily, starting not at the top floor of a skyscraper but on the ground floor. A little at a time, you work your way up, never exceeding on any one occasion a height that makes you just a little uncomfortable. Eventually, you arrive at the top floor, and that makes you only a little uncomfortable; after several visits there you are no longer uncomfortable at all.

One woman had been reared by an abnormally fearful mother who wanted her children to stay close to home, either within the house itself or within the confines of the yard. The mother had a great fear that if they went beyond, somehow something terrible might happen to them in the neighborhood. When the daughter grew up, she took over her mother's anxiety and applied it to herself.

She consulted me because she had become extremely critical of herself. "Here I am," she told me, "a grown woman, with a wonderful husband and two children coming along well, and, because of these silly reactions of mine, which make no sense to me, I have become a prisoner in my own home." And, in fact, she was able to come to see me the first time, and on several subsequent occasions, only in the company of her husband, who had to keep reassuring her all the way to my office and back home again that there was no danger and that he was there to make certain she would be safe.

It sometimes happens that some manifestations of child-of-the-past conditioning are postponed for a time and then make their appearance suddenly or are present in mild form for a long time and then become acute. At one point, the woman had been able to drive a car and get about at least a little without panic.

We started slowly. I asked her if she thought she could leave the house at all by herself without becoming overly fearful. She thought she might. Could she go beyond the yard? She didn't know. I asked her to investigate, to go as far as she could without great discomfort. In a second visit, she told me she could go about two houses down the street without becoming fearful. That was fine, I told her; we knew the present limit.

We then concentrated on having her determine and understand why she had the fears—understand that, given her conditioning, they were not silly; that neither her mother nor she herself was to be blamed; that there was to be no further self-belittlement if she could possibly avoid it.

But she still had the fears, and hers was an extreme case. She could make progress but only very slowly. It couldn't be forced—and shouldn't be. Overreaching could set her back. One day she could, without acute discomfort, go a few houses farther down the street; the next, just a few more. When she could get comfortably down the street, she was to get her car out and do the same—just drive to the end of the block and back. She did.

I asked her then what she would really like to do, want to do, outside her home if she had her choice. She wanted to be able to go to the shopping center, shop instead of phone for what she needed and stop in the drugstore for a cup of coffee. Not much—but it would mean something to her. So I suggested that since the shopping center was only three blocks away, she next undertake to continue practicing driving her car to the end of the block and continue on and walk to the shopping center. She did that and subsequently took the car to the center and back, and she gradually worked up to the point of doing all she wanted— driving to the center, doing her shopping, stopping for a cup of coffee and driving back. That, for her, was a gratifying advance, a little personal triumph. There has been much more progress since; gradually she has become able to drive downtown several miles routinely to shop and to take trips with her husband.

Developing Adult Muscles

In practicing to overcome a problem, carry out the practice without any unrealistic expectations of sudden, dramatic change. You expect only to try, and then try again and again. If you fear going to parties but they are important to you, you go to parties—and for the first time or even the first several times, you expect nothing more of yourself than that you will be physically present with no self-belittling. You don't expect to suddenly become the "life" of the party. Just to be there at all, even somewhat fearfully, is an advance. You make efforts, as soon as you can, in practice situations—parties, dances, other gatherings—to practice self-respect and, as much as you can, also gradually, to become interested in people and less worried about yourself and what impression you may make. And, with practice and time, you gradually move toward self-confidence and deep interest in others and the ability to talk and empathize with them.

You start with modest goals—but you start. And you keep going because you want to, because it is going to mean something to you that you want. And gradually you add to the goals because you want to—and because, having achieved the more modest ones, you can see that the new goals are realizable.

Beginning goals can be modest indeed. One woman traces the beginning of her growth to determining that she would put the cap back on the toothpaste tube every morning. She was living alone, recently divorced, feeling rejected and worthless. Replacing a cap on a tube may, at first blush, seem hardly supportive. But doing it reminded her that she was a person worth doing it for, that she mattered. Every morning, finding the toothpaste tube neatly capped signified to her that at least yesterday she had thought enough to do herself this courtesy; it gave her just the tiny lift she needed to start her day in the right frame of mind.

We also need practice in discovering the joys of making others happy. Most of us have been so overwhelmed by our problems that we have had little psychic energy left for other people. If we have done anything for others, it may have been out of duty, a sense of "ought to." All of us feel better about ourselves and life in general when we can be outgoing and generous. But start with little things.

One man reported that he had noted for a long time that a neighbor down the street was catching the same train into the city. It was always a race against time for him; apparently his wife was not a well-organized woman and at the last minute he would appear at the station running for the train after having been driven there by his wife, who was still in her bathrobe. He started picking the man up and got a tremendous sense of pleasure out of it and it cost him nothing. Indeed, he reaped a reward since his neighbor turned out to be a handy person who knew how to fix many things around a house and car. The point was that he had done it without expectation of reward, and this is the secret. This man went on expanding his ability to give to others and is now one of the best-liked people in the community. His real reward was that he learned to like and enjoy people, something he could never do before.

Look around you at the daily circumstances in your life. You will find many practice situations at hand—small enough not to overstrain your developing adult muscles, not so important that success or failure in them is critical, but important to you because they can help you to develop.

chapter 26

Evaluating Situations
and Your Reactions

While an important part of your job is to be aware of how child-of-the-past distortions influence your reactions in real situations, the real situations themselves need as objective evaluation as you can bring to them.

Feelings as Cues

When, for example, a self-belittler feels depressed or anxious or alienated or put upon and resentful, the feelings are cues that old distortions and reactions are at work.

A woman goes to a party, comes home and tosses and turns until 4 a.m. though she must go to work in the morning. This is a fact of life for her. The same thing happens just about every time she goes to a party. She is unable to fall asleep because she goes over the party in her mind, examining minutely everything she said and did at the party. She plays back the whole evening and finds that she is unhappy about everything that went on: the things she said weren't witty enough; her dress didn't fit quite right; she made some remark that probably turned off another person and that was a bad thing to do. She takes no pleasure in the party; all she can do is point up to herself instances of her inadequacies. It hurts—and here are cues that she is inflicting the hurt upon herself, that her reactions are from her past conditioning. The realization of that is an important step in the direction of being able to overcome the past conditioning.

But consider another example. Suppose you are a self-belittler and happen to be in a job where the boss is almost continuously critical and belittles you. There are such people in the world, and some of them are bosses.

In that situation, the childhood conditioning that led you to be self-belittling is strongly reinforced. It may not be enough, then, to say to yourself: "I am going to put my arm around myself kindly and treat myself as kindly as possible," although this is part of your work. The other part is to be realistic about the job situation, to know that with a critical, belittling boss, there is a great strain on your sprouting small powers of self-kindliness.

In such a situation, you may be like a man who is allergic and has not yet been fully desensitized but goes into a field of ragweed and then is led to criticize himself because he sneezes.

While working on your inner problems, on the distortions induced by your past conditioning, you need, in kindness to yourself, to avoid as much as possible real situations that only aggravate the problems you are trying to do something about.

For the woman who suffers so much after a party, the problem is likely to be entirely within herself, and that is where she must concentrate—unless, perhaps, there is some one individual at the parties she goes to who really belittles her and reinforces her problems, in which case she would do well to avoid that person while working on her inner problem.

For the man in the difficult job situation, the inner problem must be worked on; but if the boss puts an unduly great strain on him and if there is the possibility that he can find another job, he may be well advised to find it.

A Consideration of "Norms"

If you know that you are impulsive and realize how much your impulsiveness is taking you away from work you really want to do and adult satisfactions you want to have, you need to set limits on yourself.

It can be helpful to consider realities in terms of "norms"—in terms of the limits within which other people seem to be able to function well and not feel deprived.

Suppose, for example, you feel it necessary to keep buying suits and shoes, to have thirty suits and twenty pairs of shoes piled up in your closet. How many other people have as many? How many suits and shoes do most other people feel they need?

If you yield to impulses to go out every night, you may realize that doing so is crimping your adult living. You may get some reinforcement in setting limits if you consider what other people seem to regard as normal going-out needs.

If you find that you come home night after night, have your dinner, then plump down in front of the TV set and watch until bedtime, you may enjoy what you do even though you feel it cuts you out of doing other things you want to do. Do others do the same? Perhaps some or many do; for them, this is a norm. But, in considering norms, you have to consider, too, whether a norm is what you consider ideal and what would be considered ideal by those who may be living seemingly more creative and fulfilled lives.

What is a norm for many isn't necessarily a norm you want—but at least if you look around and see what the norms generally are, you have something in the way of relatively objective guidelines.

Getting at Realities

In relationships with other people, you may find yourself tempted to put all the blame for what happens between you and others on your own inner problems once you have recognized those problems. But that would be unrealistic and would not serve you well.

If your relationship with your wife leaves much to be desired, you may well understand how your past conditioning may contribute to the difficulties. But she, too, may have some distortions from the past and they may have something to do with the marital difficulties. There are, in fact, four people in a marriage: each spouse and each spouse's inner child of the past, and we will discuss the four and the interactions between them more fully in a later chapter.

Similarly, in your relationships with your children, it is not all you. Children are immature beings who are exploring, as they should, and they sometimes come a-cropper. Inevitably, they make mistakes and get into trouble; this is part of the learning process, the growing toward maturity. When they make their mistakes and get into trouble, they are not "awful" and you are not inevitably at fault.

Relationships—and all of life—are complex rather than simplistic. Consider a simple yet representative example in medicine. Once it was thought that if anyone came down with a cold or a throat or other infection, the reason was simple enough: an invasion of disease organisms. But we know now that there is something more. There are at least two major factors in every infection: the host or person who is infected and the organisms that do the infecting. We know now that the bugs are always there. It is easy enough to find them in the nasal passages, skin and other areas. They can be found and recovered from people in good health. They are there, plain to see, under a microscope. It is only when the host is primed for invasion, when his natural body defenses are lowered, that invasion may occur—invasion in the sense that the bugs move from their normal habitats and multiply.

It is all too easy for a self-belittling parent to blame himself or herself for everything that goes wrong with a child, especially if the child has some congenital anomaly or becomes a real behavior problem. But unwarranted self-blame does the parent no good and may do the child harm by affecting parental attitudes.

In your dealings with others—friends, boss, spouse—you need to recognize that reality impinges on them, too. However fine another person may be, however minimal his or her child-of-the-past problems, he or she has encounters with everyday problems. Another person's irritability today may not be a reflection on you at all but a reflection of the problems he has today, perhaps a stomach upset or a fight with his wife.

Unjustified Distrust of Yourself

Often a self-belittling person agonizes because of unjustified self-distrust. If, for example, he wants to sell his house, he may tell himself: "I probably am going to do poorly on this deal because I am not much of a person when it comes to selling anything and I will make a poor job of it. If I were more adequate, I would make a good deal like my friends do."

If he wants to buy a new car, he may tell himself: "I will probably be sold a bill of goods by a high-pressure salesman who will talk me into something I really don't want and I will probably pay too much for it, and that will only prove to me once more what I already know—that I am inadequate."

And, because of his self-distrust, he is inhibited—and may be so to the point that he makes no effort to sell the home or buy the car or delays a decision unduly and reinforces his self-deprecation.

And yet, what is the reality? If he feels inadequate as a buyer or seller of major items, it is no reflection on his character. He hasn't had much experience in such buying or selling. He could get advice from somebody who has had the experience. But he hesitates to get the advice because he suspects that another person might then find out how incompetent he is—and he fears that in itself and also fears that it would go to under-score for him even further his conviction that he is inadequate.

Faulty thinking? Of course. It is child-of-the-past thinking. As an adult, trying to put your arm around yourself kindly, you need to realize that nobody realistically expects you or anyone else to be expert in all areas and that seeking advice is not a sign of weakness or inadequacy but rather a strength, a recognition of reality.

Making Decisions

As children, virtually all of us saw bears in the closet. There were no bears and if a kindly parent realistically established that fact for us, assured us he understood why we might have imagined the presence of bears and did not criticize us for the imagining, we soon recognized the reality and that was that.

But some of us had less fortunate experiences. We have never gotten over the feeling that there may be bears in the closet—not literal ones, but apparitions that threaten even though unseen and that inhibit us and make us fearful, self-critical and self-deprecating.

And such bears or apparitions are especially threatening and inhibiting when it comes to making what we consider to be major decisions.

We want to ask the boss for a raise. But that, in effect, would open the closet door. We are fearful of what might happen. As long as the door remains closed and we don't ask for a raise, there is no harm; we get along, not as well as we would wish, but we get along. But to open the door is risky; we feel acutely inadequate and self-deprecating when we even think of it; and we don't open the door. Although we try to convince ourselves that we don't have to, there is no real need to, we are reasonably comfortable as is, we are not comfortable. We are aware of our fears and self-critical because of them, and we grow more and more unhappy and more and more self-deprecating.

Is there really a bear in the closet? Are we really endanger-ing our job if we ask for a raise? We have to look into ourselves and see and understand how our past conditioning is at work. And we have to try to examine the situation realistically. Are we doing a good job, one that warrants a raise? Is the boss really an ogre who would react by firing us, or are we attributing that to him automatically?

The answers don't come instantly. But we have to seek them. We may need to take time and not jump to conclusions. If we actively work at getting the answers, we can afford to take time to let the evidence soak in. We can work hard to get the answers and then relax, let a little time pass. At some point, we may suddenly realize that we have reached a decision—or, if we have not, that the time has come to make it.

If the decision turns out to be the right one, fine. But if it turns out to be the wrong one, fine, too. The immediate results of a wrong decision may not be pleasant—but the long-term ones are likely to be rewarding if the decision making is a step on our way toward becoming a good parent to ourselves. As we have said before, we have a right to be human and to make mistakes. Worst of all is to so fear the possibility of a mistake that we doom ourselves to inaction and continuing frustration.

Overcoming a Paralysis

Trite though it sounds, the old saying "First things first," if applied literally, often can help us make decisions, get moving, extricate ourselves from a kind of mental paralysis.

Edith had been divorced by her husband for a younger woman. In her depression in the months that followed, she had let everything go. When she sought help, she was almost totally unable to function, although she had two dependent children and would soon need to get a job to augment her small income. She was terribly frightened. "I don't know, the more I have to do, the less I am able to do. I know I can't go on this way," she said, "but I feel paralyzed."

In such situations I am usually quite directive, suggesting that the patient do routine tasks by rote in everything she felt she had to do and select just one to do tomorrow. If she was in doubt, she could call me for help. The next morning she called, her voice frantic. "I have a list three pages long," she began, "and I can't make up my mind which is most important. These are all things I should have done long ago. I suppose looking for a job or paying my bills should come first, but I really don't feel up to either," she wailed.

"Have you made the beds?" I asked. "Well, no," she admitted, "but . . ." "No buts," I said firmly. "Make them and call me back when you have finished." After the beds, I directed her to straighten the house, not really clean it, just make it look tidy and superficially attractive. After this, since she seemed to be going strong and gaining energy rather than relapsing into her usual lassitude, I had her pay her utility bills since she faced a threat of having service shut off. After this, she was game, even eager, to go on but I called a halt.

"Now," I told her, "as a well-deserved reward, you are going to be good to yourself. You will arrange to have dinner for yourself and the children sent in tonight. You will take a nice long bath, put on something that makes you attractive and then read, watch television or listen to music or whatever you like doing best." In a week, after a few false starts, Edith finally got through her list. She gradually learned how to apply the "first things first" principle and to realize the value of any sort of action, however small, in promoting more action.

Many of us lose more energy in fighting and putting off action than we expend if we take the action. As the saying "If you want something done, ask a busy person to do it" reflects, up to a point the more we do, the more we can do.

There are times when we must make a decision before we really feel ready to do so. In reaching the decision, we should make every effort to use our "other-centeredness." We can sort out in our minds to the best of our ability the possible alternatives. We can ask others for advice. And we can be as honest with ourselves as possible in determining what motivates us toward one choice rather than another. At this point, because our abilities may not yet be great and we may feel somewhat muddled, we can turn to our other center. We can use meditation—and we will discuss this in the following chapters on other-centeredness—to help us arrive at what is for us, at the moment, the best we can do.

Painful as such forced decisions can be, we always learn from them and sometimes find that if our first "practice" decision has to be a major—and, at the time, a somewhat terrifying—one, all others that follow are easier by comparison.

chapter 27

Other-centeredness

> "I am convinced that man's fundamental problem is his human egocentricity. . . . A living creature is a bit of the universe that has set itself up as a kind of separate counteruniverse. It tries to make the rest of the universe serve the creature's purposes and center on the creature. That is egocentricity. Of course, this is a forlorn hope. All the great historic philosophies and religions have been concerned, first and foremost, with the overcoming of egocentricity."
>
> —Historian Arnold Toynbee in *Surviving the Future*

All of us have some egocentricity. It is an attribute of childhood. As a child matures, he moves increasingly away from egocentricity and toward other-centeredness. It is a movement toward something more than complete focusing on self and toward being an agent of something bigger than self. And the movement can be considered to be under the pull of adulthood or growth or the urge of a Higher Power.

But almost any parental pathogen can impede this movement and may sometimes even abort it. The child is unduly or even exclusively focused on self, and the tendency toward concentration on self may be carried into adulthood. Yet, if we have distortions carried over from childhood, none of us is ruled entirely by them. We recognize that while there are many times when we react according to past conditioning, there are other times when we do not.

However egocentric we may be, we are not entirely so. We have within us other-centeredness, and it can be of tremendous help in overcoming the effects of parental pathogens and in becoming good parents to ourselves if we recognize and explore the other-than-self center within us. Here we can find the vision for enlarging the scope of our adultness, nourishment to help strengthen our adult muscles and potential for commitment that at once can help fulfill us and leave us less time and inclination to bow before the automatic conditioning effects of the past.

Adult Commitment

It is natural in childhood to be "I-centered."

It is characteristic of adulthood, however, even if some of us have not thought it out in these terms, to focus our lives on goals. Something tells us: "Commit yourself. You have a certain amount of daily vitality that comes because you are alive and have had a night's rest and have had breakfast; now wake up and do something." An adult's urge to work toward a goal, to go beyond mere catering to self, is normal. When it is not present, the individual finds himself restlessly seeking pleasures, finding them empty and sooner or later berating himself because he has not articulated his adultness.

Adultness is hammered out in commitment. It is as if we are given a great hunk of marble that is "us." It is undifferentiated, not shaped in any way; we have to work on the marble by working toward something; and as we do so, the marble is carved and shaped. We are not carving out a niche for ourselves but rather are giving form and shape and meaning to our lives.

To put it another way, it is characteristic of adultness that you think of yourself as an agent—an agent of something bigger than you are. Religious people think in terms of being an agent of God's purpose. The nonreligious may say, "There are things in life bigger than I am," or, "I have a mission in life that is greater than I am."

There is a feeling in adultness that you possess talents that should be applied to the outer world, to make something there grow or flower that was not growing or flowering before—another person, a relationship, children, a cause. Bigger than self for many women are the growth and development of husband and family; they have a kind of built-in awareness of mission where a man has to seek his.

You need not be religious at all, or religious in any conventional sense, to have a sense of mission. I respect very much those who "experience" God. For myself, I feel that I am not in a position to ever experience God directly for I am finite and I conceive of God as being infinite. But anytime I see something flowering in another person or situation where there may have been only weeds or barrenness before, this is my idea of what the footprints of God are like, what universal creativity is about.

Breaking the Grip of the Past

All of us need to be, and those of us affected by parental pathogens need to become, aware of other-centeredness. I strongly favor meditation for the purpose of quiet, respectful assessment of our talents and also of what around us needs to be done and what we as individuals can do to help get it done. This doesn't mean that we must necessarily find our mission in work. Work and productiveness are important but so, too, are the giving and receiving of acceptance supplies in the interpersonal relationships that further the growth of others and ourselves, that nourish them and us, that invigorate their and our other-centeredness.

If one can be pulled along by the development of one's sense of mission, talents and loving interchange, new avenues open presenting new opportunities, new insights, new satisfactions. And this is the way it should be.

But conditioning from our past can interfere—can crimp our

powers, limit and hurt us and let much of our adultness go to waste. Because of such conditioning, we may flounder ever deeper in the past and in I-centeredness.

And so an important aid in helping to break the grip of the past and in adding meaning and fulfillment to your life resides in the development of your other-centeredness.

In periods of meditation, you can achieve the receptivity—perhaps only briefly at first but increasing with time—that allows consciousness of other-centeredness to develop and grow. In meditation—accepting yourself, at least then, as an infinitely worthwhile person—you can consider, without belittling, your talents and yearnings and get a feel for your individual blueprint.

I am convinced that each of us has an individual blueprint of some kind and nobody else can tell us what it is; we have to discover it for ourselves. There are many jobs to be done, songs to be composed and sung, plays to be written and acted, shoes to be made, ditches to be dug, pipes to be fitted, TV sets to be repaired, civic projects to be worked on, crops to be grown, children to be reared, persons to be fulfilled. We need to look to our talents, whether yet used or not, and our yearnings, whether yet expressed or not or even appreciated before. And then we need to look around for where the talents and yearnings can best be applied—in an unfinished world.

Wishful, unrealistic thinking is not in order here. I know many people who yearn to be "writers" who haven't the foggiest idea of the discipline, sweat and dogged persistence it takes to fill blank pages intelligently and usefully. I know people who would dearly love to be President of the United States but only a President on vacation, with all the trappings of office but not the sweat. There is no sense in yearning for and aspiring to something you are not willing to pay for in sweat.

Some people may find a simple question useful: What would I really want to do with myself if I had a million dollars tax-free? The answer may help them discover what their real yearnings are. If a person's answer is on the order of "I would like to take a four-month vacation, get my wife a mink coat and some diamond rings, buy a new house and car, join a country club and enjoy myself, giving myself the recreation I never could afford before," that person had better think about the question awhile longer.

Anyone who must seriously answer the question that way needs to recognize that such yearnings are "I-centered" and if they are *all* the yearnings he has, he will never know what adultness means and life will pass him by.

Such a person would be well advised to consider that his yearning for play may have much to do with the fact that he has been working at something he dislikes or has been burdened with excessive responsibility—and he may indeed need a vacation, a time away, a time to get his thoughts clarified. And when he has rested and given himself opportunity for meditation, he may then again ask himself what his yearnings are. And if they then go beyond "I-centeredness," fine. And if they don't, I would urge him to take an arbitrary stand if he possibly can bring himself to do so—a stand in favor of going outside of himself and working toward something bigger than himself, of trying that and sweating at it, with the good hope that it will grow on him.

The Many Aspects of Other-centeredness

To commit ourselves to the uncommitted life, to no goals except day-to-day living and getting as much impulse satiation as we can out of each moment, is to negate essential aspects of adult life. We commit ourselves then to being bound to childhood, and, so bound, we go back to old patterns of the past that hurt us to begin with and will keep hurting us. We cannot pursue happiness directly. Happiness is the by-product of commitments to persons and goals.

Facing the realistic need to earn a living, many people may properly turn to something outside the job that more nearly allows them adult expression and fulfillment. If a job is humdrum, without satisfactions, providing only a paycheck, perhaps it can be changed now or later. If not, there is more to the day than the hours of work.

I should, and do, emphasize here that if you enjoy going to your work and relating there with the people around you and you do a good job, the job itself can give you the feeling of being in tune with the universe. One job or career or profession isn't necessarily more valuable than any other; they all can be made

pipelines to the universal if they use our talents and energies for
that which is bigger than we are.

There are many aspects to other-centeredness.

It can be the locus, the vantage point, from which we can
differentiate best and easiest between child-of-the-past conditioning and adult of the present.

It can help in the formation of close and caring relationships
with others. Particularly, it can help us form a close committed,
physical, caring relationship with another, since children don't
make love.

It can help us to see things humorously and to laugh at
ourselves and our foibles sometimes. Only an adult of the present
can chuckle at himself; a child of the past is too "I-centered" to
do this.

It can help us commit ourselves to that which is bigger than
our impulse fulfillment.

It can help us to develop a lively interest in the arts—literature, music, theater, painting, sculpture. Interest in these areas
takes us away from the I-centeredness of our childhood. It puts
us in touch with committed, other-centered people and their
works. Although some persons in the arts do shoddy work because of their own child-of-the-past impulsiveness or to exploit
that of others, the arts can be an excellent arena in which to
develop other-centeredness.

And, hardly least of all, other-centeredness can help us to
develop appreciation, a sense of wonder, an ability to see things
as they are, see them brightly, see the moon through all the neon
signs around, see things in their lastingness and true beauty
rather than dimly and transiently.

Many of you reading this book will wonder why I am
describing other-centeredness and its various aspects in such
detail. You will have grown smoothly from childhood into adultness. You take your mission, your sense of purpose in life, for
granted. You have been living with it for years. You can laugh at
yourself sometimes; you have a spouse that you love. Bear with
those of us who are not so fortunate.

Some of us lose sight of adultness and what it is, or we see it
only dimly. This is usually because the child of our past is so

strong within us and we are spending so much time and energy in self-deprecation or self-aggrandizement that we are alienated from our adult selves. We have to struggle to keep in this other center, to keep from sliding back into the old familiar but painful home-of-the-past feeling. How do we work at it?

Meditation, as I have said, is one way. A regular retreat from the day's activities not only gives us a welcome respite but allows us to kindly check on ourselves. You can sometimes ask, "Am I using old, hurting methods on myself today or am I using *my* methods? Am I keeping my relationship with my spouse well nourished with respect and with reasonable limits when infringements occur? Am I taking myself too seriously? Am I comfortably committed to using my special talents, to making a project, a piece of land, a relationship flower?"

If you make it a practice to have a self-accepting quiet time each day, you will soon discover how helpful it can be, the extra dimension it can bring to your life. It is a simple practice but not an easy one to keep up on a regular basis. You are late in the morning, tired at night, have endless excuses. Maybe setting the alarm for five minutes earlier in the morning will get you started. At night, even if it is late and you are very tired, a short meditation time will help you sleep. I know many who started a quiet time practice reluctantly and were given to occasional lapses until they noted how much more tense, angry or oversensitive they felt after the lapses. For most of us there are many days of particular stress when taking some short quiet times can be vital in keeping us from hasty, inconsiderate action or in keeping us from being overwhelmed by negative feelings.

Perhaps the person who needs a quiet time during the day most, and may find it hardest to come by, is the busy mother and housewife. Indeed, the woman who has small children often feels it is impossible to find time to do everything that needs doing, let alone to find any time left for herself. But, with determination aided by a realistic appraisal of, to use a much-abused word, priorities, time can be found. Finding time for other-centeredness will help her put her endless chores in logical order and perspective. It will help her see that she has to respect her own rights as well as those of her children, that just as she must limit herself when she wishes to scold and belittle them, so must she limit them when their demands infringe upon her.

One mother of three children under five found the right way. "I had to," she confessed, "because I was going out of my mind and driving everyone else out of theirs!" One morning, she looked at her situation. The four-year-old was pulling out all her pots and pans, the three-year-old was chasing the cat, the baby needed changing, the wash cycle had come to an end and it was time to transfer to the dryer, she had a splitting headache and an equally strong desire to split heads. It was exactly ten minutes of ten and her day had just started although she had been up since six.

"Suddenly, I felt," she said, "that I just *had* to get away, if only for a few minutes. I decided the baby and the wash could stay wet for just a few more minutes. I plunked the other two children down on chairs opposite the clock, gave them each a lollipop, and told them to call me when the long hand pointed straight up. I said that it was a new game called 'Mommy quiet time' during which nobody was to speak above a whisper and that when they called me I would come. I told them that I was really counting on them to call me, right on the minute. Not before, not after. Something about my inner determination must have impressed them, for they did exactly that. Indeed, they were inordinately pleased with and proud of themselves for calling me just when I had asked.

"As a matter of fact," she went on to say, " 'Mommy quiet time' became something they would suggest themselves, not only because I always found time later to play a game with them but also because they knew I would be a kinder, nicer mother after I came out. An unexpected dividend was that all the kids learned to tell time early!"

What does she do with her quiet times? "Well, sometimes I just close my eyes and rest and think of something nice I am looking forward to. But often I review the tasks of the day ahead and reduce them to manageable proportions. Whatever I do, I feel much better. The feeling that I am controlling my own life, if only for five minutes, is such a relief. Or rather, I suppose I should say that I have discovered that I always have another life to which I can retreat in times of stress."

Busy executives often ask their secretaries to hold all calls, allow no disturbances, while they are working on a special problem. They can do the same for a needed quick contact with another way of looking at things.

For some of us a first acquaintance with other-centeredness begins during illness. Then we are slowed down, often alone and thrown upon our inner resources. Our routine "busy-ness" does not wall us off so completely.

One woman I know has a neuromuscular disorder that has restricted her activities, largely cutting her off from work and social and recreational interests she once enjoyed. For a long period, feeling dejected and hopeless, she was preoccupied with the single I-centered question "Why did this have to happen to me?" Finally, at one point, she tried meditation and in her meditation considered the question "What can I do just as I am . . . how can I be useful, helpful? How can I be an agent?"

"A few days after I began asking myself this question," she says, "some friends picked me up and took me to a bridge party. At the party were a couple of women who in earlier years had spread some false gossip about me and I hadn't spoken to either of them for a long time. That day, in confronting these women, I suddenly had the strange urge to see them as suffering human beings rather than as objects to be ignored or cut down. I spent considerable time with them, asking each about herself and showing interest in the replies. Both soon were telling me about their troubles and seemed to feel that I had helped. I came home feeling richly fulfilled in a way that I haven't been for a long time."

Sickness can be particularly painful if one is I-centered, and it tends to pull us there. When we are sick, we feel like "going home." To the question "Why did this happen to me?" the I-centered person often answers, "Fate is against me" or "I am no good, therefore I deserve this." If we can get outside ourselves and become other-centered, we have better perspective. We may see that it would be as logical to ask, "Why not to me?" as "Why me?" We may reflect that if something good happens to us, we do not usually question why. We are apt to ascribe the good fortune to a "lucky break" and think no more about it.

Other-centeredness does not, as many believe, imply just

forgetting about oneself and devoting oneself to others. With other-centeredness we respect ourselves and do everything possible, if we are physically ill for instance, to make ourselves comfortable physically and to restore our health. But, hopefully, we can also respect and care for others even if we aren't feeling well ourselves and, through being able to understand and share their concerns, we diminish our concentration upon our own. I-centeredness tends to increase physical pain and disability. Other-centeredness respects both "I" and others and encourages mutually respectful relationships. In this atmosphere, pain and disability tend to decrease and the restoration of physical health, to whatever degree possible, is aided and accelerated. The whole practice of faith healing is based on other-centeredness. Faith can't do everything; it should not be counted on to replace modern medicine or surgery; but it can work in harmony with them to contribute to healing.

All this does not mean that we can, or are supposed to, live all of our lives solely in other-centeredness. We are human and seek only to be fully this, not saints. We will often go back temporarily to childhood orientations. It is refreshing to do so as long as we do not infringe upon the rights of others, upon our own dignity or upon our adult goals in the process.

But other-centeredness can be our most valuable tool in many situations where we might not, offhand, think of applying it.

It can help us develop composure and ability to tolerate losing out. Just as the athlete who has developed good sportsmanship can acknowledge and admire the play of a victorious opponent without feeling diminished himself, we can stand off and see that in any contest there must be a winner—but when we don't win we are not really, necessarily, "losers" in a self-deprecating sense.

It can help us to be fair, to distinguish correctly between our rights and those of others and to respect both. The really good business executive is able to recognize the rights of employees, understand their aspirations, sympathize with any complaints they may have and be helpful, standing firm only when not to do so would mean infringement of his own legitimate rights and the legitimate goals of the company.

It can help us especially in controlling our inner child in trying circumstances. I know a scientist whose supervisor tried to direct every aspect of his research. The scientist came from a home where he had been critically directed in his daily life by his mother. Because of this, he reacted to the supervisor as he had to his mother, either complying resentfully or rebelling with consequent fear and guilt. When he was able to achieve some other-centeredness and to see himself in objective focus, he could, much to his surprise, manage the situation without any difficulty, paying respectful attention to the supervisor, taking from the latter's directives those which made sense and then proceeding to do his experiments largely in his own way and without anxiety.

Finally, other-centeredness can keep us feeling that we are one with the universe, that others are too and that one of our reasons for being, one that gives real meaning to our lives, is to help ourselves and others grow.

chapter **28**

Allowing Yourself to Be Creative

The phenomenon is known at times to some of the most creative artists, writers and composers: the block, the impasse. Suddenly, it seems, the stream of creativity dries up and nothing can be done. Struggle though the victim may, nothing goes well; often, nothing goes at all.

Blocks and Creativity

Frequently, the problem turns out to be a miring down in self-criticism. It is almost axiomatic that one cannot be critical and creative at the same time. Having done his work, a creative person can stand back, view it and bring his critical faculties to bear upon it in an effort to make improvements. But if he tries to bring, or somehow finds himself bringing, a critical view to what he is doing while he is in the process of doing it, he may find himself blocked, unable to proceed.

Creativity has many definitions. The essence of it in any area lies in bringing into existence something new, in working diverse elements with one's own personality and one's individual approach to form a new entity. It is possible to be tremendously creative on a rundown farm, as a shoe cobbler, as a businessman refashioning a relatively chaotic organization into a smooth-working, productive entity.

To put it another way, to be creative, one has to assess what his particular talents and tools are and then, finding some patch of garden that is choked with weeds, bring his talents and tools to bear and make the patch flower.

At some time or other, almost everyone has had the experience of getting a sudden flash of vision, an unexpected insight. Perhaps you have had a blind spot for something, a lack of understanding, an inability to see an answer, difficulty in finding a solution to a problem in school or on the job or in a relationship. And then suddenly, there it is: you see it clearly. Somehow the bars have been let down and your creative faculty has emerged.

Until then, you may have been critical of the problem, may have dismissed it as not worth trying to solve. Or you may have been critical of yourself, dismissed yourself as not being worthwhile enough, not well enough endowed, to see the solution.

Self-belittlement gets in the way of creativity for many of us. And when we can begin to see that we have no valid cause for self-belittlement, that it is an attitude we have been endowed with from the past, we can begin to be creative or more creative. And a realization of the link between self-esteem and creativity can help us realize why we have not been creative, or as creative as we would have liked to be, before and can buttress our efforts at establishing self-esteem.

Opportunities for being creative lie all about. And you can almost certainly count on the fact that as you get your self-critical self off your hands sufficiently to allow your unique personality to look about, you are likely to find opportunities where perhaps you never before thought they existed—whether in making a home, composing, organizing a department, or selling shoes. As your creative self becomes strengthened, you can consider situations and envision possible solutions and set out to test them.

To be creative, you need to believe in yourself.

Other attitudes in addition to self-belittling may stand in the way of creativity.

The overcoerced person cannot find his full potential for creativity as long as he yields to the command-resistance cycle, barking orders at himself and using evasion and other means to resist them.

The impulsive person may have potentially excellent ideas but has a hard time making sustained efforts, and nothing ever seems to get finished.

It is worth emphasizing here that one of the ways of bringing creativity to bear upon a difficult problem is to soak yourself in the problem, work at it hard, tire yourself with it, never coercing yourself but grappling, grappling, grappling, and then letting go, relaxing for a while, and in that period of relaxation or temporary concern with other matters, the insight often comes. But such tiring hard work does not come naturally to impulsive people or, it must be said, to many others.

Impulsives and many others as well need to beware of another problem—a delusion that self-discipline is a bar to creativity. To be creative, they mistakenly believe, there must be freedom from discipline. If they see themselves, for example, as potential artists, they fancy that their artistry would be likely to flower best if they could go down to Greenwich Village and, freed of all discipline and all confining rules, throw paints onto a canvas on the floor. Perhaps without realizing what such thinking implies, they see creativity as something haphazard, which it is not at all. After years of study and discipline, someone who knows what he is about may, indeed, go down to Greenwich Village and throw paints onto a canvas, and may be creative because there is some order and direction to his paint throwing.

Building Toward Creativity

To arrive at adult freedoms without discipline is an impossibility. You can't have any elbow room as an adult unless you control the impulsive or self-belittling child of your past—not stifle but control. And when you enter into any profession, art or craft, it is a help not a hindrance to discipline yourself in it, to make use of what has been learned in the past, not to slavishly follow old guidelines but to know what they are and where you feel you should, and want to, depart from them for a creative purpose. But if you neglect them entirely and never give yourself the opportunity to learn them, you are doomed to repeat history and to bind yourself to the childhood of the art, profession or craft.

To be creative, you need self-esteem and self-control, and as you work toward achieving these you will find that your creativity begins to emerge and, as it emerges, it will help to reinforce your further efforts to build self-esteem and self-control.

chapter 29

Man and Woman—1 + 1 = 4

The most intimate of human relationships, that between a man and a woman, deserves a chapter of its own. For convenience, I will be talking here of married couples but what is said will apply equally to those who have not gone through the marriage ceremony.

When two people marry, it isn't just two people who make their presence felt in the actual marital situation. Because each of us has within himself a child of the past, four persons must adjust to each other in some manner.

The two adults are "in love," which usually means that they are reasonably companionable and physically attracted to each other. Often, too, it means that the child of the past of each sees in the other adult the promise of fulfillment of past longings.

Each adult in the marriage sees the relationship in the light of adult experiences and goals. Each child of the past sees it in accordance with previously developed reactions and responses— submissive, rebellious, impulsive or other—to attitudes prevalent during childhood.

After the honeymoon, which is fairly simple because in that period the adults are very much to the fore and are in a not-at-home situation, a home is established. And, because the establishment of the home seems to the inner child of each spouse to promise the familiar "at home" feelings of childhood, the inner children rush forward.

Now each person tends to treat himself as he was treated in his old home life. Often, he tends to view his spouse as if she were treating him with old home methods whether or not she is actually doing so. And there is often a pronounced tendency to invite the spouse to do so.

It would undoubtedly be helpful if young people were taught that four are indeed involved in any marriage; understanding this, they might be more realistic about, and less disturbed by, the difficulties that almost inevitably occur.

The most common complaint from one marriage partner about the other is that the other is "so childish" or "acts just like a kid." The discovery of childishness in some aspects of living would not come as such a surprise and shock if, for example, the wife understood that her husband has within him a boy who never picked up after himself and didn't appear at the dinner table instantly when summoned. Nor would it be a shock if, on the other side, the husband understood that, for example, within his wife is a girl who may have needed to be reassured that she was attractive and capable.

Without such understanding, there may be bitter conflict over what seem to be trivial matters. I recall a young couple who reached the point of seeking help because the husband, as soon as he got home from work, removed his shoes and insisted upon walking around in his stockinged feet. This incensed the wife, who viewed the habit as indicative of total disrespect for their home. Indignantly, she kept pointing out that he didn't remove his shoes in the office, only at home, and "Why should I work hard to make and keep the house looking beautiful if you're going to sit around and walk around in your stockinged feet?" To this the husband replied indignantly: "Good Lord, what can be wrong with being comfortable when you're home?"

The husband had come from a home where it was customary for the hard-working father to arrive back from work at night, take off his shoes, relax and be comforted by the mother. On the other hand, the wife came from a home where housekeeping standards were strict, the mother was inflexible and there were rigid rules that nobody appeared in the living or family room without being "properly" dressed.

There can be many misunderstandings in marriage based on differences in child-of-the-past conditioning. Sometimes, the misunderstandings are moralized. "Because my wife doesn't respond in the way I want her to or because she responds differently than I do, she is wrong . . . or bad. And, in fact, if she only loved me, she would change," a husband may think. Or so a wife may think. Or either may put a different complexion on a conflict, still moralizing, but now taking the blame upon himself or herself, saying, "There must be something wrong with me." Whether it is "shame on me" or "shame on you," it is moralizing through misunderstanding and what is really at work is past conditioning.

There may be conflicts over money. One spouse, having grown up in a poverty-stricken home, may be terribly anxious if money is not put away in the bank regularly. The other, raised in a home where the expenditure of money was equated with love, may become anxious if money is not spent freely.

There may be conflicts over child rearing and over sexual relations. In the close, intimate relationship of marriage, conflict may develop over a wide variety of day-to-day activities. And unless the source of conflict is recognized, one or both partners may feel deeply hurt and aggrieved.

I have seen couples in conflict over show of affection. A woman raised in a home where the parents were generous with material things but never displayed (even though they felt it) as much affection toward her as she wished marries a man whose parents—and grandparents—doted on him, showered him with affection, to the point where he felt almost suffocated by it. When, after the honeymoon, he backs off somewhat from intense, almost-continuous displays of affection from his wife, the marriage becomes unhappy.

Reinforcement Patterns

There are many combinations of marital partners who unknowingly help each other to re-create childhood emotional patterns.

In one, for example, the coupling of a self-indulgent, belittling husband and a self-critical, striving-to-please wife, the
husband caters to his own whims much as they were catered to
by his parents. Without meaningful experience in considering the
rights of others since his parents never insisted upon having their
rights respected, he does not consider his wife's rights or dignity.
He tends, in fact, to pick a wife whose background has been
characterized by parental demanding and criticizing and who,
consequently, as an adult, is self-critical and desirous of pleasing. She often puts up with the excessive demands and criticism
of her self-indulgent husband because, despite the discomfort
they bring, they re-create for her the old home atmosphere of her
childhood. There may come a point, nevertheless, where the
marriage becomes intolerable for her.

There can be considerable variation in reactions and in their
severity, as two cases will illustrate.

Mrs. X grew up trying to please a cold, critical mother and a
perfectionistic father without ever succeeding. She now treats
herself as her parents did with their belittling criticisms of her,
and she has selected a husband who is a somewhat indulged man
and who criticizes her. When he does this, she finds herself with-
drawing under the attack, feeling incompetent and unable to
relate to him even though she caters to his wants. Characteristically, Mr. X picked a wife who would cater to him but he does
not understand that his wife, in catering to him, is reviving a
painful childhood atmosphere in which she strove for but never
achieved acceptance. The four people or personalities in this
marriage are in moderate conflict over many day-to-day aspects
of living together and a clash has developed in the sexual area, a
strong emotional focusing point. Mr. and Mrs. X need to understand the role their children of the past play in their lives and
need to learn how to respect each other's rights. When they do

so, the four-way clashes in their daily interactions and in their sexual relations will come less and less frequently.

With Mr. and Mrs. Y the conflict is more acute. Mrs. Y was raised in a striving-to-please atmosphere and resisted and rebelled against perfectionistic drives. She married an impulse-ridden, demanding, critical man whom she tries to please. He recreates her childhood environment by demanding performance and service. She responds to the demands, belittles herself and at the same time rebels against and rails at her husband for being too demanding. Mr. Y's temper and impulsiveness, stemming from his child of the past, contribute greatly to aggravating the couple's conflict. If he learns to set limits on his temper and impulsiveness, the way may be opened to development of a less rebellious wife and a less discordant marriage with increasing opportunity for the two adults to understand and keep in check their respective children of the past.

At this point, I would like to inject a caution. Even if you consider your marriage unhappy, perhaps even less promising than the one we have just described, do not consider breaking it off immediately. To repeat what we have said elsewhere, for it is even more important in connection with deciding whether or not to break up a marriage, most of us who have not been good parents to ourselves simply do not have the ability yet to make the judgments or the skills to effectively change matters. Generally, it takes a year or more to develop the ability and skills.

Particularly in a hurtful marriage situation that has endured for some years, both partners have been so emotionally bruised that it takes time to recover properly from the wounds. Even if the situation no longer is actively painful, there may still be lingering suspicion and wariness for a time and difficulty in believing that the other person has changed. Even with change, there may be temporary relapses into old behavior patterns.

It is not wise to rush a decision to break off a marriage for all of these reasons and also because there are avenues to be explored, new ways in which we can live, if only temporarily, far more peacefully with our mates. When the steps I will outline have been tried wholeheartedly, not only have many couples

decided that their marriages seemed worth saving but often they
have succeeded in developing an exciting new relationship that
has made it almost seem as if they had actually changed partners.

It is vital to remember that in trying to work out marital
difficulties as in trying to work out any others, your motivation
should be to bring about change in yourself, in your own attitudes. We are powerless to change anyone else, including a
spouse. Change must come from inner willingness, over which in
another person we have no control. But the power of example is
great. Often, when one partner in a marriage makes progress, the
other is impressed and sets about the task too. But we cannot
count on it. It would be ideal if both partners in a marriage
undertook to do the same thing at the same time. But this happens only sometimes. I do assure you, however, that if you
faithfully stick to your efforts to change yourself, no matter what
the provocation from your spouse, the day will come when you
will be rewarded either by your spouse's willingness and efforts
to change or by a certain knowledge that, for whatever reason,
your partner is incapable of doing so.

Meanwhile, the first thing to do is to act to smooth the
way.

Smoothing the Way

I like to call it "the rule of adult courtesy." It can be used—and
often has been most successfully—in marital situations at least
temporarily, until one or both partners can achieve the state of
good self-parenthood. It serves as a guideline for holding in check
each child of the past and for establishing at least a temporarily
workable mutual-respect relationship.

All of us as adults have conventional ways of reacting to
other adults. When, for example, an adult guest comes into our
home, we are polite. We may have differences of opinion but we
either accept the differences or work to resolve them in a respectful way. Overall, in a casual adult situation, each adult respects
the other and the interchange is respectful. Limits are imposed
firmly but without belittling.

The rule of adult courtesy applied to the marital situation is simply that you do not say or do anything to your spouse that would hurt or embarrass an adult guest in your home if it were said or done to him.

In a marital situation, one spouse or the other, however well intentioned, will inadvertently break the rule of courtesy since child-of-the-past urges and demands are much more intense than in a house guest situation.

So you need some way to let your spouse know when you have been infringed upon and vice-versa, and this is very much part of the rule of courtesy. When one spouse inadvertently breaks the rule, the other is supposed to say: "Look, this hurts me; please stop." Just that. No retaliation. Only an indication of hurt and a polite request for a halt.

If the other's child of the past comes on very strong and refuses to stop infringing, then you need to break off the relationship temporarily, repectfully, saying: "I will be back." And you go to another room, or take a walk, or do anything you can think of, to give the breezes time to blow in the relationship, and then you come back as if nothing has happened.

And if, when you return, the child of the past is still coming on strong, then you need to ricochet away again—temporarily.

The rule of courtesy is not a panacea, only a helpful guideline for keeping the marriage from degenerating into open, retaliative warfare between two children of the past.

There often may be a temptation for one spouse to respond to the other's quiet remark, "Look this hurts me; please stop," in a critical way. The fact is that both spouses, by this time, have been sensitized, have open wounds. "You have the nerve to say I hurt you" may be an almost-automatic rejoinder. But there would be no such rejoinder to a guest in the home.

And if you establish the rule of courtesy in advance between you, it is always possible to point to the rule and to reply in return to such a rejoinder: "Please, you may think I am trying to criticize you but I am not; I am simply trying to observe the rule. I may be wrong, possibly, in doing so but that is what I am trying to do."

The rule does not preclude some disagreements that may make it difficult to carry on the relationship. And it may be necessary in some cases, if the marriage is to continue even temporarily, to seek help—from a good friend, minister, physician, counselor or another respected third party—in resolving or compromising such disagreements because the two children of the past still are getting too much in the way for the partners to compromise or resolve them by themselves.

But when the rule breaks down, it is often because "Look, this hurts me" is spoken in a way that, calculatedly or not, arouses the wrong response. The hurt partner may be saying in effect, not necessarily in words but by tone of voice, attitude or manner: "Look, can't you see how you hurt me?" The implication is that the other spouse is a devil with horns and tail. There may be a deep thrust into the other person's guilt feelings and he may react by becoming defensively aggressive, hurt by the play on his guilt feelings.

But if you can avoid this, if you can establish the rule, if you can be deeply courteous and considerate to the other person and his past conditioning and if he tries to be as courteous and considerate in return, you have gone a long way to help resolve something that has stood between you.

While the rule of courtesy is no substitute for the patient work we must do to change our inner attitudes, it does help to cushion against the reopening of old wounds and provides invaluable practice, too, in "acting as though." Hopefully, it may permit you and your spouse to examine together some of the very real problems in your marriage, the most important of which is likely to be sex. But even if the time has not yet come when you can discuss this topic calmly and frankly with your partner, it is helpful for you, at least, to begin to understand more about it.

It is not that I consider sex, as some do, to be the most important element in a marriage. I subscribe rather to the saying that while sex may be credited as being 10 percent of the reason for the success of a good marriage, it will be blamed for 90 percent of what is wrong in a bad marriage.

When I tell people that, almost literally, there are four people in the marriage bed, the idea startles some, amuses others who perceive a rollicking foursome. But there may be little or no rollicking, more combat than orgy.

Before going on to the negative aspects of the intrusion of

the inner children in the marriage bed, I should like to say that this is one area where our inner child, if properly limited, can make vital contributions to a really good sex life. For it is in childhood that we develop feelings of tenderness and love for another. It is then that we may learn joy and uninhibited abandonment. And, if restrained by adult unselfishness and mutuality, it is in the sex situation as in all situations calling for wholehearted enjoyment that our inner child can come into his own again and can be welcomed.

But too often, our inner child's feelings of love and tenderness have never been given the chance to develop properly or there has been exposure to faulty attitudes about the sexual act, or the inner child is rampant, intent as totally unlimited children are, on self-satisfactions with little or no thought for anyone else. Frequently, the inner child of each partner, because of past distortions, may feel embarrassment, shame, resentment or even desire for revenge. One inner child may seek to exploit the other.

A child of the past, conditioned by a home atmosphere that produced anxious, guilty feelings about sex may make adult sexual functioning difficult or, in the extreme, impossible. In many cases, until they have learned to set limits on the child of the past, women liberated in other ways approach sex with a feeling that it is animallike and disgusting and are never able to enjoy it. They may go through the motions dutifully but may develop resentment at being expected to do so.

There are performance-oriented men so driven by a child of the past expected to "achieve" that they look upon sex as a contest, a performance arena, and are unable to enjoy it, cannot approach it as a warm, loving, intimate relationship until they can set limits on the striving inner child.

First Aid for the Sexual Relationship

Ideally, sex is to be regarded as no entity in itself but rather a warm, intimate component of a close interpersonal relationship, and in sex two adults should be free to playfully, joyfully, and fulfillingly exchange love and acceptance supplies. When the two children of the past are strident and uncontrolled, almost inevitably there are problems in the marriage bed as there are elsewhere in the marital relationship. And, as problems in other areas are overcome, those in the sex relationship are likely to be.

But it can be helpful not to wait for the spillover from the solutions of other problems and to work specifically, too, at the sex problems.

When you know the pathogens that afflict you, perhaps have a good idea of those that afflict your spouse and are aware of the conditioned responses that each of you has to your own pathogens and to the possible reactions that may stem from the interactions of pathogens between you, you can make a start by trying to keep your own child of the past from dominating you in the marriage bed. It would be all the more helpful if your spouse would undertake to do the same—but even failing that, you can make some inroads on the problems and perhaps encourage him to do the same as he senses your efforts and progress.

One attitude often stands in the way of even an attempt to work out sex problems. "But how can I think about anything else when I am thinking about sex? It will turn me off if I have to be considering my attitudes," many people protest.

Yet it is possible to consider those attitudes, to make an effort to differentiate between child-of-the-past feelings and your own adult wishes and potential, and to limit the child-of-the-past demands that intrude in sex. And you cannot really afford not to try to do so for it is your child of the past who has played a very large role in turning you off, in preventing sexual enjoyment and fulfillment.

Particularly in men, self-belittling undermines sexual response. A man who has been conditioned in childhood to believe that he is inadequate or that his sexual feelings are bad may have trouble with potency. The trouble may be compounded if the wife is critical or leads him to believe that he is inadequate for her sexual fulfillment.

It is especially easy for some men to get into a critical cycle that blocks sexual response. If they try to have sex when tired and they fail, they may turn on themselves critically rather than

pass the incident off as one of those things that result now and
then from fatigue. The next time they attempt intercourse, they
may enter into it with doubts about their ability, remembering
vividly the last unhappy episode. The distrust of capability gets
in the way of performance the second time. A wife may wonder
what is wrong and ask about it and this may increase the
husband's doubts about himself and the cycle can continue.

Often, it is possible to work out of such a cycle with patience
and kindly good humor. Adequate rest is a help. Another is
simply to relax for several nights, with each partner stroking the
other as they lie close together, but with no effort to go on to the
sexual act. After several such sessions, intercourse may be resumed but not with any purpose of performing to achieve pre-
conceived orgastic heights. Rather, the idea should be to take sex
out of the self-critical performance arena and put it where it
belongs—in a self-respecting, caring, sharing fun arena.

Self-belittling is usually not as great a factor in blocking a
woman's sexual response. Many women who are cripplingly self-
belittling in other areas are responsive sexually. They find that a
loving man can come between them and their self-belittling,
enabling them to achieve symptomatic relief at least for a little
while and at the same time permitting them to satisfy their need
for closeness.

Women are more often blocked in sexual responsiveness by
childhood conditioning that inflicts on them the attitude that sex
is wrong or bad. Such conditioning is no longer as common as it
was a few generations ago. Women—and men as well—who have
been indulged in childhood often lack sexual drive since sex
demands energetic adult giving and they are conditioned to be
passive and to take. As they overcome such conditioning and its
manifestations in other areas, the sexual drive is likely to increase, but an understanding of the origins of their problem may
help in the sex area even before the conditioning is overcome in
all areas.

At present, the most common type of automatic, conditioned
response in women that blocks sex is adolescent resistance or
rebellion persisting into adult life. Women so conditioned tend to
be aggressively insistent on their "rights" and may be excessively
preoccupied with the development of their individuality. They

may feel uncomfortable in a sexual situation because it calls for a certain amount of individual surrender, which they look upon as threatening. Understanding this and understanding too that there is, or should be, joint surrender in sex and that this is what makes the sexual relationship most worthwhile for both partners often can help overcome the block.

It is not my intention to go further into the clinical aspects of sexual disorders. These are beyond the scope of this book and there are now many excellent sources of help (*Human Sexual Inadequacy*, William H. Masters and Virginia E. Johnson, Little, Brown & Co., Boston 1970, among others) if you decide that your problem lies primarily with some sexual dysfunction. Today, many problems once thought to be responsive, if at all, only to years of deep analysis—among them frigidity in women and premature ejaculation and impotence in men—are among those that are often successfully handled by experts in the field within relatively brief periods of time.

For the purposes of this book, I will confine myself to addressing those problems that can be worked out without outside help given the willingness and cooperation of both partners.

Perhaps even more common than any real sexual block is lack of interest. The lack of interest is often ascribed to being too "used" to the other person, who no longer provokes sexual excitement, or to being too physically tired, or to getting "too old for that sort of thing."

Let's consider the last two "reasons" first. As most of us know by now, given good health and normal freedom from excessive stress, many people continue their sex life well into advanced age. This is an individual matter but certainly age is not likely to be a real factor in any decline in sexual interest until well past the middle years.

As to physical tiredness, this is more often an excuse for disinclination due to other reasons, but occasionally it may be a factor. If a medical checkup reveals no cause for the tiredness, perhaps an evaluation of your energy expenditures is in order. Sometimes a husband will exhaust himself in making money or a wife in being a perfect mother or housekeeper when both, if they really understood what they were doing, would be far happier to settle for fewer material comforts and perfectionistic strivings in favor of a good sex relationship. Often a frank discussion will reveal that both partners have thought they were pleasing each other, that each felt that sex meant less to the other than it actually did. This can go on for years without being discovered, except through frank discussion, because many people feel ashamed of wanting more sex than they believe a partner may wish for.

One such couple told me that they felt that their real sex life started only after their last child left for college. "It is even better," the wife told me, "than in our honeymoon days, for we were both so young and shy then. Soon the babies came and George felt he had to work hard to give us everything. When the children started to school, I wanted to take a job and help out, but he wouldn't hear of it. I tried to work as hard as he did, keeping the house nice, making all my clothes and the children's, and trying to entertain for him. As the years went by, we had less and less sex. One or the other of us was really so tired it was an effort, although at times I used to feel he found me unattractive and I felt that I loved him more than he did me, which hurt."

George took up the story. "But when John went off to college, she finally persuaded me that she needed a part-time job to keep occupied. Although she didn't earn a great deal, and at first I wanted her to spend it on herself, I found after a time that the difference her earnings meant could let me be home more and allow us to take trips together. I didn't feel I needed to drive myself so hard. It started slowly at first but soon we were like a couple of kids!"

This was an example of inclination hampered by true tiredness and stress. But far more often disinclination is real enough though usually not for the reasons given.

The idea that we need a new partner to stimulate our sexual appetites is one that has until recently generally been ascribed to men and more or less condoned by society on that basis, although from my practice I can assure you that many women feel the same way. We often have fantasies about another partner or may actually seek one when we grow weary of trying to adjust our past conditioning to our spouse. Such a partner has the advantage, temporarily, of being in an "away from home" atmosphere, and there are only two, not four, in the relationship at first. Those lacking in basic self-esteem or self-control sometimes feel they "need" someone new to become aroused. Sex can be used to continue our "I-centeredness" so that our partner becomes for us, then, an impersonal opiate or pep pill.

As anyone who has ever had a really good sex relationship knows, the deepest joys and excitements are reached only after there has been time enough to really get to know the other thoroughly, to learn to trust one another fully, not possible in fleeting relationships. For those who are still largely living in their past conditioning, much effort must be exerted to rein in the child of the past while working constantly to increase the ability to interchange love and tenderness and to catch up on the long-term experiences in this area that were lacking before. At first, they may not be able to achieve this directly but I assure you that they cannot help sharing in the happiness and joy they see they are giving, and in time they come to see that this was what was lacking before and the reason why they did not experience the fullest pleasures of sex. Again, children don't really make love— and neither can child-of-the-past-driven adults.

But for those who can remember a time when they did have deep sharing and full pleasure but seem to have lost them, or seem to have grown "bored" with each other or with sex itself, almost certainly the trouble does not lie exclusively in the sex area although there are symptoms there. Yet it is these couples who will insist most strongly that sex is the "only" thing wrong, or the basic cause of all else. Whether they quarrel bitterly on all topics or, as some unhappy couples do, boast that they never argue about anything, many are convinced that if their sex life could be restored to what it was in the happy days, everything else would fall into place. In a sense, they are right, but they are putting the cart before the horse. The fact is that unless there has been some traumatic event that has interrupted it, a good sex relationship once developed between two people usually remains that way if things are right in the rest of the marriage. Indeed, there are quite a few couples who remain married far longer than they should in spite of disagreeing in most other departments simply because sex is the only thing they do have in common, but sex alone is not enough to cement a marriage enduringly.

Those who want to win back their once-good sex life must

concentrate on finding and correcting attitudes that have so impinged, in other areas of their marriage, on their original trust of each other as to dissipate it if not provoke actual anger and resentment. Where lack of consideration and respect has led to alienation and retreat, the partners who once had tender knowledge of each other may now feel married to hostile strangers. And all the more for having once known sex with love, they now find that sex without love is neither nourishing nor pleasurable and it is no wonder that sex seems to be the most important problem. But if they will look over their pathogens and those of their mates, they will soon pinpoint many infringements that over the years have grown worse, exacerbated by the interactions of their children of the past. For these people especially, the observance of the rule of courtesy will go far in helping to restore mutual esteem and trust.

Mildred and Jim

The story of Mildred and Jim has an unusually happy ending. They had been married twenty-five years and by the time Mildred came to see me, they were one of those couples who almost never quarreled. Indeed, they were not close enough even to do that. With no discussion, sex had been tacitly dropped from their lives some years before, although both were only in their early fifties. Although they lived in the same house and went through the motions of sharing a life, they were, in terms of normal marriage, as divorced as if they lived in separate cities.

Oddly enough, although they came from widely disparate backgrounds and had quite different pathogens, they were in many ways absurdly alike. On the plus side, both were highly intelligent, talented people, with strength and determination. On the negative, the strength often was manifested by pride and stubbornness and an inability to see any but their own point of view or, when they could see it, by a feeling that it was nevertheless "weak" to give in. Outwardly both were rather cool, undemonstrative people but they had an inner need for love and badly needed reassurance of being loved before they felt free to express it themselves.

Both were hypersensitive and very vulnerable to criticism from the other, expressed or implied. By the time Mildred came to me, they were living together like anxious strangers, each taking the temperature of the atmosphere of the other, so to speak, and adjusting their communication according to the warmth that could be sensed at the moment. They had not always been so.

In the beginning, they had been delighted with their similarities of outlook. When it came to ideas, tastes, goals, these two usually agreed with each other completely. *How* these were to be attained was the rock upon which they split. Here their inner children diverged sharply. She had been criticized but indulged at home; he had been subjected to punitive overresponsibility. She was much more outgoing, generous and loving than he; he was far less self-indulgent and much harder working than she. Over the years in spite of the fact that they really loved and respected each other and had had a very good sex relationship, they had, with their knowledge of what would hurt most and their caustic tongues, so battered and bruised the ego of each other that both had retired from the lists. In doing so, they retired from all forms of sharing. Neither had changed views but each secretly felt hurt and rejected.

Mildred was the first to come to me. She was in a painful state of confusion. "For years I told myself that the only reason I was staying in this travesty of a marriage was for the sake of the children. Given our income, if we separated, their education would most certainly have suffered, especially since my husband has great anxieties about money and even now is most reluctant to spend anything not absolutely necessary. I told myself that once the youngest was in college, I would leave. But now that the day has arrived, I find I am panicked at the thought. It is not financial; I have money of my own and, actually, should we be divorced, he would probably have to give me more than he spends on me now. Can it be that I still love him? And, if so, what kind of self-respect do I have to love a man who treats me so?" She began to cry bitterly and to belittle and upbraid herself for being so emotionally dependent on a man who cared nothing for her feelings.

After listening to her story, I ventured: "But are you sure he doesn't love you, however poorly he shows it?" "No, but if he does," she said, "it is such a hurtful love I hate myself for clinging to it. Anyway, he doesn't respect me; he has told me so over and over again." "Do you think he feels that you respect him?" I asked. "Well, he certainly *ought* to, I'm always giving in and catering to him!" But her tone was defensive.

I then asked her if Jim would be willing to talk to me and she said that she didn't know but would ask him. Jim, being a highly intelligent man who did, as I suspected, really love his wife and want to improve their marriage, duly appeared. Talking to him confirmed my impression that these two were like race-horses hitched to a wagon. If they happened to want to run in the same direction, they made a marvelous team, but if they diverged, woe betide the wagon, in this case the inner structure of their marriage.

What this couple needed was for each to rebuild faith in the other's basic love and respect. As things were, what love each still was conscious of feeling for the other only made them vulnerable to hurt, and their very real basic respect for the other was felt mostly as respect for the other's ability to wound. Each had retired into an inner storm shelter.

For them, the rule of courtesy had to be extended to initiating and maintaining conversations in which each would refrain from covertly attempting to advance his or her point of view as superior and would simultaneously refrain from reading into any disagreement a criticism where often none was meant. They both subscribed to a sort of inner domino theory in which if one admitted to being wrong on any point, it followed that he or she was "all wrong." They had to learn to admit mistakes with no loss of self-esteem and no fear that the other would seize upon the admission to use. Obviously, this could not be done overnight.

Jim, especially, had difficulty in maintaining conversations since he was normally not much of a talker and if preoccupied, hurt or displeased tended to relapse into long periods of silence. If Mildred attempted to interrupt these, he was apt to retaliate with contemptuous irritation. She had to learn not to go on and on with a topic, beyond Jim's capacity to be interested or to care.

But, in time, they both managed to respect each other's weaknesses, understand each other's conditioning from the past and begin to see each other as well intentioned at least. This was the real breakthrough for them. Once they stopped being afraid of each other, they could, through use of all the other tools we have been talking about in this book, begin to act as a team again.

Sex was the last citadel to fall. Since these were people to whom sex without love meant nothing, they each had confessed to me to being secretly relieved when they had finally stopped even their sporadic attempts at intercourse. Both had also felt sad and rejected, but as Mildred said, "It was so unlike what we used to have, I actually felt as if I were being unfaithful!"

Finally the day came when, as Jim put it, "We went to bed almost without thinking about it. We had been unusually close and warm all day and somehow I just found myself making love to her."

Mildred told me: "It was the most exciting relationship I have ever had." Since she had been briefly married once before her marriage to Jim and had had two very profound love affairs between the marriages, I knew she was talking from experience.

"It is hard to describe," she told me, "but it is like having all the joy of first being in love with someone, and at the same time knowing them well. Especially thrilling is the discovery of new facets of Jim I never knew were there. I am not talking about sex techniques. It is more like finding that, much as in the fairy tale, Jim has turned into Prince Charming! At least, he is if I can remember to be his princess," she ended on a more realistic note.

Lest you think all my stories have such conventional happy endings, that of Ann and Don worked out quite differently.

Don and Ann

Ann's parents had both been perfectionists. She had grown up to be a very striving-to-please, self-belittling person. She was enormously flattered when handsome Don proposed since she sincerely felt he was too good for her. Soon after the honeymoon it became obvious that he shared her opinion, for nothing she did was ever good enough. This fitted in with the way her parents had treated her so, although she suffered, she accepted the evaluation. When she came to me she was deeply depressed.

"I don't know what is wrong with me," she said. "Don is right to complain. I can hardly drag one foot after the other. Even the simplest thing seems too much for me. When I look ahead I feel I can't bear to go on living!"

Because of her strict religious background, this woman could never consciously contemplate suicide but she displayed some of the symptoms of those who want to take their own lives. This, however, was not the reason she had come to me. It was because in the last year, whenever Don had made love to her, she had become hysterical. She blamed herself bitterly for this. She had tried to submit to his demands, but so great was her emotional resistance that she had developed vaginal spasm so that even Don had to realize that something was wrong. When the gynecologist could find no physical reason, he had referred her to me. Don was loudly contemptuous of her having to go to a "shrink" but was anxious enough to have his sex life restored to permit it even though he would have nothing to do with coming himself.

From Ann I pieced enough information together to get an idea of his pathogens. They were not promising. His mother, too, had been strongly religious, but where Ann's parents had also given her love, his mother had neglected his need for affection in favor of what she called "the good of his soul." His father had been overtly punitive, physically punishing him for the slightest infraction of rules. The father was an alcoholic, and Don grew up both fearing and despising him. The boy had taken refuge in being a "loner" and had worked out one standard for himself and quite another for the rest of the world. He could not see this, and anyone who resisted his self-righteous arrogance seemed to him to be an enemy attacking his very being. It was precisely because of this that he had been attracted to worshipful Ann. As long as she went along with him in all things, he was more or less satisfied. His feeling for her could hardly be called love; he was not capable of it except in the sense that one loves one's own leg. He gave her as little thought or attention as one would to such an extension of oneself until it fails to function as one expects. He was both as outraged and as frightened as he would have been if his leg had suddenly refused to function properly when she suddenly refused him.

It was obvious to me early that this marriage was not likely to endure. This was confirmed by Don's utter refusal to discuss, much less face, some of the real stresses his behavior had put upon the marriage. He reacted with fury and felt that Ann was blaming him for her own failures as a wife. He dismissed any suggestions such as the rule of courtesy as "nonsense" and even regarded it as an attack on him. He was so defensive that he could not permit himself to remember things he had declared vehemently even five minutes before. If others supported Ann by saying that they had also heard him make a statement, he would dismiss the matter with a muttered "I guess I belong in a lunatic asylum," obviously meaning that *they* did.

I believe that his self-deception, based on his inner insecurities, was so deep that he actually believed he was speaking the truth. In other situations, his rule of "do as I say, not as I do" came to his rescue. For instance, he would grow livid and highly moralistic if Ann or any of the children used what he called a four-letter word in his hearing, yet even before the children were old enough to understand, he would denounce Ann before them as "a stinking bitch" and freely used that sort of language to the children as well when enraged.

This was an obviously loveless marriage. Don had succeeded in killing Ann's original love for him, although at this point she was not consciously aware of this, only that her body had rebelled. With her background, the idea that she did not love her husband, the father of her children, was deeply shocking, and divorce or separation was frightening and unthinkable. She gradually realized for herself that she would be far happier without him. She had to work first on her self-belittlement and then she decided to move away from the destructive relationship.

Slowly she learned to treat herself in her own way. She freed herself of her borrowed parental attitudes and the fears instilled by her maternally imposed religious instruction. She learned not to react to Don's tirades and threats. As she did so, the tirades and threats lessened some. As a matter of fact, when she finally got a job and announced that she was leaving him, it was he who revealed his dependence on her. He begged her to stay but she was now ready for a far deeper, more fulfilling relationship than Don, even if he had been truly willing, would ever have been able to offer her. She did eventually marry again, though a good many years later, so this story has a happy ending, too—at least for Ann.

Here, once again, although the presenting symptom was sexual, the real trouble lay elsewhere.

Before concluding this chapter, I want to urge patience once more. You may feel that there are no great problems, sexual or otherwise. You may be able to honestly say that you have done all you could but your marriage remains stalemated. You may be right in feeling that your spouse is not motivated as you are. Still, if you keep taking steadfast action, working toward your goals in other areas, your spouse's attitudes may be influenced. The case of Don was extreme and coupled with inability to cooperate, the prognosis of failure was apparent much sooner than it usually is.

"Miracles" From the Outside

Sometimes aid may come from the outside and, together with the power of example, may work seeming miracles. A number of examples of this appeared in an article in *The New York Times Magazine*. Written by Susan Jacoby, the article concerned the impact of "women's liberation" on a group of middle-aged house-wives in the Bronx, New York. This is a lower-middle-class area largely inhabited by second- and third-generation Jewish and Italian families. Twelve women who had known each other for many years had banded together to hold "consciousness raising" sessions, and the major question discussed was "Now that our children are grown, what will we do with the rest of our lives?"

I have no way of knowing what parental pathogens might have been involved, but the women came from groups that generally are resistant to sweeping change and, because of their close-knit nature and modest education, may be among the last to be infiltrated by new social attitudes, even those widely accepted by mainstream America.

Nevertheless, the women agreed to meet on a regular basis.

That produced the first storm of objection from their husbands. Typical was one woman's comment: "My husband expects me to be home every evening unless he decides to go bowling; then I am free to go to the movies or visit my family or friends." One husband showed his basic opposition by having a series of minor accidents requiring his wife's attention just before it was time for her to leave for a meeting. But, with each other's support, the women held firm.

Unsurprisingly, their version of women's liberation differed from that of some of their sisters higher up on the socioeconomic ladder. The freedom and opportunity to hold *any* job was what was important to them. They realized that they had neither the education nor the skills to worry about female "tokenism."

Similarly, they loved their blue-collar husbands and did not want to be "liberated" by separating from them. Being of an older, more reserved generation, they did not talk about their right to orgasm but did spend many early sessions on the unfulfilled sexual desires that seem the lot of many middle-aged women in America. The unluckiest woman in the group said that her husband reserved sex for birthdays and holidays. "It's more like a monument than an act of love," she said ruefully. The sexual problems turned out to be the result of ignorance and embarrassment in most cases, for when, supported by their sisters, they plucked up courage to talk to their husbands about their needs, they found relieved and gratifying responses. Typical was one husband's comment: "You know, Rose, we were brought up pretty ignorant. This Masters and Johnson thing you were telling me about . . . I thought you'd think I was a dirty old man if I kept trying to take you to bed when we are fifty years old!"

When it came to jobs or going to college, as some of the women decided to do, there was much stiffer opposition. "College!" snorted one husband. "You haven't the brains to clean the house properly, let alone go to college." But, with persistence, they all won out, with a dividend of better marriages as well. Two cases are particularly striking.

Both of these women opted for college. Alice decided upon speech and reading therapy as a career since there was a shortage in the field and entree for an older woman might be easier. Her husband, a hard-hat, contradicted the stereotype, after the first shock wore off, by not only being less opposed than the other husbands but by deciding to follow her example. He had secretly thought about architectural engineering for years and believed that he knew more about putting up buildings than most engineers on the job. When he was young, there had been no money for college and he had had to help support his family. Now, he decided, if she could do it, so could he. They have it all planned out. She will get her degree before he will, but then he will have a pension since he has been in the union eighteen years. They'll have enough money to get along on while he looks for an employer who won't think he is too old to start a new career at forty. Quite obviously, this marriage, as well as the individuals in it, has taken a new lease on life.

Joan, who is entering college to become a statistician, has done the books and income taxes for her husband in his delicatessen business ever since they were married. In spite of this he has been doling out household money each week. Although they have a joint checking account, she has never used it and has never bought anything without consulting him. Abe apparently had been doing some thinking on his own about women's liberation because one night he suddenly said to her: "Look, Joan, it's really stupid of me to go on doling out money to you, a woman who has kept my books better than I could for twenty years. I'm not going to tell you how to spend money any more. You just go on and take what you need. I never really wanted to be cheap. It was just the way my parents always did things."

I was especially delighted by that last sentence, for here was a man with minimum education and not well read who had never heard of my theory or anything like it, yet he had put his finger squarely on the real culprit: his childhood way of looking at things.

But we must give credit to the determination and the persevering action of Joan and the other women that sparked his insight. There is every reason to suppose that the reader of this book can be equally helped by the power of example and the revolutionary impact of new ideas.

chapter 30

Relating Now to Your Parents

To achieve full adulthood it's essential for you to be—or become—accepting toward your parents as human beings and able to relate to them kindly and well. If you find that you blame them and feel resentment and hostility, it means that you are still back in the child-of-the-past framework and are not viewing them from an adult standpoint, seeing them as people who hurt you but not because they set out to do so. They were driven by their own problems and distortions.

You may find that any tendency to be resentful and hostile toward them—or to become self-belittling again or return otherwise to your old child-of-the-past attitudes—becomes most pronounced and painful when you visit them.

Many make the transition with their adult children from parent-child to friend-friend easily and a warm fulfilling relationship develops between them.

But some parents continue to feel that they must retain their parental function long after their children are grown. So when you return to the home of your parents for a visit, you may find yourself being subtly or not so subtly directed, lectured, criticized, overindulged or otherwise treated as you were in childhood. Although you have no wish to hurt their feelings, you may find yourself upset as their actions and attitudes impinge again on an area inside you that was rubbed raw in childhood and that you yourself have rubbed through much of your adult life.

There is a vast difference between living at home with your parents in childhood and a short return visit now. No longer do your parents have any actual hold on your life. They may continue to direct and criticize, but part of you can now see, or at least begin to see, them as people with problems. Since you still have some hypersensitivity to the atmosphere they may create, you may need to keep your visits brief, polite and relatively superficial. Otherwise, the child of your past may take over and you may find yourself feeling as hurt, resentful and guilty as you did long ago.

Your parents may be hurt if you don't go along with their wishes for you. You will have to say "no" sometimes but you can do so politely, just as politely as you can possibly manage. You are as tied to your parents if you have to rebel against them as if you have to comply. Rather than rebel and storm angrily, you are usually better off to put space between you and them temporarily.

If, for example, your mother becomes critical, perhaps complains that you don't write her often enough or visit her often enough, you may be well advised to say, simply and politely: "Mother, I know I haven't written or visited as much as you would like, but as you know I am very busy and life has a way of pressing its demands on us." There is much in favor of using polite, conventional responses to assuage any hurt she may feel and to keep yourself from being dragged back into child-of-the-past patterns to the greater hurt of both of you.

If such a response is not sufficient for her, you may have to limit her with a polite, "Please don't." If that fails, you will have to put space between the two of you, removing yourself temporarily from the situation, excusing yourself and saying you will be back shortly, then taking a walk or going off into another room for a few minutes, and returning later as if nothing had happened.

And if this doesn't work and you find it harder and harder to remain an adult of the present, tending more and more to slip back into the old grooves of childhood, you may need to make some excuse and cut the visit short, saying, for example: "Mother, I have to go now. I'm sorry. I just remembered an appointment I must get to."

By all means, avoid breaking off the relationship completely. That would be hurtful both to your parents and to yourself. If you break it off, you are encouraging your child of the past. You are, in effect, saying to yourself: "This parent, this human being, is so formidable and I am so weak that I cannot endure a relationship." Don't break it off—but keep your contacts, if you must, infrequent, brief, polite and superficial.

If a parent lives with you, you will have to set firm limits, insisting that there must, for the benefit of all, be a mutual-respect relationship in the home, with the adults of each generation respected in their right to pursue their lives in their own way but with no infringement on the rights and dignity of others. There may be some hurt feelings but the hurt will be far less than if mutual respect is not firmly established as the principle.

It sometimes happens that a mutual-respect relationship cannot be established successfully and separate living arrangements for the two generations are needed. If such arrangements do in fact become necessary, they will, in the end, be best for all and they should be carried out with as much respect and kindly, understanding feelings as possible.

However, if you would really like to have a better relationship with your parents—more loving and less guarded—you may find help in the next chapter, although sometimes your desire and willingness alone may not be enough to overcome the entrenched patterns of a lifetime.

chapter 31

The Essential Self-honesty

Developing the habit of being rigorously honest with ourselves, even though it may not be wise or possible to be so with others at all times, is of incalculable value in helping ourselves in good parenthood.

It can be painful, though the rewards far offset the pain. Often, it can seem impossible. For sometimes, hard as we try, we cannot judge what is the truth—which, for example, of two or more conflicting ideas about ourselves is the true one, or the truest. Yet, as we go along, the process becomes easier, for as we establish some truths about ourselves we can more readily discern and discard what have been seeming truths but do not really fit. It will be a lifetime process, and happily so, for if we were ever "finished" with it, we would lose much of the excitement of our voyage of self-discovery, the joy of finding new talents and interests, the relief from discarding constricting, and outgrown, attitudes.

More than a century ago, a Catholic priest, Frederick Faber, who wrote a book called *Self-Deceit*, warned that it was the one thing we would suffer from all our lives in some measure no matter how much we progressed. He remarked that it was the hardest thing of all to see ourselves clearly. He did offer one guideline. Self-deception, he said, had an Achilles heel: it hated to have itself revealed. Thus, he counseled, whenever we find ourselves reacting with inordinate heat to any accusation, we would be well advised to look there, and if we are really thorough, we will find the self-deception hidden somewhere there.

If we are certain we are not guilty of an accusation and our extreme anger grows out of the threat we see in the accusation to the good opinion others hold of us, then the reaction indicates we are more concerned with the appearance than the fact and this is an area in which we need more self-esteem. We need to know that what we are will emerge as the truth no matter what people say and that the only really important opinion is the one we hold of ourselves.

Before we can begin to deal with the reality of our situation, we must disentangle it from any false view that may be caused by seeing ourselves as we suppose other people do.

One woman whose husband's death was shortly followed by the departure of her older daughter for a job in the West and of her younger to college felt understandably adrift, lonely and sorry for herself. A certain amount of feeling sorry for herself was natural. Aside from her grief, she was living entirely alone for the first time in her life. Quite apart from, as she put it, "not having a man to depend on," she sorely missed having anyone to be companionably there, to share her meals.

As time went on, she continued to be consumed by self-pity because of her lonely state in spite of the fact that she had many friends. Although she was ecstatic at first when the daughter in college came home on vacation or the other came for a visit, I noticed that after a week or so she began to complain about them. They were very minor complaints but it was obvious to me, at least, that in reality she enjoyed living her own life and that her daughters, much as she loved and enjoyed them, got in her way. She enjoyed freedom and privacy and, much as she had loved her husband, being without him was in some ways deeply satisfying. She would never admit this to herself, much less to her friends, who, although she suspected them of pitying her, frequently expressed envy of her "freedom." She resented such expressions.

"They only say that to be nice to me," she complained. "They say they wish they had time to paint"—she had recently resumed

her interest in art, which she had dropped when she married—
"but they know that it's the only thing I have in my life. They feel
sorry for me and often I refuse invitations because I know a
woman alone is a fifth wheel."

It was on the heels of one such typical outburst that I
decided to point out gently that she was a victim of her own
imposed picture of herself as the unwanted lone woman. I said
that it was more than likely that the women who told her that
they envied her genuinely did, or thought they did. Could she
not remember feeling the same way many times when she was
hemmed in by family responsibilities? Hadn't she then, at times,
envied other freer women? She had to admit she had.

Then, I went a bit further and told her that I noticed that
she really valued and enjoyed doing as she pleased and that
while she loved to see her daughters come, she often seemed
relieved when they left. That was a bit harder for her to admit.
Indeed, it was not until several sessions later that she told me she
had thought it over and had to confess I was right.

I had also told her on a previous occasion that I very much
doubted that her friends continued to invite her because they felt
sorry for her. The period of active mourning was over and she
was a most attractive woman with a good mind and sense of
humor that would make her a desirable guest and companion. I
noted that few occasions nowadays called for a "balanced"
dinner table, that most people no longer subscribed to the ark
theory of two of each when inviting friends for enjoyment. This,
too, she had given some thought to, and she said: "I guess I just
thought that was the way people always felt about an 'extra'
woman."

Later, she also came to see that many times when she had
thought she felt lonely it was only because she saw herself as
such through other people's eyes and that many times when she
had refused invitations it was because she really preferred to go
on doing what she was doing. She learned that while she enjoyed
people and they enjoyed her, she really had no great dependency
upon them. She learned to differentiate between being alone by
choice and being lonely.

This story has a little postscript. Some years later, after she
had remarried, I met her and she said: "Remember all that wail-

ing I did about 'not having a man to depend on'? Well, I discovered that I was really far more practical than my first husband had been and that after his death the house and my affairs were much better managed than when I 'depended' on him. As a matter of fact, my present husband isn't any better so I attend to that sort of thing. I wish I had known this in my first marriage. It would have saved us both a lot of irritation."

One fine man, a minister, consulted me in an extreme depression about his marriage. He confessed that at times he felt that he actively disliked, even hated, his wife but he was miserable when he thought of separating from her. Indeed, he often was miserable when, reciprocating his coldness, she would increasingly reject him—not just sexually but by seeming to withdraw her love and attention. "I must be crazy," he said, "but I really don't know whether I love her or hate her. I feel so emotionally dependent on her."

I discovered that he was the neglected child of overbusy, remote, cold parents. He felt, as he put it, "as if I have a tight band around my chest when I try to feel things." He was deeply self-deprecating about his ministry, feeling that he did not have the proper love of God. He saw both his marriage and his life work as shams.

Both his marriage and his ministry had started out as love affairs but, gradually, he had retreated further and further into himself, putting forth a mechanical person who just went through the motions of both marriage and ministry. "I have often thought I must be schizophrenic," he said, "for the husband and priest seemed like another man I was watching." He was a successful minister and that only deepened his feelings of guilt. He also had kept his marriage going through seventeen years and two children by alternately wooing his wife with lavish attention when she withdrew from him, then retreating when she turned to him again. "We are like those little good and bad weather figures," he said ruefully. "When she goes in, I come out."

The reason he had finally come for help was that his wife was thinking of divorce and he was thinking of getting out of the ministry. Both prospects filled him with dismay, but he conceded he could no longer go on as he had been going.

As usual, I advised him not to leave the ministry and if at all possible to avoid divorce for at least a year. During that time, indeed long before that time was over, he came to see that it was his fear of acting out his overdependent feelings that had resulted in his belief that he was cut off from true feeling. He began to develop feeling, slowly, progressively, and to find the process rewarding. One day he said joyfully: "I was like a man with a bad ear who nevertheless craved to play the violin. I still haven't an ear good enough for that but I can play the piano and I love the music I make!"

He was encouraged to have open and honest talks about his deepest thoughts and feelings with his wife. She was the daughter of an overdominant father and was delighted to discover during their conversations that his outward cold self-righteousness had covered a little boy longing for great warmth and affection. She had never really been able to develop her full womanhood since he had reaffirmed her childhood tapes, which insisted that one appeased men by reflecting their mood, whatever it was at the moment. Their sex life, which had deteriorated because of his off-again-on-again approach, began to return to what it had been in the beginning. She confessed that she had felt that she had either "outgrown" sex or become frigid since she had not enjoyed it in years. In fact, she told him, she had felt that he had turned away from her even shortly after the honeymoon because she was more loving than he.

It was no easy process. He had first to face the fact that if, after a year, he found he didn't really love her, he would have to learn to do without her, if only for her sake. It was hard, but she helped him not to withdraw when he felt her becoming too close and thus threatening what he used to refer to as his "manhood" but in reality was his fear of breaking down and repeatedly confessing his dependence. The hardest thing of all was to prevent himself from rewarding her little-girl temper tantrums or careless self-centeredness with his former anxious assuagements. Indeed, in time he was able to see that very often he had provoked the reactions in her simply in order to permit himself to come close to her again.

The ability of this proud man to be rigorously honest with himself was heartening to see. Here was a man who was outwardly successful, who, though powerless to help himself, never-theless had helped many around him and was admired and loved for this. He could easily have gone on deceiving himself and others. Many, I venture to think, might have done so in his shoes. But it was his basic honesty, and with it the necessary humility, that made it possible for him to face himself as he really was.

chapter 32

Humor: A Powerful Ally

Most of us have come to accept the popular notion that when man is confronted with stress, he is basically still a jungle animal with only two alternatives open to him: "fight or flight." And, so the theory goes, not allowed by modern society to do either, he must provide himself the safety valve of expressing outwardly his aggressive or fear reactions, even in outbursts of temper or floods of tears, if he is not to become victim to anything from ulcers to impaired mental health. I don't accept this theory.

There is another alternative, a third thing he can do: laugh. If he cannot go quite that far, he can at least learn to smile at how seriously he is taking himself, and this can be a potent aid in making unnecessary "acting out," which, as we have seen, can be so self-destructive.

Most of us, when friends have tried to point out the humorous aspects of some upsetting situation, have often responded with increased fury and hurt that "There is nothing to laugh at!" while we have been totally in the grip of our inner-child-of-the-past conditioning. But few of us have not had the experience of thinking otherwise later and saying, "I couldn't see the humor of it then but now I can laugh."

Virtually no one is totally humorless although at times we

may think some people are. The trouble is that we often confuse humor with wisecracking. Not all of us have the gift of wit but most of us can appreciate it. Humor, as the dictionary defines it, is "a state of temper, of mind . . . flexibility . . . an ability to perceive absurdities." Joke making may or may not be a product of this. Humor can also be defined quite simply, as perspective—and, since this is one of our long-range goals, the development of humor is vital to our growth as well as excellent first aid in bad situations.

Often we object that humor is impossible because of the reality of a situation. "But I really am being unjustly treated, deprived of what I need and deserve, misunderstood," etc. We are frustrated because of our inability, whether related to outward circumstances or inner immaturity, to do something to correct the situation. Yet we forget that humor has ever been developed and nourished in just such situations in order to ensure survival. Luckily, we do have more resources than our jungle ancestors.

When we think of cruelly oppressed ethnic groups we are likely to attribute their survival to their different cultural strengths—the "fight" of the Irish, the "genius" and supposedly superior "intelligence" of the Jews, the "long-suffering good nature" of the blacks. We forget that just as not all groups are equally strongly favored with any such quality or attribute, so not all individuals in any one group are equally endowed. It appears to me to be more likely that an important reason why such oppressed peoples did not go under or all develop ulcers if not madness was that they have in common a strong sense of humor. But do not make the mistake of thinking that this was innate; it was developed because of their plight.

It is probable that not many Jews in the Pale had the wit of Tevye in *Fiddler on the Roof,* who could observe so pithily that "For a Jew to eat a chicken, one of them must be sick." But what was true was that his listeners were able to laugh, though it brought them no nearer to a chicken dinner. What humor did do, aside from lightening the moment, was to provide the inner resources for many humble, powerless Jews to go on living and reproducing until a Freud, an Einstein or a Herzl appeared and could help change the attitudes of the world. Similarly, with humor, we can keep ourselves going until we have developed our adulthood sufficiently to be able to act effectively to change our circumstances or attitudes.

How to develop or encourage humor? By using all the tools described in this book. Most importantly, by not permitting ourselves to indulge our habitual overreactions and by turning away from our negative feelings, especially self-pity, in favor of a consideration that, devastated though we are, this is probably not the end of the world, not even ours. If we cannot control our thoughts as yet, we can remind ourselves that in the past, in similar circumstances, we have with time been able to see things in perspective and so we will allow ourselves time before we decide that all is lost. Even catching ourselves using such an exaggerated phrase may make us smile, if only wanly.

One woman expressed her changed attitude most amusingly. "I haven't had one good bout of self-pity in ages. You know I used to sort of save up my woes and then retire to my room. There I would pull down the shades, get a clean hanky and turn down the bed so I could cry into my pillow. Now, even before I start for the hanky, the whole thing strikes me as funny and half the time I begin to giggle at myself. Do you know, though—for an instant I feel almost cheated. I see now that I did use to enjoy it in some way."

Another example of how absurd our thinking is when in the grip of uncontrolled emotion and how the ability to see this can "snap us out of it" was a man I know who was given to indulging himself in fits of temper. During these, he reached for every profanity he knew and would deliver it at the top of his voice. Aside from upsetting his wife and the household, he afterward not only became extremely remorseful but actually felt physically ill. One Saturday morning he called me up.

"I want you to listen to what I have just been telling my wife here. This is the last straw," he opened and was off, the phone crackling with his rage.

"So what are you going to do about it?" I interposed practically, as soon as possible.

"Well, I have to leave at ten to play golf," he began. I glanced at the clock.

"So that gives you ten more minutes in which to cuss your wife out," I observed pleasantly.

"*Yes!* And furthermore . . ." His sudden silence showed that he had seen how foolish he was being, and shortly he joined me in a hearty laugh as we both hung up.

Do not think that I am suggesting that we should, even if we could, dismiss all our resentments and hurts with a laugh and a shrug. But humor can provide us the flexibility to be able to listen and consider another point of view. The man I have just cited was able on this occasion to permit his wife to explain about the conduct that had so enraged him, and his rage, he saw, was actually the result of a misunderstanding. He was able this time to allow the explanation before, rather than after, his golf date. Thus, his wife did not develop a resentment while he was off playing golf, and he had a far more pleasurable outing untroubled by incipient feelings of guilt.

Even if we have genuine reason for our resentment, humor can place a cool poultice where it really hurts. It is not so much, as a rule, another's conduct itself that is so hurtful as the feeling that the conduct was deliberate, due to a lack of love or to basic animosity rather than to some perfectly human shortcoming due to faulty childhood conditioning.

At the very least, development of humor can prevent us from adding self-insult to injury.

chapter 33

Fear and Distrust: The Inhibitors

Fear, a most destructive emotion, lies at the root of much of our self-destructive behavior, our seeming inability to change, no matter how compelling or perhaps even partially true the other reasons we give ourselves.

Obviously, there are realistic human fears—but in this chapter we shall try to deal with feelings that are often considered to be real fears when in actuality they are not. Much like the child's fear of an imaginary bear in the closet, which we discussed earlier, these are feelings that are products of generalized fear of the unknown. Unlike our real fears, which are often concerned with physical threats to our bodies, these are concerned with possible failures that may or may not result in actual physical harm.

Many of our judgments about the possible consequences of some action may be based more on opinion than on fact. For instance, one man once declared dramatically to me: "I have just been fired from the best job there is in this town for someone in my field. I'll never get another that good. I'll probably lose my house and anyway I will have to move. I'm a total failure!" I said to him quietly that his first statement was the only factual one, all the rest only his opinions. He glared at me and said, as so many do: "But, Doctor, you just don't understand!"

But by the end of our talk that day he had agreed reluctantly not to confine his job seeking to his own field, to make a real survey of all opportunities the town offered. It took him some months, during which he did have to borrow money for his house payments, but he finally landed a job with a local hospital. There, he paid with his bookkeeping and accountancy skills for on-the-job training as a medical purchasing agent. Later he was to specialize in this field, travel all over the country as a salesman for one of the big medical-supply houses and then become an executive of the company at many times the salary he had ever dreamed of earning. Best of all, he was happier in his work than he had ever been because he had always had a secret hankering to be a physician and this, he felt, was the next best thing.

But, perhaps unfortunately, most of us are not forced by the lash of necessity to take chances on ourselves, to overcome our self-distrust. Many of us sit enviously, on the sidelines, saying to ourselves: "I wish *I* dared do that . . . I wish I thought I could succeed in some new endeavor or hobby that beckons . . . I wish I had that ability."

But to insist upon assurances of success before we permit ourselves to try something is to demand the impossible and even actually undesirable if we want to be rewarded by feeling the expansion of our powers.

While I belong to that group of people whose appetites are not particularly whetted by the spice of physical danger, who remain somewhat more puzzled than enlightened by the explanation of the mountaineer that he climbs mountains because "they are there," nevertheless I could fully identify with Sir Edmund Hillary, the conqueror of Mount Everest, and the response he gave when he was interviewed recently. He was asked: "Did you know that you would succeed before you started?" "No, of course not," Sir Edmund replied, looking somewhat surprised and puzzled. "If I had, I wouldn't have done it. What would be the point?" And there you have it: he was doing it to prove something to himself, not the world. On the other hand, he obviously felt that the odds were good for success; he certainly did not have our common preconviction of failure.

As a matter of fact, most of us display a similar attitude in terms of daily physical risk. Statistics tell us that it is dangerous

even to cross a street and among the single most dangerous
things we can do is drive a car. Yet we all cross streets and most
of us drive cars, and we do so without second thought. We feel,
rightly or wrongly, that the odds are with us, that no harm will
come to us.

Pathogen-produced Fears

Most of us are similarly rather healthily optimistic in most areas
other than those in which our particular pathogens operate.
Thus, few of us would conclude, as does the hypochondriac, that
if we get our feet wet or become chilled, we will immediately
contract pneumonia.

How can we know, you may ask, if our fear of failure is
really due to reality factors or is the result of a pathogen?

One clue to pathogen-produced fear of failure is to be found
in those areas where we have little or no factual evidence to go
on but nevertheless feel we are experts. In other matters, we are
normally open to reason or willing to admit our ignorance, but
here we "know" that we are uniquely unable. We are sure we are
less talented, weaker, less attractive than others. Even when
others profess their faith in our abilities, we cannot believe them.
We feel, at best, that we have done a pretty good job of hiding
from them the shameful secret of our basic inadequacy and are
all the more determined not to risk its exposure.

In our current culture, we are led to believe that nobody
should undertake anything in which he cannot attain expertise,
that a small talent is not worth developing for one's own pleasure
and that of one's family and friends. We need to revise the old
saying so that it becomes "A thing worth doing is worth doing,
even poorly if we enjoy it." And, in fact, who knows: talent is
only one ingredient in success, and even that can expand.

Listening to our childhood tapes, we project onto tomorrow
the conviction of failure, perhaps because we did fail in the past
or because we were always told, and believed, that we were
incapable of such development. Yet a vital part of a whole school
of psychiatry, the Adlerian, has been based on a theory of

compensation; that is, that some people, just *because* they lack talent or are handicapped in a certain area, are spurred to greater effort than others and thus succeed where the more talented but less motivated fail.

As a matter of fact, the woman I mentioned earlier who resumed her early interest in painting did so with no thought other than to distract herself from her widowhood. But, in time, she developed a real talent as a watercolorist, and many of her friends have been glad to buy her charming pictures to replace prints or reproductions of better-known artists with her original work. I am no art critic but I have had many hours of pleasure from one of her studies of a dogwood spray. Perhaps some day people will pay large sums for her work. But if that day never comes, she has gained and given pleasure through her "small" talent and, as a totally unexpected by-product, has made some money from it.

One of the most common and most unfounded fears among many people I see is that if they meddle with "the way they are," their personality may vanish; that if they try to "change," they may no longer be "themselves." Sometimes, particularly if they are oversubmitted to or overindulged, they fear that they may be committing themselves to futures full of boring, unremitting labor that they will hate; or, if they are perfectionistic or overresponsible, that they will turn into lotus-eaters; or, if they have been punitively treated, that they will become doormats to be trampled upon. Nothing could be further from the truth.

The only things that ever really diminish in significance in our lives are those we have truly outgrown, and we must usually make an effort to see them as outgrown before we are willing to give them up. Generally, we are more like those people with attics full of outmoded or useless objects, kept because of some feeling they may come in "handy" some day or because they have been useful in the past.

A good example of this is our hanging on to destructive old ways of doing things even when we may already know that there are better ways. One frequently held on to is anger. Even though we know how costly it is to us and even though we may have succeeded in curbing public outbursts of temper, we may still rely upon it to goad us into action or mask fear. Many of us feel too unsure of our rights to ask for them calmly; we must work ourselves up with anger to dare to demand them in tones of outrage or to galvanize ourselves out of inertia into action against "injustice." It is rather like giving ourselves dutch courage with a few neat shots of whisky. As a method of ensuring that we get our own way it is very likely to backfire or, even if it succeeds, to generate needless resentment.

More often, it is like exhausting ourselves dragging the cannon into place when the gates of the city stand open. There will be time enough for the artillery when we have been refused. And even then, it is far better if we can learn to stand up for our rights without becoming emotionally upset.

But isn't there such a thing as righteous indignation? you may protest. Of course there is, or at least so it appears, but it is an expensive luxury for most of us. Actually, more often, if we look closely, the truth is that we become upset not when we are sure of our rights but rather when we are doubtful, or at least doubtful that our opponents will see things our way.

Nowhere is the twenty-four-hour principle more important than in handling our fears. By looking ahead, we sap ourselves of the energy we need to take the important step of practicing in small ways, so that little by little we can replace self-distrust with sufficient self-esteem to enable us to reach for what we have always felt was beyond our grasp. But, as we have noted, the gaining of self-esteem is not something we can measure quantitatively or even feel for long periods, and there may be times, during the gaining, when we even think we have lost ground. Unlike the stamp collector who can see the empty spaces being filled, however slowly, and know he is making progress, our realization of progress more often seems to come not steadily but in uneven chunks or sometimes even suddenly.

The Woman Who "Couldn't" Leave Home

"Yesterday morning, like out of the blue, I said to myself, and *meant* it, 'Today is the day,'" one woman said, beaming. I had been seeing her on and off for several years and even I had begun to doubt that she would ever muster the "courage to change the things she could."

This woman, who was already near sixty when I first saw her, had literally never left home. The only man she had ever wanted to marry had been killed in an accident, and she had never met anyone else she preferred to her parents. Aside from a brief period when she worked as secretary to an attorney in town, she had put her secretarial skills to work for her father, who was a writer on scientific subjects. She took care of her parents during their last illnesses and when her father died, shortly before I first saw her, she was left with the house, free and clear, and a small income sufficient to live on modestly. Superficially, she hadn't a problem in the world. But underneath she was aware that in some ways she had never grown up, never really lived. Although, as she was to tell me again and again in the years that followed, "I am too old, it is too late, I am too afraid to start now," she was nevertheless aware that if she didn't do something "now" she would die in the same house in which she had been born and in a sense would never have experienced anything that was not contained within its four walls.

She did have an alternative that she longed to have the courage to embrace. An old friend who had moved to California, where she owned a combination house and gift shop, had urged her to sell the old family home and go into business with her. The prospect had intrigued and frightened her. Most of her friends thought she was crazy to even consider the idea. But, after talking with her, and in spite of all the risk of possible disappointment, I felt sure that going to join her friend was what she really wanted to do and if she failed to do it she would never really be content.

She had hardly had to incorporate her parents' attitudes; she had had them right there all her life. Moreover, unlike many parents of people with problems, hers were extremely loving, intelligent people with few pathogens so far as I could determine. It could almost be said that their main fault was that they had been too nice; it was little wonder that their daughter, who was rather a plain woman, did not find a sufficiently attractive man to lure her away from them. Nor, since her life was both interesting and comfortable within narrow boundaries, was she tempted to leave home because of any lack of harmony there. Yet, with all this, now that her parents were dead she felt a yearning for wider experience.

Almost immediately we disposed of her original objections to joining her friend. First to go was the notion that she was too old. For there is no more untrue old saw than the one that "you cannot teach an old dog new tricks." The daily newspapers are full of examples to the contrary. She conceded that she could probably rent the house instead of selling immediately and could borrow sufficient money to try living with her friend for six months before burning all her bridges behind her, as she put it. She had never had to learn to depend upon her own judgment after trial and error, as most of us do, for her parents had always been there for her to turn to if she was in doubt.

I encouraged her to plan and put into action many projects, big and small, in the community, in which she had to make her own decisions. I steadfastly refused to give her any advice even when she begged for it, although I did commiserate with her failures and applaud her triumphs. Although she became increasingly happy and busy with all this, she seemed no nearer to being able to make up her mind about joining her friend, and, as I noted earlier in this account, I was about to decide that this was probably as far as she could, or ought to, go until the day she rushed happily into my office.

"I called my friend first thing and asked her if she still wanted me. She said yes, and I'm not even going to wait to sell or rent the house. I've arranged with the bank for a mortgage and, who knows, Doctor," she said, looking at me with eyes twinkling, "maybe with all the project experience I've had lately I might make so much money out there I won't even have to sell or rent it!" I was truly amazed, for just the previous week she had spent our session drearily shifting from one horn of her dilemma to the other, just as she had done a hundred times before.

Few of us will have to invest as large a percentage of our remaining years in gaining inner courage as did this woman. But some patience is necessary.

chapter 34

Helping Yourself Through
Sharing With Others

Although sharing with others is one of the most valuable measures for increasing and deepening our self-knowledge and adulthood, with rewards in learning how to relate to others and in adding greatly to our self-esteem, I have left it toward the last because it must be approached with caution.

Before we have recognized our own inner child and his demands, we are too entrapped in our old conditioning to really see and appreciate other people and their needs. Or we may be motivated to go out to them for self-aggrandizement: behold me, the doer of good! Or perhaps we may be motivated by a noble ideal of self-sacrifice, not realizing that people do not want self-sacrifice because it puts too much of a burden on them and what they really want is overflow. If we really want to sacrifice ourselves for others, we had better look to our own needs and fulfill these first or we will be using others to support the demands of our childhood tapes.

Happily, however, there comes a time when we are ready to share with others. When it comes is an individual matter. We all have our own rates of growth, some of us moving faster than others, although often the slow starters pull ahead later on.

Only you can judge when the time has come. There are some

rules of thumb. You are likely to be ready when you have made headway with recognizing and coping with your own pathogens and can begin to spot them and others in the people around you without even trying; when the feeling you have toward others is neither pity nor superiority because of your "better" insight but instead is one of outgoing sympathy and understanding of their difficulties and a truly unselfish desire to share with them what you have learned so far. This is true overflow. If you then act to share, the rewards will be so tremendous that you will feel, as you should, grateful to the other person rather than expectant of gratitude and love, although you are likely to receive both.

There is no harm in accepting these emotional supplies and letting them expand our self-esteem so long as we do not come to maintain the relationship because of these dividends, however delightful. For once we do that, we are in danger of letting our old I-centeredness revive and before long the relationship will deteriorate as so many did in the past. No, no matter how fervently our new friends assure us that we have helped them, that we seem the very founts of wisdom, we must ever remember that although our help is given unselfishly, the only reward we should seek is very selfish indeed, the highest form of selfishness: self-growth.

The Best Way to Learn

Educators have long known that the best way to learn is to teach. We realize the truth of this sometimes when we share some new way of looking at things with another and see it transform the other's life, perhaps even seeming to work better than it did for us. This is because we often have reservations that prevent us from fully using our new knowledge, but as we hear ourselves state the facts aloud and see their impact we find our reservations dissolving and we are able to experience the deep feeling of truth we have been seeking. Moreover, when we are honestly seeking to understand and help another, we have only our own experience, strength and hope to call upon—or, sometimes, the reverse: our sad experience with trying to hold on to our old distortions. In

either case, we often find ourselves saying things that are true, or
we believe to be true, about ourselves that we did not realize we
thought or felt. So, even if we should not be successful in reaching the other person—and often we are not or at least can see no
immediate response—we have still gained much in additional
knowledge of parts of our own nature previously unsuspected.

One man elected to work as a volunteer in his local mental
hospital. Originally, he felt that aside from having sympathy for
and desire to help patients there, he might, through observation,
learn something about how the sick mind works, and so what to
avoid.

"I learned all right," he said later, "but in a most surprising
way. At first, in order to 'get down to their level,' as I put it to
myself, I found myself telling what I considered to be benign
lies; I would claim to have had thoughts and experiences which I
thought I never had had, in order to relate to them. But, invariably, on the way home, I would realize that if I had perhaps
fabricated the actual events or settings, the basic truth was that
these things *had* happened to me, though I had never realized it
before!"

In trying to respond to their need, he had reached deep
down into himself and fetched up things that were invaluable to
him in his growth. As he always remarked when he was thanked
for his donation of time and effort, he could not be sure that
anyone but himself had benefited and he should be, and was, the
grateful one.

The Results of Sharing

A most deeply satisfying result of this sort of sharing is that
through it we can finally straighten out what has been wrong in
our interpersonal affairs. With our view of others distorted by our
old attitudes, we were forever in trouble in this area. Either we
demanded too much of those we loved so that in the end they
rebelled against our overdomination or overdependence to our
bitter hurt, or, fearing such hurt, we retreated into ourselves and
sulked or cowered and led people to believe that we were cold
and did not care. Whether we loudly expressed or hid our resent-

ments and sad belief that nobody loved us, the result was the same: we felt bitterly alone and misunderstood.

But, as we begin to understand our own distorted views, we see that all of us are to some extent emotionally troubled as well as frequently wrong and that it is pointless to permit ourselves to be hurt and angered by the behavior of people who, like ourselves, are suffering from the pains of maturing. Moreover, we learn to separate the behavior from the person. We are not our behavior any more than our unique adult selves are what our childhood tapes have always seemed to prove we are. Indeed, most of our interpersonal difficulties arose from a collision of our childhood tapes with another person's.

Choosing a person with whom you can share your insights makes your inner work progress more rapidly. I think here would be a good place to caution against at first choosing a member of one's own family, or even an old friend, with whom to initiate such a sharing and mutually helpful relationship. We have already had too many collisions between our tapes and theirs for either of us to see the other without some bias; that is, we always tend to feel that a person close to us is too predisposed either in favor of or against us to be properly objective. Very likely this is true and it is a reason why physicians are advised not to treat their own families. However, a sympathetic understanding of what is going on inside your nearest and dearest will certainly be a big help eventually in improving your relationships with them, even if in this early period a relationship of the type we are discussing may be more helpful directly.

Another reason for surrounding ourselves with as many people as we can for whom we feel empathy and can exchange overflow supplies of love and help is to safeguard ourselves from relapsing into old ways: we can never consider ourselves permanently "cured." The inner child will reassert himself whenever we are under pressure or in situations that are similar to our "at home" situations. Our friends will detect in us, as we will in them, the beginnings of lapses long before they become obvious to us, which too often is not until we have done something that we regret. Often, with a gentle hint, they will be able to remind us to get busy on our attitudes again before we run into trouble.

There is a saying that "We have to give it away to keep it." I can think of no better way to delineate the ideal basis for inter-personal relationship. We cannot retain enjoyment or satisfaction unless we share it. With such a basis, the relationship is one of true equality, with each participant at once giver and receiver and with no necessity for gratitude on the one side or hurt for lack of it on the other.

This is the ideal and this is far from an ideal world and we are not saints. So the relationship will not always be that ideally balanced. Sometimes one person will be giving more in response to the other's greater need of the moment, but then the tables will be turned. Still, there will be many shared times of simple enjoyment of each other, with neither giving more than the other.

This is true friendship. For some of us, it will be the first really true friendship we have ever experienced. Warmed and sustained by even just one such relationship, we can face our problems and our other relationships with renewed hope and strength, knowing that if we can find love and acceptance on an adult level with even just one person, we can be sure that they are there for us in other relationships if we will but make the effort.

Initiating Relationships

How does one go about initiating such a relationship? Each of us will work out the method that suits us best. Generally, a sympathetic remark, showing that we understand and care, is often enough to lead to the pouring out of what is troubling another person. Then—or, to begin with, with more reserved persons—we will tell of our experience with what we suspect could be their difficulty: how we used to suffer from our old way of looking at things; how relieved we were when we found that so often our problems were not due to the unkindness of the world or some hideous defect in ourselves but rather to something we could correct if we wanted to enough. More than by what we say, the other person will be impressed and attracted by our evident peace of mind, however partial we may feel our attainment of it is. And perhaps they will be led to ask our help most of all because of our hope based on even our limited experience of the joys of our hard-won new attitudes.

If our help is asked, we must explain that while we will give it freely, the other person will be helping us by permitting us to learn more about ourselves. We will probably see to it that they initiate the techniques we have been using ourselves. Often, we may find that another person will outstrip us from the beginning in some areas since all of us have some particular areas of strength. One of our first lessons from the relationship may very well be in learning to accept help as freely as we give it, for this is difficult for some of us. For others of us, learning that "To give is more blessed than to receive" is, quite literally, true will be a great reward. There are always people to give to, and to be able to do so implies we have something to give. And when we have that, it means that we have finally found the joy of self-respect.

chapter 35

Who Are You?

For those of you who not only have read but have worked your way through to this chapter, "Congratulations!" Not that you will need them from me.

Your reward will be that you will be able to begin to answer the all-important question "Who are you?" It is only with the hard-won knowledge of who we are that we can effectively begin to reorder our lives, either by finally making those decisions we have been putting off or by recognizing that now that we have altered our inner attitudes, little need be changed outwardly.

Now that you have an ever-firmer grasp of the principles of good self-parenthood, you have become increasingly able to depend upon your ability to tone down, if not completely control, your childhood tapes when they threaten to interfere with your adult goals. Now that your self-esteem has increased, you are able, more and more of the time, to avoid belittling yourself and, when self-belittling does start, to switch it off. Even on bad days—and we all have them—you are encouraged by the knowledge that the good days are more and more frequent.

The time has arrived when you may be starting to question old goals, old relationships, old values. Just because the questioning has begun does not mean that you are ready yet to arrive at final answers and to act on the answers. Nor is there need to at this time. There will be later stocktakings, and the time for definitive answers and actions based on them will come.

A Personal Inventory

As a preliminary to deciding whether or not you are ready, an honest and searching inventory of your assets and liabilities, of just where you think you stand, is essential.

This is not a sitting-in-judgment procedure. By now, you realize that, even if you wished to sit in judgment, you cannot—for you know now that you cannot speak for who you will be tomorrow and, whatever the errors of yesterday, you cannot validly blame yourself for them, for you did the best you knew how to do. Without fear or criticism, you look at yourself and your record to date, surveying your interpersonal relationships, job, ideals, goals, the areas of most importance to you.

So get out your tape recorder or notebook. Once again, I urge you not to try to shortcut this procedure by "doing it in your head." Not only will you overlook much vital material; you will deprive yourself of a valuable method of measuring progress. To prove this to yourself and because it will help and encourage you in your present quest, take out your very first record, your pathogen identification.

Most of you, mentally if not otherwise, will already have added to or amended this first attempt. But when you contrast your present attitudes with those of months ago, you will be immensely heartened by the gains. In all probability, there will also be areas where you will see that you were either too hard or too easy on yourself. Now, with your growing self-esteem and ability to be really honest with yourself, you can rid yourself of many crippling ideas. It would be wise to note these areas, for it is likely they need special scrutiny in the assessment you are about to make. All in all, a brief review of that first record should convince you how valuable a permanent record of today's evaluation will be in your next stocktaking.

There is no one set way to go about an assessment. Most

people find that a good way to begin is by listing their assets and what they consider to be their character difficulties and then to see how these apply to current goals. Finally, they decide what they can do, what course they can take, *today*.

In looking at what you consider to be your shortcomings, it is important to try as hard as you possibly can to establish whether you really think they are shortcomings or only feel you "ought" to think they are. For, as we have seen, self-manipulation based on self-deception often backfires.

Frank, an overresponsible, had fallen into the trap. In going over his inventory with him, I noted that he had written in capital letters: "BE MORE UNSELFISH, SPEND MORE TIME WITH FAMILY, EVEN IF IT KILLS ME." He had realized that his compulsion to overwork had robbed his family and himself of the reward of shared family life. He had made real attempts during the past year to correct this. But, impatient with his slow progress in feeling comfortable when he worked less and spent more time with his family, he had relapsed into his old self-belittling attitude. His family couldn't help sensing his discomfort and the family outings and times together were becoming less and less successful.

Frank needed to remember that his efforts to overwork less and be with his family more were for himself, that there was no moral issue involved and that, in the long run, however genuinely unselfish his desire to make his family happy, it was really for his own gain that he was putting himself out. It was his enjoyment of his family that was important, not what he did for their enjoyment.

Although he could see this intellectually, he really couldn't feel it at gut level. For underneath, his inner child still had him convinced that working was the unselfish thing and "playing with his family" was really self-indulgent. After we had discussed this, Frank went off aware that he had better work on his inner attitude, that to try to get his satisfaction from a family outing by seeing himself as a "noble, unselfish soul" could not work because there was no validity in it and, worse, it was preventing him from really learning how to "let go."

Discovering Your Own Attitudes and Goals

Perhaps you will find that you have already outgrown an old goal, that you are discovering a new set of values, that the job you have—no matter how successful you have been in it or are becoming in it—is not what you truly want. Or your job may have taken on a new meaning and dimension for you. Or perhaps you may find that, because of old longings to be popular, you have forced yourself in the past to go to and give parties and be gregarious when, in reality, what you like best are quiet evenings at home with a few choice people.

You now realize that if you are to be happy and successful in whatever life you elect, you must get on your own side and stop the civil war within caused by old pathogens.

One woman I know had carried over a childhood ambition to be a nurse. Although she was temperamentally unfitted to be a nurse, she entered nursing school. Fortunately, she had married before finishing her probationship. However, she continued to see herself as a frustrated Florence Nightingale, although she was the bane of the family's existence whenever anyone fell ill. She moved in and took over. Never happier than when someone was ailing, she made incipient hypochondriacs out of her children. Believing herself to be a soothing person in the sickroom, she was deeply hurt by what she termed the ingratitude of the recipients of her kindly, unselfish ministrations.

In time she came to see that the reason she was such an unsuccessful nurse was that she was basically bored and repelled by sickroom routine. It was only the drama, and a feeling of being needed, that attracted her; thus, she kept herself and her patients busy in a turmoil of overconcern and overefficiency. She was a genuinely outgoing person and did want to help others. When she transferred her attentions to the needs of healthy people, she became a genuine mainstay of civic groups and one of the happiest as well as busiest members of the community. Had this woman become a nurse, she might have spent her life unhappily enslaved by a false picture of her own nature.

There was nothing wrong with Tom's goal, only his methods of trying to achieve it. He genuinely loved his work and both believed in and was happy working for the large corporation that employed him. Tom was a perfectionist and, although he drove himself hard, promotions were slow in coming. Each time he was passed over, he would redouble his efforts, working harder and later, but with apparently even less recognition of his abilities.

Tom backed into the realization of what had been wrong with his techniques. At the time of his inventory, a coveted promotion lay between him and another man. During the year, he had been working hard on driving himself less but he had not dared to apply this new way of treating himself to his job. During his stocktaking, he decided—wrongly, as it turned out—that he probably wouldn't get the promotion but that in any case he would cease worrying about it. Moreover, he decided that he was doing a good job and that so much overtime was really unnecessary. He went even further and determined that he would stop weighing every word he said for its possible effect on his superiors.

An immediate result of his new relaxation was that he permitted himself to voice opinions and suggestions at meetings that he had previously censored, feeling they might sound silly or presumptuous. This was a side of Tom his superiors had never seen. While fully appreciating his ability to follow orders, they had been doubtful that he possessed enough creativity to solve problems and initiate programs on his own. Even an uncharacteristic "goof-off" helped him.

Tom told me about it when he called to tell me of getting the promotion. "I'd said to myself, 'what the hell,' and had taken off a little early to play golf, which I had been doing a lot of lately in the time I used to spend working late. It seems that the boss saw me there and was delighted. The new job had an important social angle to it, and they had had a feeling that I was such a sober-sides that I never played anything, let alone golf."

I was delighted for him and told him so. But I was even more pleased when he added: "You know, Doctor, what I really think did it? I think they sensed some of the new feeling I have inside—about me. I have more confidence in me, so they do."

Sometimes, "lowering" our sights is what is needed, even if

this may seem to go against popular notions of what is supposed to be the American "success story." Jerry found this out.

Jerry had been an excellent foreman. He enjoyed his work, was popular with his men and had the admiration and respect of everyone from top to bottom in the large construction company for which he worked. But his wife was after him to be a "white-collar" man. She wanted to join the country club and mingle with executives' wives, and she kept telling him that he owed it to the children to "better himself."

It was not a matter of money. Jerry had assured seniority and earned a large salary. Indeed, with overtime and many side benefits, he really wouldn't be doing any better, certainly not at first, on the office side.

Though reluctant, Jerry finally gave in, for it was part of his cultural background as well that a man go as far as he can. But "as far as he can" was too far for Jerry. It was not that paper work was too difficult for him; being an intelligent man, he soon mastered it. It was just that it didn't suit him. He missed the sense of direct contact with the job he was working on, missed the men, missed the physical activity. By the time the company doctor referred him to me he had an incipient ulcer and was moody and depressed. His relief was enormous when I suggested that he consider returning to his old job. But he was worried about his wife. "I don't care, neither do the kids, but she enjoys all that social stuff." He needn't have worried though. His wife had already discovered that she was far more at ease with her old friends than with the country club set. As for the children, they had been welcome long before as guests at the country club since many of their friends were children of members. For them, which color collar their father wore was a matter of total irrelevance.

It is the matter of finding out who we are and accepting ourselves, at least for today, as we are that is a fundamental goal of our inventory.

Up to now, we have not freed ourselves enough from old conditioning to be able to work on much more than our superficial behavior in whatever situations we have found ourselves in. Now we can begin to discover attitudes and goals that are not really our own. And by so doing we can begin to discover the goals that are truly our own. We will begin to see that our self-acceptance and outside approval do not depend upon our jumping through idealized hoops.

Our measuring rod is only ourself. We should not measure our growth against outside standards, religious or cultural, but in terms of what seems "comfortable" to us. Nor need we worry that this will turn us into a "moral slob." Most of us will spend the rest of our lives evaluating and rooting out the results of early conditioning. For impulsives, for example, such evaluation will show how far the inner child has taken them from "norms" that most people need to reach in order to get along at all with others—and, without moralizing, permit them to see more clearly areas in which they need, as a practical matter, to amend behavior.

Let's consider three housewives. The first, a perfectionist, has been practicing letting things go a bit in order to have more time for her husband and children, but she still doesn't feel really comfortable inside. Now, perhaps, she can begin to understand why at gut level. If she can really see that her acceptance is not at all dependent upon maintaining a spotless house, she will add to her freedom within and begin to feel really comfortable. The second housewife, an impulsive, feels perfectly comfortable if her house is not spotless if the cleaning depends upon her. Indeed, she feels that she deserves a maid even if her husband can't afford one. However, she doesn't enjoy the reactions of her husband and friends to her sloppy house. Clearly, she must concentrate on her behavior in this area and take her unwilling child of the past with her to do more things that make her adult self more satisfied. The third, an overcoerced woman, must gently get herself to do that work which she resists and then reward herself frequently as she breaks through her resistance in little ways.

Resolutions of Remaining Problems

To get at overidealized pictures of ourselves demands our most rigorous honesty. We have deceptive egos, and a good test is to ask ourselves when we feel particularly ashamed of some behavior: "What would be my reaction if a friend came and told me he or she had done that?" Nine times out of ten, we would dismiss it as of no importance. Why, then, do we regard it as so shameful in ourselves? It could be—if we face up to it—because we may consider ourselves better or finer, or feel we should be better or finer, than our friend.

All this does not mean that we need to be satisfied with ourselves as we are. We can keep on growing—not so much by changing ourselves as by uncovering who and what we really are, by rooting out weeds so our true personalities can flower. On the other hand, once we give up certain, long-cherished grandiose notions about what we "ought" to be, we may find that we are quite happy to settle for values we have and consider important.

If we have feelings of guilt, we may be able at this point to make a list of people whom we think we may have harmed. Perhaps, on reconsideration, we cross some of them off the list, either because we see we didn't do them real harm or because there is nothing we can do about what we did except behave in our new way toward them from now on—and this is often the case with family and friends. However, with others, we may acknowledge that after all we do owe that money or we have done damage through irresponsible action. If we feel real guilt, it is good to try to become ready to make amends on a practical level, for failure to do so can hold us back and hurt our self-esteem.

If you do not feel the willingness or courage as yet to admit error and make restitution where possible, do not force yourself. Simply acknowledge that you want to become willing.

Even more practically, never try to make amends for the sake of your own clean conscience when to do so would harm another. Obviously, to apologize to someone for dallying with his wife is to make a bad matter worse. Or to pay a debt fully right now if it would entail hardship for your family is really to be selfish. However, you may want to inform your creditor that you do plan to pay your debt and you may put something on account.

But it may be wise not to do any of this until you feel a goodly amount of self-esteem, since there may be some people who will not accept your amends and, if they do not, you will be tempted to use this as an excuse to throw in the towel and fall victim again to old pathogens. However, you can expect most people to gladly accept and forgive, and your friendship with them will become deeper and better than it ever was in the past. Even when this does not prove to be the case, remember that, as with all we practice doing, you are making amends for *your* sake. Once again, you are responsible only for the effort, not for the results.

Whether or not our spouses' pathogens are strongly involved, once we make progress on our inner problems, our families may need much patience, if not help themselves, in adjusting to us. Even if the change is welcome, it can be unsettling. At the very least, it can make our spouses and our children feel somewhat foolish and out of step, somewhat like continuing to waltz when your partner and the music have changed to a tango.

Children especially need time. One twelve-year-old's remark to his father was revealing. "Gee, Dad, it's hard for me to get used to the way you are these days. It's great that you talk to me so calm and all instead of blowing your top and yelling. But used to be you'd forget all about it then and I could get away with lots more. I like it much better this way but I keep forgetting that you keep track of everything nowadays." This father was wise enough, when he found his son disobeying him, to withhold punishment for a time and just quietly remind the boy that "nowadays" no really meant no. He was fair enough to acknowledge that for a while his son might have trouble "remembering" because of his own former inconsistency.

Sometimes the trouble may be due to a perfectly understandable even though to us hurtful inability of our partners to believe that we have really changed or that the change is permanent—or to a very human though not laudable desire for revenge. As we have seen elsewhere, attitudes that we have built up in others by our behavior over the years are not erased in a moment, and our heartfelt expressions of contrition may be greeted with skepticism or a desire to let us "stew in our own juices" for a while.

Richard's wife had such attitudes. He was the product of childhood neglect and had indulged in a series of extramarital affairs over the years, seeking that "ideal" love he craved. When he came to see that he truly loved his wife and his best happiness lay in developing his emotional relationship with her, he was shocked to find that she did not believe him and was not disposed to cooperate with him in any way.

"She says she had learned to fill her life with other interests, her bridge club, the community playhouse, her friends, and she is not about to give up all that for me. She doesn't want to any more, she claims; I hurt her too much."

I advised him to be patient and give her time to discover that he really meant it. But when, after a reasonable period, it became apparent that she was enjoying the situation of the boot being on the other foot and when he remarked disconsolately one day that "I was better off the way I was. Now that I have learned to feel things more, what am I going to do with it all?" I decided it was time for him to act.

"You have to begin to face the possibility that what your wife tells you is true," I suggested to him. "That she really doesn't care enough about you any more to help improve the relationship between you. In which case, you might have to start thinking about freeing yourself from Nancy and looking for someone else who can return your love. On the other hand, it is quite possible that she really doesn't know how she feels. I suggest that you separate for a time before you make any decision."

Richard agreed, as did Nancy, who maintained that "it won't make any difference to me" although she was obviously shaken. She even told herself, he found out later, that he was getting "restless" again but just didn't want her to know. Richard moved to a small apartment across town and, as the weeks wore on and his name was linked to no other woman's, Nancy had to admit that her suspicions had been unjustified. Busy as her life was, she found herself missing him more and more. Finally she faced the truth, which was that she had never stopped loving him but had feared being hurt again, feared that if she was betrayed once more she would not be able to salvage her pride and rebuild her life. She also was honest enough to admit that she had enjoyed "paying him back." Long before the six months were up, she sought him out and asked him to come home. That was quite a while ago and they are still together.

The biggest reason for a tentative approach to making a major outward change in our lives is that it is quite possible that we still do not know what we really want, that we can mislead ourselves. This can be so not so much in spite of as because of our new adulthood and insights. Most of us will have periods of euphoria as we free ourselves from the grip of our pathogens. I believe that this is one way we help and encourage ourselves to carry through the time-consuming and often painful process of change. These feelings of euphoria are all to the good if, in our delight at being freed from some of our old problems, we do not confuse this with being freed from all of them, or freed from having to wrestle with them for all time, or freed from all of the ordinary problems and reverses of life.

Normally, these extreme feelings of being on cloud 9 subside, but in some people they may be unduly prolonged and action taken in an unrealistic, euphoric state can lead to trouble. This is especially likely to be true of overdocile or overpunished people. Understandably, they are anxious to use their new independence. The joy they feel in their unfamiliar ability to assert themselves is likely to blind them to their other real feelings. Mary was one such case.

Mary's parents had been both overcoercive and somewhat punitive, but they also loved their daughter deeply. Mary thus associated love with domineering, which she mistook for strength. She had depended on it to force herself to act as she felt she should. After she married Joe, who was basically an easygoing man, her inner child subtly maneuvered Joe into treating her as her parents had done. When after much work Mary finally freed herself of her need to be dominated and threatened by anyone, she found herself married to a husband who did both. She made the mistake of confusing Joe himself with the behavior she had previously demanded of him. This way of treating her had become habit with Joe. He needed time to adjust. Mary did not have the patience. In fact, as so many of us are likely to do in similar situations, she turned the situation into an additional excuse for making a "clean break."

"I'm afraid, Doctor, that if I stay with Joe, I'll fall back into my old ways," she declared. It seemed clear to me after further discussion that Mary was "high" on her new sense of power and this hid from her the fact that she really did love and need Joe. However, she would not listen, and later when she did realize this, it was too late. Joe had married someone else.

Happily, most of us end up feeling unsure, unable to decide whether or not we are seeing ourselves and our real needs clearly. We should be glad of this, for not only will it help prevent premature action but it also shows that we know there will always be new things we learn about ourselves and that we are aware that it is much easier to see others in perspective than ourselves.

New Perspectives

There is something you can do at this point. If you have developed one of the mutually helpful friendships we discussed in the preceding chapter, you can ask the friend to help you review your present position and he or she will probably be able to give you a clearer picture of your present strengths and weaknesses. Or, if some parts of your self-searching seem too personal to share with anyone you know, you may want to obtain professional help from a marriage counselor, psychologist or psychiatrist.

I would like to emphasize the value of getting professional help to aid us in seeing ourselves in perspective. We cannot always get perspective by ourselves, and if we feel that we still need help after we have put forth our own best efforts, we may find that professional help is exactly what we need for further growth.

chapter 36

Special Problems

Certain problems—those to be discussed briefly here—require more help than any book can provide. If you have one of them, I strongly urge that you seek additional help. Your family physician may be able to provide it or, if not, can refer you to a psychiatrist or other specialist. Or you may find valuable help in a group.

There *are* special groups capable of being enormously helpful for some problems. But a word of caution about groups.

The value of group therapy depends very much on the group's orientation and procedure. Meeting regularly in a group, getting to know one another intimately, individuals can respect each other, provide insights for each other and offer each other a kind of support that often allows the burgeoning of strengths and the solving of problems that otherwise may seem forbidding and beyond solution.

But there are groups in which members belittle and deprecate each other, often in sincere attempts to be "honest." Certainly, it is true that reality has to be faced. But if, in the process of facing it, you are pushed further to the conclusion that you are "bad" or "lesser" or "no good," or if anyone in a group tells you this and you feel belittled by the group, you are being harmed, and the group may be worse than useless to you.

You can have your mistakes pointed out. You may have to face the fact that your behavior is destructive in some way or infringes on someone else's rights. But just because you have some unfortunate behavior habits that hurt you or someone else does not mean that you are bad. With all your habits, you are an infinitely valuable human being. If you belittle yourself or allow a group to belittle you about these habits, not only will you find your inner pain increased but you will feel alienated and cut off from the acceptance you need. Besides, you will work successfully on your habits only in an atmosphere of respect. In an atmosphere of disrespect, it is difficult and even impossible to change anything. So if you feel that the group members are disrespectful, get out of the group.

Suicidal Thoughts

I particularly urge those who have suicidal thoughts to seek prompt help.

This is not to say that many, perhaps even most, of us do not have fleeting moments of seemingly deep depression and despondency when our problems may seem too painful and too overwhelming and when the thought of ending our lives as a way out crosses our minds.

But for most of us the thought is held very briefly. We recognize that today is a day of particular gloom; yesterday was not that bad; nor is tomorrow likely to be.

And, particularly as we develop sharper insights and move progressively toward understanding the sources of our problems and toward putting an arm around ourselves kindly so we can begin to work on the sources, the days of deep gloom, while they may not disappear entirely, do become fewer and the gloom less deep; we are buttressed by thoughts of the progress we are making overall.

But what if you think often of suicide? If, perhaps, you get some feeling of comfort and security out of secret plans you make and keep elaborating for ending your life? If, perhaps, you even go as far as to secrete a loaded gun or a hoard of pills?

This is child-of-the-past thinking. It is never useful. It does

not supply real comfort or security ever. But if you have been
working on the principles set forth in this book and such thinking
persists nevertheless, you must take immediate action. Such
thinking is an urgent signal that this book is not enough to help
you, does not provide enough of the help you need immediately.
It may be useful to you later; you can return to it later; but now,
without delay, you need to look for and become a patient of a
well-qualified psychiatrist in your community. Your family physician will advise you in selecting one.

Obesity

Although obesity may be a problem of diverse origins, in the final
analysis we gain excess weight because we eat too much. There
are constitutional differences: some of us gain more easily than
others because our metabolism runs at a slower pace. Nevertheless, if we eat less, we will take off pounds. Some of us gain more
readily than others because our lives are more sedentary and,
expending less energy, we store some of our intake as fat. While
we need and could benefit greatly from increased physical activity, we may need to eat less, too.

Eating less is not easy.

Eating habits that make for obesity may be culturally induced. Some of us, because of rich cultural influences, have
special fondness for high-calorie dishes. Some of us came from
deprived cultures and we have a hungry child of the past with us
no matter what our present circumstances are. And our modern
American culture surrounds us with temptations: everywhere
around us are invitations to eat. In addition to family meals,
there are coffee breaks with doughnuts or Danish; candy
counters and peanut, soft drink and other types of vending
machines in office buildings; business and club luncheons; popcorn and soft drinks in movie houses; and so on, ad infinitum.

Our food and eating habits and attitudes are, to a large
extent, formed in childhood, and parental influences play a great
role.

In some homes, mothers enjoy showing family members how

much they love them by the food they prepare. They may cook large quantities of gourmet foods to demonstrate their love. And family members then sometimes eat large quantities not solely because of enjoyment but also because they feel a need to show Mother that they appreciate her loving care.

When children are overindulged, food is often a prime area for the overindulgence. Oversubmissive parents cater to food demands and whims.

Other parental pathogenic attitudes may be influences either for undue weight gain or for great difficulty in adhering to any diet intended to take off and keep off excess weight. If, for example, you came from an overcoercive home and there was overcoercion at the table as well as in other areas—directions to eat this and not eat that, to eat more of this and less of that; insistent directions; repeated directions—you may have gained weight out of rebellion or you may find it difficult to stick with any reducing diet that may be imposed on you or that you impose on yourself because almost any command, any bit of coercion, arouses resistance in you.

The perfectionist adult, raised by perfectionist parents, may turn on himself belittlingly—shame on me, I am too fat, I can't accept myself as I am; if I just lose some weight, maybe I can accept and like myself better—and, when he does this, may become caught up in a kind of rat race. The more we turn on ourselves belittlingly, the greater the emotional hollow or void in our chests—and the aching void, we find, may be at least partially relieved by food, whereupon we eat more than we wish to eat at meals, nibble between, deprecate ourselves still more for having done so, create more ache, then go on almost automatically to try again to ease the self-deprecation with food.

What do we do?

To resort to diets alone provides no answer. Fad diets, in any case, are self-defeating. Even when they lead to weight loss, there is little or no chance to maintain the loss because such diets, almost invariably crash diets, cannot be maintained. They are neither palatable nor sufficiently well balanced and nutritious for prolonged use.

But even well-balanced, carefully planned, physician-prescribed reducing diets may not do the trick, because we do not stick with them.

Drugs are no answer. Pills to help reducing may under some circumstances serve as a useful temporary crutch—but they are no more than that.

There are some new, relatively simple, techniques of behavior modification that are showing promise for many of the obese. If obesity is a problem for you, you would be well advised to consider them, particularly in conjunction with the efforts you make to become a good parent to yourself overall.

Because investigators have found that many obese people often eat in response to environmental cues—accessibility of food, odors, and so on—reducing these cues is of some value.

At the University of Kentucky College of Medicine, for example, Dr. Hugh A. Storrow, professor of psychiatry, has found it helpful to direct patients to remove from their homes calorie-rich foods that can be eaten without preparation; to pause and lay down utensils after each bite of food; never to eat when doing anything else such as reading or watching TV; and to engage in pleasurable alternative activities when they get the urge to eat between meals.

At the University of Pennsylvania, Dr. Albert Stunkard and his psychiatric team ask patients to keep detailed daily records so they can become aware of how much they eat and the circumstances associated with their eating. Because many habitually eat in different places at many different times during the day, they are encouraged to confine any eating, including snacking, to just one place. They are also asked to use a distinctive table setting, including an unusual-colored place mat and napkin, and to make their eating a pure experience involving no other activity such as reading or TV watching. In addition, they are asked to do such exercises as count each mouthful of food and put utensils back on the plate after every third mouthful until that mouthful is thoroughly chewed and swallowed. Among patients following this course of treatment, 53 percent have lost more than twenty pounds and 13 percent more than forty pounds, results better than for those receiving psychotherapy and among the best ever reported in the medical literature.

Many obese people find it helpful to join groups of those

having the same problem and dedicated to supporting each other in their efforts to reduce and maintain the reduction.

Efforts to modify eating behavior or to obtain group support, or both, may be all the more helpful when coupled with your work to put limits on your child of the past and the inner attitudes and conflicts you have carried over from your past home life and that influence your weight as well as other areas of your life.

If you have been overcoerced, for example, you need to become less harsh in your arm twisting of yourself. It you have been overindulged, you need to become less indulgent of yourself and, as you begin to do so in other areas, there will be some spillover in the weight area. If you tend to be self-critical, moralistic, perfectionistic, you need to make an effort not to spoon in self-criticism with every bite of food. The more you criticize and belittle yourself for your eating and weight problem, the less you are going to be able to act constructively. Control always depends upon self-respect.

You will do best with your weight problem as you move increasingly toward other-centeredness. "Should I eat or shouldn't I eat?" is an I-centered conflict. The weight loss problem becomes much less difficult when you act as an agent for your adult purposes and look upon weight loss as a means of making yourself a more effective agent because the excess weight is getting in the way of achieving your goals as an adult.

Some people consult me because of obesity. Others may be obese but they come because of other problems that overwhelm them. And as they work toward the solution of these other problems, their obesity problem often becomes easier to solve.

I think of a woman who came with a marital problem. She was obese, as it turned out, largely because of the marital problem. She was married to a dependent, somewhat ineffective man who leaned on her heavily and unrealistically. Lonely and frustrated, she was annoyed by her husband's dependence and his inability to provide her with much in the way of satisfaction. She had turned to food as compensation for the lack of adult satisfactions and hated herself because she was not attractive.

She had come from a home where she had been neglected, left alone a good part of the time. And she had married a man who had been overcoerced in childhood and had an uncanny knack for finding work under bosses who would twist his arm so that he would resist and do a mediocre job, prompting more arm twisting from the boss, which only made him more resistant. He came home nightly full of feelings of how mean his boss was, wrapped up with those feelings, and unable to give any attention to his wife or her needs.

She had to examine her marriage and decide what she wanted to do about it: did she really want to leave, as she believed when she first came to see me, or did she think she might, if nothing else, achieve a satisfactory life by finding interests of her own and fulfilling her desires without making her husband such a central part of her life?

She looked into herself, examined the influences of her childhood. She remained married, worked at becoming a good parent to herself, decided to join a well-known weight control group, became very much involved in the group program and gradually lost her excess weight. She became a lecturer for the group, grew increasingly tolerant of herself, with some spillover of tolerance in her relations with her husband. Encouraged by the change in her, her husband sought help and began to work on his own inner-child problems. Slowly the interaction between husband and wife improved; their social life expanded; he eventually found a job that gave him more satisfaction than any he had ever held before.

Alcoholism

A drink or two on occasion can help to produce an aura of relaxation and contentment, allowing cares and responsibilities to be forgotten temporarily and encouraging sociability. Many people find this helpful and desirable and recognize that it is so only as a temporary state.

Some people, however, feel it necessary to extend the state, to cling to and accentuate it. When they yield to the desire, drinking more and more and even almost continuously, they become alcoholics, addicted to drink.

Once alcoholism has developed, it can be an extremely difficult problem to overcome. But it is not hopeless. It can be solved and indeed it must if permanent damage and possibly death to the alcoholic, and incalculable hurt to spouse and family, are to be prevented.

There is still no definitive answer to the question of what causes alcoholism. Physical factors have been cited. People who become excessive drinkers may be prone to become so because of some predisposing metabolic or other physical difference. Psychological factors also have been cited. Nor are the two concepts of possible causation mutually exclusive. Both types of factors may be involved in at least some if not all cases. It is now increasingly recognized that alcoholism is a disease and thus differs from other problems for which willpower has some use.

If a problem of alcoholism is to be solved, it cannot be approached in simplistic fashion. Every aspect of the problem, which means every aspect of the alcoholic's life, must receive attention.

An alcoholic needs to recognize, accept and understand his illness—and must feel, or be helped to feel, that he is no pariah, no outlaw or outcast, but a worthwhile person who has a severe but manageable difficulty. Treatment should be multifaceted: physical, psychological, social and spiritual. On the physical side, for example, because an alcoholic often drinks to the exclusion of eating and may be seriously malnourished, his diet can be a vital consideration.

Many forms of treatment have been tried. In some cases, there has been some success with medication in stopping the abuse of alcohol and avoiding the complications of alcoholism. Antabuse, a drug that can make one violently ill when it is followed by drinking, has proved useful for some well-motivated alcoholics. Hypnotism has been found to be of limited usefulness, helping some alcoholics to the extent of teaching them to relax. Psychoanalysis generally has produced disappointing results.

In the view of many authorities who have devoted lifetimes to the problems of alcoholism, Alcoholics Anonymous has had the greatest success in the rehabilitation of alcoholics.

Alcoholics Anonymous—AA—is an unusual, self-supporting

organization of people who have given up or are attempting to give up their compulsive drinking and who work to help others with the same problem. From their own very personal experiences, they have learned how to stimulate and encourage others in their desire to stop drinking. In AA meetings and discussions, there are opportunities for the airing of problems, a most useful form of psychotherapy. Attending such meetings and discussions, the alcoholic loses his feeling of isolation and begins to see that there is hope for him. He or she finds in AA a pragmatic, simplified, spiritual approach to life, a prescription for living.

The organization has branches in many communities across the country and members are welcomed wherever they travel. Anyone may attend open meetings of AA without obligation and with no pressure of any kind exerted on him. He is welcome if he wishes to join, welcome if he does not wish to do so. He joins only if he feels he may find help and he himself must persuade himself; others will not even try to do so. Even if he has not joined and even if has never attended a meeting, if he finds himself in an acute situation and is desperate for help, a call to a local AA branch will bring it *to him* immediately. The national headquarters of AA is P.O. Box 459, Grand Central Annex, New York, N.Y. 10017.

I have great respect and admiration for AA—for its whole approach and for its achievements. I recommend it often to patients. For many, it is the extra help, the continuing support, they need to go along with their efforts to understand themselves and the influences of their inner child, and to set limits. And I have known many AA members who have chosen to supplement their AA work with the work of coming to appreciate inner-child influences as they apply to their drinking problem and to other problems, which, like nondrinkers, they very often have.

As we have seen throughout this book, attitudes carried over from old home life can play significant roles in uncontrolled drinking. We have considered them under the various parental pathogens and need not do so again here.

Suffice it here to recall that the oversubmitted-to person, for example, has a hard time saying no to himself—to his temper, his demands, his whims and often his drinking. Drinking loosens his controls, which were flimsy to begin with, and one drink often leads to another. The overcoerced person, particularly if brought up with strict thou-shalt-nots, often becomes resistant to them and, once out from under parental control, may take to drinking in excess as a form of defiance. The overindulged, leading a jaded life, searching for what will give him a kick, seeking passive pleasures, may drift toward alcoholism. The perfectionist, unable to accept himself as is, always trying a little harder with the hope of being acceptable if he betters his performance, finds that no matter how hard he tries, he cannot accept himself—and may weary and find in drinking the anesthetic to quiet the critic within. And so, too, other pathogens may lead to alcoholism.

If the inner child, the carrier of the pathogens, is understood and if limits can be set on him, all areas in which the pathogenic attitudes are detrimental influences, including excessive drinking, can be expected to show improvement.

But drinking can be a special problem. Resort to it can retard the whole process of becoming a good parent to oneself. And any extra help that can be applied to the drinking problem can be beneficial for the whole process. AA, I like to think, and so, indeed, many patients have found, can help to support the work of becoming a good parent to yourself and the latter can provide support for the efforts of AA. Except in rare instances, I have found that alcoholics need outside help. They usually will not give up alcohol and continue to abstain and achieve a happy life without support from AA or another source. Certainly, no book, however helpful it may be, can be relied upon to do the whole job.

Drug Addiction

Drug addiction is often thought of in simplistic terms—as a habituation that follows accidental or deliberate exposure to a drug. But it is not simplistic at all.

Drug use frequently begins in adolescence. Adolescents are experimenters and most of them will try marijuana or amphetamines or other agents experimentally. But they generally will not persist in drug use, in my experience, unless they are having to cope with serious, rather flagrant departures from mutual respect in the home, either current or internalized from earlier life.

Almost all of the pathogenic parental attitudes, if they are severe enough, are commonly involved in predisposing adolescents—and adults—toward persistent, serious drug abuse.

The oversubmitted-to person—who has had parental capitulation to his childish whims and demands and grows up capitulating to them himself and, without capacity for self-control, who is accustomed to immediate gratifications and well practiced in inability to say no to his own impulsiveness—may give in quickly to a drug habit.

The overindulged person—who has had a parental showering of goods and services and grows up bored and blasé, expecting a cornucopia of satisfaction without effort, and restlessly seeking for impulse satisfaction and new pleasures and experience—may turn to drugs and find in them a way to recapture the passive, effortless satisfaction learned in childhood.

The overcoerced person—subject in childhood to constant parental direction and redirection and grown resistive and rebellious—may think that drugs will expand his individuality and free him from parental constraints.

The self-belittling person—whose personality or accomplishments have been made light of by parents, whose sense of worth and self-respect has been minimized or obliterated, who was given in adulthood to downgrading himself and to feeling hopeless and depressed often—may turn to drugs for at least temporary relief, via their anesthetic effect, from the pain of self-devaluation.

The person who has been victimized by parental distrust—a parental expectation of his inadequacy—may grow into adolescence and adulthood with a tendency to resort to the very things that are objects of the parental distrust.

The person who has been neglected—given little or no parental attention and interest—often drifts into relationships with any contemporaries willing to form them with him and if these peers happen to be drug users, he may emulate them.

It is extremely difficult, if not impossible, for a drug-addicted person to give up drugs entirely by himself, without any kind of numan support.

It can be of great help if he is living at home when parental attitudes can be modified; when parents can come to understand how, although meaning no harm, they may have caused harm and how modifications of their attitudes now can play a vital role in helping the adolescent.

It can be of great help for the adolescent or adult drug user to understand the influence of pathogenic attitudes and to undertake to begin to become a good parent to himself.

But he will still need support. He will benefit from the interested concern and active treatment—with medication or other means—of a physician or clinic. Often, he can benefit from psychiatric counseling. Group therapy is likely to be of great value for him. Sometimes institutionalization may be necessary.

To be permanently freed of the addiction problem, other-centeredness is as essential as it is for other problems. But the development of other-centeredness takes time, and time for drug addicts, time before they do themselves irreparable harm, can be very short. Right now, immediately, a drug addict needs as much support as he can give himself, as much as those around him can provide and as much as physician, clinic or group can possibly offer.

Hypochondriasis

We have considered hypochondriasis earlier; we should touch on it again here, briefly.

It is a common problem, this ballooning up of minor aches and pains and normal body sensations and functions to the point of worry and discomfort. It accounts for a large proportion of the millions of dollars spent on patent medicines, laxatives and assorted other pills and remedies each year—and for the incalculable misery and despairing incapacitation suffered by people who, although they should be well on physical grounds, feel so sick, weak and tired they cannot enjoy life.

If you're a victim of hypochondriasis, you may have sought medical help many times in the past—and felt you found none.

Perhaps you now have realized, from the earlier discussion, that your inner child of the past was subjected to parental hypochondriasis.

Perhaps you've considered such questions as these: Did your parents enjoy good health or complain much of the time about poor health? Did they, perhaps, repeatedly tell you about "germs" and sickness and the need to protect themselves and you? Did they insist that you take precautions against inclement weather that far exceeded any taken by your schoolmates? Did they frequently make you stay home from school because they thought you might be sick or "coming down" with something? Did you perhaps use their concern about your health to stay away from school, escape chores, avoid social or other obligations?

If your answers to these questions make you realize that your parents were unduly concerned about health, unduly preoccupied with the possibilities and hazards of disease, you will probably find that you have continued their hypochondriacal attitudes.

But you may also have another unfortunate carryover that must be taken into account. You may have consulted physicians many times, seeking some physical explanation for your complaints and, when none could be found, you could believe only that the examination was not thorough enough. Every physician has had the experience of seeing patients, free of physical signs of illness, who insisted upon expensive, time-consuming tests for which there was no need. Every physician has known many patients who also have insisted upon medications for which there was no need—and even for surgery for which there was no basis. Unfortunately, some physicians allow themselves to be coerced by such patients into collaboration. Nor is this necessarily for financial gain. A physician may give in, may carry out tests he really thinks are not indicated, may prescribe medications he really thinks are not clearly indicated and cannot help and even may permit surgery out of anxiety to be a "good" doctor and out of frustration at being unable to pinpoint the cause of mysterious symptoms.

You need to go to work on your inner child, yes. If you are ever to be freed from the burden of hypochondriasis, that is essential. You may also benefit from one more medical checkup—but approached now in a different way. You may benefit from a checkup that is made without undue demands on your part, made to reassure you that a physician of excellent repute finds you physically OK, finds as he most likely will that there was nothing wrong at any point and nothing has gone wrong since the last checkup. Then you are ready to practice being a good, firm parent to your complaining child of the past, and insist on pursuing your adult goals without letting the child take over.

Homosexuality

There are those who believe that there is a constitutional factor involved in homosexuality and I would agree that there are probably persons who are constitutionally more prone than others to become homosexual. However, I don't believe that constitution alone, something innate in protoplasm, often if ever makes for homosexuality. I do believe that what happens in early family life is much more significant.

Nor do I have any sympathy for the argument that homosexuals should try to change, willy-nilly, and must change if they are to be happy, productive human beings. Homosexuals do have strikes against them—but they are cultural strikes. Wrongfully, this particular symptom of child-of-the-past conditioning is more damning culturally than any other.

The homosexual usually has to deal with three self-esteem problems that reinforce each other, to his detriment. He carries with him, internalized from childhood, deprecating attitudes toward him of parents and playmates. He is faced with belittling attitudes that the "straight" culture has toward the homosexual, which often coincide with his self-belittling estimate of himself. And he may internalize and turn against himself, whenever he has sexual feelings, the scorn displayed by society toward his homosexuality.

The homosexual may or may not wish to achieve heterosexuality. If he does wish to, he may find that an understanding of what influence his early home life may have had on his sexual development can help, particularly when it leads him to seek and obtain support from another person who can, and wishes to, provide that understanding. If he does not want to become heterosexual, the understanding may help him to live more comfortably with his homosexuality as it helps him to solve other problems that he may have as the result of his past conditioning.

Origins of Homosexual Tendencies

A popular idea has it that normal children are often made homosexual because of seduction by homosexuals. Yet entrapment through seduction is improbable. In one follow-up study that was carried out with 108 boys who had been homosexually seduced between the ages of seven and sixteen, not one became homosexual as the result of the experience.

Sexual impulse can be likened to the flow of a river. The direction of the riverbed over which this river flows is determined by the individual's childhood conditioning within his family group. In a family situation radiating mutual respect, particularly respect for a boy's boyness and a girl's girlness, the river follows a course of heterosexual development; in a distorted family situation, the riverbed may be diverted toward homosexual adjustment.

If a male child happens to light in a family where the father is extremely busy, aloof, somewhat critical and distant from his wife emotionally and pays very little attention to his son because he is so busy or because he does not care for his son's characteristics; and if the mother, being deprived of the love of her husband because of his criticism, punitiveness or aloofness, becomes starved for loving and swaddles the very young male child with all her love, concern, care and catering and anxious protection because of her frustrated adult needs for loving, the child will have great difficulty growing up to become an individual on his own.

Enveloped by his mother's excessive feelings, his striving for experimentation and independence may be stifled. He may not get a chance to play at and enjoy masculine games and interests. In a hothouse atmosphere of cloying closeness, the boy may fail to develop skills needed to earn the respect of playmates.

He may go sometimes to play with the boys but, lacking the play skills and techniques they have developed, he will be a target for their teasing. He will feel himself inferior and weak as a boy and may rush home to further catering, protection and excessive loving care from his mother, which will perpetuate his difficulty in developing the robust skills of boyhood.

Critical of himself as a boy, he may become vulnerable in later childhood to larger adolescent boys who may use him in sexual episodes. Virtually all children at puberty or in early adolescence begin to experiment sexually and the beginning experiments may take homosexual forms. For the self-critical child who otherwise feels "out of it," a willingness to engage in homosexual experimentation may become a means of achieving acceptance and vicarious participation in the older boy's strength. Such a boy may become fair game for older boys and homosexual men. And the boy is attracted because of his hunger for male approval and friendship.

But if a pattern of homosexual relationships develops, the boy's feelings of inferiority often deepen. "I am doing this awful thing," he may say to himself. And, labeling himself homosexual, he labels himself with the cultural scorn and this compounds his difficulty and locks him into the only kind of relationships he can establish. When he goes to girls, making fumbling adolescent attempts, he is half-hearted about it and self-defeating. He feels he is so inferior that no girl will have anything to do with him. He feels fearful of girls, anyhow, because he has learned, through his early life with his mother, that if you get close to someone of the female sex, you get stripped of any kind of individuality.

Often, girls who become Lesbians are turned off by men because of experience with extremely belittling or punitive fathers or older brothers. Some may even have been assaulted sexually. They may come to think of men as aggressive, exploiting, hurting persons. They may turn to the softer, gentler sex epitomized by their mother, who was reasonable and not "exploitive" as men are.

These are just two examples of what can happen—and what commonly does happen—to produce homosexuality. They are certainly not the only ways that homosexuality may develop.

Options

Some persons choose to lead the homosexual life and certainly have the right to do so. All the onerous, belitting criticism from the culture is out of place and hopefully there will be less and less of it in the future.

For those, male or female, who wish to change, change is often, though not always, possible. They need to understand how they carry within them, in their inner child, the old home attitudes they were exposed to during childhood. They need to think of themselves as not being cripples—because they are not. They need to think of themselves as not being inferior—because they are not.

For those who do not wish to change their sexuality but do wish to find solutions to problems they have in common with many who are not homosexual, the solutions can be found—and without interference with their choice of remaining homosexual. As we have shown throughout, insight in itself is not enough. There must be practice in setting limits on the child of the past and in becoming a good parent to oneself, and the practice must be in specific areas. If the choice is to practice in many areas but not in the area of sexuality, there is no danger of being converted automatically to heterosexuality if one doesn't wish to be.

If the choice is for heterosexuality, there must be deliberate practice in trying to achieve it. In addition to work with one's inner child another person is needed—if possible, a person who cares for and loves the homosexual as he is and who is not belittling. While the homosexual will need to wrestle repeatedly with his own self-belittling, there must be no belittlement from her; instead, he needs from her support in overcoming his self-belittling.

Many homosexuals have the opportunity to find, or may even already know, someone of the opposite sex who cares for them. With the help of that other person, there can be a gradual introduction, in progressive stages, to heterosexual activity. The techniques developed by Masters and Johnson to help heterosexuals with sexual difficulties have much to commend them for this purpose too.

There will need to be understanding and much give and take of warmth and acceptance. In bed, there should be no rush to achieve sexual union. Instead, lying close together, without anticipation of an attempt at union until much later, the two partners can gently caress each other first in nonerogenous areas, simply enjoying sensual warmth. Later, slowly, there can be stroking of erogenous areas—and always the emphasis should be on allowing full sexual expression to come spontaneously and gradually without being forced.

Excessive Sexual Stimulation

If you seem to misjudge the role of sex, find yourself emphasizing the physical aspects, are unable to form or maintain a loving sexual relationship, often become preoccupied with sexual fantasies and feel that your intimacies are unsatisfying and almost impersonal, excessive sexual stimulation of your inner child of the past may well be the cause.

Such stimulation in the past may have taken the form of prohibitions, which led to excessive sexual fantasies, or they may have been intentionally or unwittingly seductive in nature.

Our society has been becoming less and less prudish. Yet some parents, even though aware of how much of their unhappiness came from prudish prohibitions and restraints, from concepts that sex is sinful, dirty, bestial, and so on, have so internalized their parents' attitudes that they exhibit prudish anxiety toward their own children in turn.

When a child is made to feel guilty about his sexual feelings, the guilt may become an important factor in his adult sex life. It may, for example, lead him to feel more "at home" in illicit love affairs with the guilt feelings attaching to them than in married love.

But, even more likely, prohibitions and restraints stimulate curiosity and sexual fantasies. What is prohibited—and punished when expressed—may be tried out safely in fantasy. But while fantasies greatly reduce the risk of parental punishment, the child feels guilty about them, condemns himself, then hungers for more fantasying.

The fantasies overstimulate the child's sexual feelings, tend to become his way of expressing sexuality and may provide in adult life the "at home" feeling the inner child seeks. Sexual satisfaction in fantasy prevents the development of normal sexual relationships.

With prohibitions and restraints on childhood sexual feelings, sexual curiosity may be expressed in adulthood in fascination with "girlie" magazines and pornography. These become sources for fantasies; the persons fantasied about are unknown and unknowable; the sexual activity is depersonalized. Masturbation may be continued. Such activities prevent the development of the capacity to participate in a full sexual caring relationship with deep satisfaction.

In contrast to parents who impose prohibitions, some parents directly stimulate sexuality. They may do so unwittingly in a "modern" belief that openness is emotionally healthy and so may ignore conventional modesty, respect no bathroom privacy, go about the house in the nude.

Many parents take young children to bed with them on occasion. Most stop doing so by the time a child has reached school age. But in some cases, the custom may be continued even long after it has become clear that it is excessively stimulating. When it is carried into the teenage period, it can provoke extreme stimulation. One study found that 15 percent of delinquent girls had had sexual relations with their fathers. Some mothers may lie with sons even though aware of the sexual excitement they are provoking.

An adult who was subjected to excessive direct sexual stimulation by a parent or another adult as a child may have within him a child of the past with feelings of frustration, rage and guilt against members of the opposite sex. He suffers from a deep sense of having had his affection betrayed. But it is not impossible for such an adult to develop the capacity for a loving, satisfying sexual relationship.

You can understand the confusion of your inner child yet set limits on how that affects your adult life. You may be able to do much on your own, using the procedures for dealing with other parental pathogens described earlier. If you feel you need help beyond what this book can provide, do not hesitate to seek it from your family physician, who, if he cannot provide it, can find a psychiatrist trained to deal with complex emotional problems.

If your sexual development was inhibited by parental prohibitions that led to excessive fantasying, to depersonalized sex, to purely physical sexual relationships, it is not too late to foster further development. By using the techniques described earlier for setting limits on the effects of other parental pathogens, you can set limits on your sexual fantasies. You can recognize that many of the fantasies are catered to and stirred up by the excessive emphasis given to sex in some media. You can begin to make yourself less sensitive to such provocation as you understand the real nature of your problem, respect yourself, set firm limits on your inner child and allow your adult of the present the opportunity to find and develop what he wants: a warm, rewarding sexual relationship associated with love and with a desire for the partner's welfare, growth and development as a person. As you associate, gradually, your sexuality with deep emotional attachment, the exaggerated promises of fantasy will have no attraction for you. And here, too, if you feel you need help beyond what this book can provide, you should have no hesitation about seeking it.

Best Wishes

I hope you have enjoyed this book and have found it somewhat useful even at first reading. It may be particularly helpful now to go back over it, marking the parts that seem to fit you most accurately. There are great sections of this book that aren't meant for you, but for other persons with other problems.

My deepest hope is that the specific sections that you find applicable to yourself and the persistent work that they suggest can help carry you far toward increased inner caring and greater personal fulfillment.